Sex Trafficking and Human Rights

Sex Trafficking and Human Rights

The Status of Women
and State Responses

HEATHER SMITH-CANNOY, PATRICIA C. RODDA,
AND CHARLES ANTHONY SMITH

GEORGETOWN UNIVERSITY PRESS | WASHINGTON, DC

The publisher is not responsible for third-party websites or their content. URL links were active at time of publication.

Library of Congress Cataloging-in-Publication Data

Names: Smith-Cannoy, Heather M., author. | Rodda, Patricia C., author. | Smith, Charles Anthony, 1961– author.
Title: Sex trafficking and human rights: the status of women and state responses / Heather Smith-Cannoy, Patricia C. Rodda, Charles Anthony Smith.
Description: Washington, DC: Georgetown University Press, 2022. | Includes bibliographical references and index.
Identifiers: LCCN 2021046441 (print) | LCCN 2021046442 (ebook) | ISBN 9781647122614 (paperback) | ISBN 9781647122607 (hardcover) | ISBN 9781647122621 (ebook)
Subjects: LCSH: Human trafficking. | Human trafficking victims. | Human trafficking victims—Civil rights. | Women's rights.
Classification: LCC HQ281 .S685 2022 (print) | LCC HQ281 (ebook) | DDC 364.15/51—dc23/eng/20211230
LC record available at https://lccn.loc.gov/2021046441
LC ebook record available at https://lccn.loc.gov/2021046442

♾ This book is printed on acid-free paper meeting the requirements of the American National Standard for Permanence in Paper for Printed Library Materials.

23 22   9 8 7 6 5 4 3 2 First printing

Printed in the United States of America

Cover design by Erin Kirk
Interior design by BookComp, Inc.

Contents

Illustrations

Figures

Tables

Preface

For many, the topic of sex trafficking conjures particular images of desperate, bound, helpless, young female victims. Images tell a powerful story about how a subject came to be victimized—that evil men have coerced her into an unimaginable fate punctuated by physical and sexual violence. These images of desperate (often minority) girls, looking at the viewer with their hands bound, their mouths taped shut, and other overt evidence of their misery and helplessness, draws in the viewer, tugs at the heartstrings, and calls out to the viewer for rescue. These types of images are used (often by well-meaning government agencies and nonprofit organizations) to elicit public sympathy and compel action to combat sex trafficking. Feminist scholars of human trafficking have a name for these types of images: the rescue narrative.

The body of images that collectively constitute the rescue narrative, while undoubtedly powerful, are damaging because they crowd out much of the complexity of sex trafficking around the world. In this work we set out to study the experience of women and girls but we could not ignore the sizable populations of men and boys, and trans and LGBTQ+ victim populations. Undocumented victims, refugees, and civilians displaced due to civil conflict are especially prone to becoming sex-trafficking victims. Girls become sex-trafficking victims not only (and not often) because they are kidnapped but because they are sold by their parents out of an expectation that they are to be married off to older men. None of these victims fit with popular perceptions about what sex-trafficking victims look like. In short, we were motivated to begin this project by a belief that the rescue narrative captures public and scholarly attention to the detriment of a more complete understanding of the problem. The interaction of social, economic, and cultural systems defines the parameters not only of sex trafficking but also of the ways states define and respond to the problem. Our motivation for writing this book stemmed from a desire to push back against these misconceptions and analytical omissions.

The rescue narrative does not just get the identity of victims wrong; we show that in some parts of the world women are as likely to be traffickers as men, duping friends and even family with promises of better lives. The misconceptions about the identity of victims and traffickers, and accordingly also the causes and consequences of sex trafficking, are so ingrained in the public consciousness that they routinely inform and shape national-level policy.

In particular, sex-trafficking services are mostly made available exclusively to women and girls, and victim services are housed in domestic violence shelters. In some cases male and trans victims are not included in national victim counts, which deprives them of being considered in future funding decisions. And generally, "rescue" takes precedence over social, economic, and cultural reform, which could help prevent future sex trafficking.

Sex trafficking is much more than the desperate kidnapped women chained to beds. Part of our purpose in writing this book is to survey how sex trafficking happens around the world in order to push back against this erroneous and dangerously misleading narrative. Victims around the world aren't always helpless and the concept of rescue may not be useful for them. In some instances those who have been trafficked become the heads of anti-trafficking organizations that help other victims and advocate for victim-centered trafficking legislation that goes far beyond the rescue narrative.

The cover art for this book has been carefully selected to avoid falling prey to the perpetuation of the gendered, racialized, patriarchal tropes that reinforce popular misperceptions about trafficking victims. The perpetuation of these images has grave repercussions for how we think about trafficking victims and how states attempt to ameliorate the problem.

Our work offers a hint at a way forward that does not depend on dramatic rescues from brothels—to prevent human trafficking what is needed are national legal protections to secure the economic rights of women and girls.

Acknowledgments

The authors are grateful to many people that have supported our work and the completion of this project. We are especially grateful to Don Jacobs, acquisitions editor at Georgetown University Press, for his keen vision and endless patience. Two external reviewers provided insightful and constructive feedback that much improved the manuscript. Robin Moore, Alexis M. Rodriguez, and Heather Heath, all undergraduates at Arizona State University, provided superb research assistance. The authors collectively wish to thank the many colleagues who reviewed versions of the manuscript. We are grateful for their comments and suggestions, which undoubtedly made the work better. Finally, we owe a large debt to the victim-support organizations that shared their time and data with us. Though we name those organizations and individuals where appropriate, we also wish to acknowledge them here: in India, Apne Aap World Wide (AAWW); Prajwala in Thailand; NightLight Bangkok; the Safehouse Foundation in Russia; the NAME Organization in Nigeria; and Thaddeus Blancehtte, professor of anthropology, Universidad Federal do Rio de Janeiro-Macaé and activist for the rights of Brazil's sex workers.

We also want to make individual acknowledgments to the people who helped us:

Heather Smith-Cannoy: I am grateful to my wonderful coauthors for their fabulous work and good humor throughout this process. In my experience long projects like this one require a loving family and supportive colleagues; I am lucky to have both. At ASU I am grateful to the Global Human Rights Hub executive committee—Dr. Tricia Redeker-Hepner, Dr. Magda Hinojosa, Dr. Audrey Comstock, Dr. Kendall Funk, and Dr. Malay Firoz. My mom, Adele Smith, is always quietly finding extraordinary ways to support me and cheer me on. To my Dad, Larry Smith, and my stepmom, Dr. Veronika Tracy-Smith: your love and support mean the world to me. To Stacy, Michael, Emma, and Riley Maldonado: thank you for always "getting it!" And finally to my loves—David "DC" Cannoy, Cole Landry Cannoy, and Buster—thank you for being my loves, and my whole world.

Patricia C. Rodda: My first thanks are to my two amazing coauthors, both for inviting me to be a part of this project and for their unwavering support as we have completed this journey. I owe eternal gratitude to my parents, Steve and Debi, and my late grandparents, Gordon and Donna, who never once questioned that I could be exactly what I wanted to be, even when I was not sure of that myself. Finally, I would be nowhere without my best friend, Benjamin Gunning, who is the most perfect source of support, kindness, and inappropriate jokes a person could ever ask for.

Charles Anthony Smith: I am grateful to these outstanding coauthors as well as all the folks at Georgetown University Press. I feel fortunate we were able to do this project together. I owe a debt to the late professor Enrique Baloyra, who first introduced me to political science as well as the field of human rights when I was an undergraduate. Finally, my husband, Julio Rodriguez, helps make my work and life feel like a vacation every day, thanks to his patience, good humor, creativity, tenacity, brains, and love.

Introduction

When writing a book on sex trafficking, one comes across a lot of tragic stories—so many tragic stories that it can be hard to know where to begin or whose story to tell first. During our research for this book we learned about the child-bride trafficking routes that transport young girls from relatively poorer states in eastern India to much more prosperous states in the north. Girls, like Roshini from Jharkhand in eastern India, are sold by their parents to bride traffickers at the age of thirteen in order to help feed the other children in the family. Roshini became a *molki*[1] to be used for sexual services by all the men in her new household, forced to cook, clean, and care for children and the elderly—and then she was sold by her in-laws when she was no longer wanted. Molki generally come from the lowest caste in the social hierarchy in India, the Dalits, or untouchables. Female children in rural India are often seen as a burden to the family because, in order for them to be married, the family must pay a dowry to the husband's family. Dowries can be more than double a family's annual income, making female children a costly liability. Selling a daughter to bride traffickers, as Roshini's parents did, can help impoverished families alleviate this economic burden.

In Nigeria, internal conflict between the government and the terrorist group Boko Haram has displaced thousands of people from their homes, confining them to camps in the name of safety, all while undermining economic opportunities, especially for women. Much attention has been paid to the plight of the Chibok girls, stolen in April 2014 from their boarding school and "married" off to members of Boko Haram. Following a negotiated settlement with Boko Haram, many, but not all, of these girls returned home. Beyond the headlines of the Boko Haram story, for a large proportion of the female population in Nigeria conflict and instability have caused them to seek employment opportunities abroad, which has led many to be entangled in human trafficking. For example, Destiny, a young Nigerian woman, took a job in Spain ostensibly to be a housekeeper after other Nigerian women returned home from Spain to show off their earnings. She explained that those who returned "told us they had to have sex sometimes . . . we are not stupid, but I did not know I would be beaten

1

and raped and have to have sex every night of the week" (Vasileyva 2019). Nigeria has become a major source country for sex-trafficking victims enslaved in Europe. Though authorities in Italy are well aware that many Nigerian women and girls are sex-trafficking victims, the authorities are often unable to compel victims to cooperate. Many Nigerian sex-trafficking victims are subject to a religious ritual performed before they depart, linking their obedience to traffickers to their religious beliefs and ultimately the safety and honor of their families back home. Fear of retaliation, death, poverty, and returning home all act as barriers to obtaining cooperation with authorities (Iacono 2014).

As scholars of human rights, writing this book has challenged the foundation of our understanding of the status of rights, especially women's rights, in the world. How can it be that, in our time, women and girls are beaten, raped, and sold like property, often by their own families, under the guise of marriage? This is not where we were supposed to be twenty-plus years into a new millennium.

Following World War II, the international community, led by the Allied powers, developed an impressive edifice of international human rights law, designed to avoid or at least mitigate the horrors of that era (Lauren 1998). The International Covenant on Civil and Political Rights, signed and ratified by 171 (of 195) countries, guarantees freedom from slavery (Article 8), the right to freedom of movement (Article 12), and equality before the law (Article 14). The Convention on the Elimination of All Forms of Discrimination Against Women (CEDAW) is notable for its unusually high rate of ratification by the international community (189 countries). The CEDAW provides for equality between the sexes in education (Article 10), in employment (Article 11), and in participation in voting and government (Article 7). This burst in the development of international human rights law has been used to explain states' commitment to the newest global anti-trafficking treaty, the UN Protocol to Prevent, Suppress and Punish Trafficking in Persons, Especially Women and Children (hereafter the UN Anti-Trafficking Protocol) (Charnysh, Lloyd, and Simmons 2015).

Throughout the early postwar period, the Allied powers pushed the global human rights agenda but a series of factors, including racism within the victorious nations, colonial oppression, and superpower conflict derailed their commitment (Tsutsui and Wotipka 2004). Motivated by their newfound independence, economically developing countries became the new champions of the global human rights movement, until their own human rights practices became the target of the movement. It was not until the 1970s, when both developed and developing states turned away or became opponents of the global human rights regime, that a global human rights movement composed of nongovernmental organizations (NGOs) and civil society actors agitated to give these treaties life and meaning. Between 1975 and 1998, 305 human rights

NGOs were established, compared with just 77 between 1945 and 1975 (Tsutsui and Wotipka 2004). These organizations all promoted various human rights issues, including women's rights, racial equality, and labor rights, among others (Keck and Sikkink 1998; Risse, Ropp, and Sikkink 1999).

Throughout the 1970s and into the 1990s, a splintered women's rights movement started to coalesce. In the early days of the modern women's rights movement, various groups around the world agitated to address very narrowly construed rights violations: female genital mutilation in Africa, sex tourism in Southeast Asia, rape and domestic violence in the United States and Western Europe (Keck and Sikkink 1998, 174). Efforts to reframe these narrow campaigns under a broader banner—violence against women—developed slowly over a series of UN Women's Conferences. In 1981, at the first feminist Encounter for Latin America and the Caribbean, participants proposed a day to commemorate violence against women (Keck and Sikkink 1998, 177). And in 1983 a conference on female slavery/trafficking was held in Rotterdam, with participants from twenty-four countries. As often happens when the issue of trafficking is raised, conflicts emerged over how to address prostitution: should they fight to abolish it, or should they encourage governments to regulate it in order to better protect the health and well-being of sex workers (Keck and Sikkink 1998)?

These conflicts over how to address the rights of sex workers and assist trafficking victims have long generated powerful, emotional responses. Indeed, one of our goals is to reframe the narrative around sex trafficking free of the religious undertones or "moral panic" that often lurk around the edges of this topic (Kempadoo 2012, xii). The early history of the abolitionist/anti-trafficking movement is embedded with racism and religious zealotry: the first global anti-trafficking treaty was titled the International Agreement for the Suppression of the "White Slave Traffic" (1904). Its purpose was to criminalize the trade in white women and girls for "immoral acts." Its successor, negotiated in 1910, similarly focused on protecting white women and girls from trafficking through "fraud, violence, threats, abuse of authority, or any other method of compulsion, [which] procured, enticed or led away a woman or girl for immoral purposes" (Gallagher 2010, 14). Curiously lacking was an attempt to criminalize such acts when perpetuated against women of other races (Gallagher 2010).

These efforts to preserve the virtue of white women and girls were advanced by elite Western women, who also campaigned for the elimination of prostitution. Their efforts dovetailed with radical feminists involved in the fight to abolish trafficking and modern slavery and prostitution among the many institutions that did violence to women's liberation (Kempadoo 2012). More recently, the elimination of sex trafficking and prostitution has created a unique alliance between liberal and radical feminists on the one hand and neoconservative governments and Christian fundamentalists on the other (Kempadoo 2012).

Following aggressive efforts by women agitating for the rights of the Korean comfort women enslaved by the Japanese military, and the many females advocating to end violence against women across Latin America, the concept of preventing violence against women became inextricably bound up with women's human rights. The UN Conference for Women's Rights in Vienna (1992) served as a focal point for the disparate women's groups around the world working to transform the framing of their movement, from preventing discrimination against women to preventing violence against women (Keck and Sikkink 1998, 180). The movement aspired to transform the world's understanding about human rights: from thinking narrowly about issues plaguing women at the local level to networking with transnational groups to finding the common thread that could be used to advance the cause of women's rights in the world. It was at the Fourth World Conference on Women in Beijing (1995) that Hillary Clinton, then First Lady of the United States, argued that "women's rights are human rights, and human rights are women's rights."[2] Though Clinton's idea that women's rights and human rights are one and the same was not new, it came at an important moment in the push for women's rights. We invoke this moment because we find that where women's rights are protected, sex trafficking is less prevalent, that is, when women's basic human rights are protected they are less likely to be victimized by traffickers. In some instances, women are their own saviors, generating progressive anti-trafficking legislation that serves their interests far better than what their male contemporaries can conceive.

Our work sheds light on the factors that make some women and girls more susceptible to traffickers than others and highlights representative stories of victims to give readers a sense about how victimization unfolds. Across the globe, approximately 99 percent of the sex-trafficking victims accessing relief services, including healthcare, shelter, and protection from their traffickers, are female (Walk Free Foundation 2017, 22). Yet women and girls are not merely passive victims of male traffickers; in many parts of the world women and girls *are* the traffickers, responsible for recruiting and deceiving others.[3] A critical paradox we confront is the outsized role that women play in perpetuating global sex trafficking. However, women are not just involved in the crime of trafficking as victims and perpetrators. Women, who often are former victims themselves, frequently run victim-service organizations. And female legislators have emerged as critical actors in developing anti-trafficking legislation at national and subnational levels around the world. Their efforts have helped to stem the tide of turning the focus on anti-trafficking legislation that prioritizes the prosecution of traffickers at the expense of victims' human rights. We focus on the experiences of women because we argue that understanding women's roles in their respective societies is critical in explaining all aspects of sex trafficking. We also highlight patterns of victimization against members of the trans community who self-identify as women, and in some cases members of the LGBTQ+ community because these groups have been largely missing from studies of sex trafficking. Understanding how prevailing systems of social dominance serve to subjugate particular populations of women and girls helps us to identify victims, while examining women's representation in government helps explain whether trafficking legislation primarily protects victims or sacrifices their rights in the name of securing trafficker convictions.

Scholars have argued that "human trafficking is more than sex trafficking and prostitution" and indeed in chapter 2 we survey existing data to show that today other forms of trafficking may be more prevalent than sex trafficking (Alvarez and Alessi 2012). However, all available data shows that sex-trafficking victims are overwhelmingly female, necessitating, in our opinion, a focus on the experiences of women.

The Argument in Brief

Any comprehensive analysis of global sex trafficking must be framed with an understanding of the embedded hierarchy, which has the effect of objectifying and commodifying the bodies of women and girls. That is, both the status of women culturally and politically must be assessed to understand how or when states attempt to combat human trafficking. Sex trafficking and sex slavery are crimes that disproportionately rob women and girls of their dignity, autonomy, and basic human rights. There is no corner of the globe untouched by this crime. Though our global analysis shows cross-national variation in the identity of those trafficked for sex, we find that from Russia to Brazil, from Nigeria to Thailand there are consistent patterns associated with sex trafficking. These patterns must be better understood if the international community and national governments are to curb trafficking and protect the rights of sex-trafficking victims.

This book addresses two primary questions through the lens of economic, sociocultural, and political factors. First is who is likely to become a sex-trafficking victim and what factors help to predict who may be more or less vulnerable to becoming a sex-trafficking victim? In countries where women's human rights are not protected we expect to see higher rates of sex trafficking than in countries where women's human rights are protected. Second, in each case study we ask whether national anti-trafficking legislation prioritizes prosecuting traffickers through a criminal justice approach over protecting victims through a rights-based approach. The more empowered women are in the legislative process (as both legislators and NGO advocates), the more likely we are to see a victim-centered approach rather than a criminal justice approach to trafficking.

We draw on Crawford (2017) to argue that understanding the nexus of gender with systems of social dominance are critical for explaining the genesis of sex trafficking. For example, where dominant religious beliefs create a rigid gender hierarchy, sex trafficking is more prevalent. In our case studies we focus on the ways gender intersects with these other systems of dominance, recognizing that although the systems themselves vary from country to country, many of the same features are apparent. We use quantitative analysis to show that where women's economic rights are protected, a lower probability of sex trafficking results. In short, understanding how women are treated overall is the key to understanding patterns of sex trafficking.

In response to the most recent global anti-trafficking treaty, 158 countries have passed national legislation to combat trafficking (UNODC 2016, 48). We ask how well these laws work to ensure that victims' basic human rights are protected. Even in countries that appear to have adopted a progressive, victim-centered approach to trafficking, many times victims' human rights are nevertheless severely violated. We build on an emerging area of research to show that victims' human rights are better protected where women are engaged and empowered in the legislative process (DiRienzo 2018; Bartilow 2012; Cho, Dreher, and Neumayer 2014; Schonhofer 2017; Wooditch 2012). When appropriate, we highlight the role that women play in the development of national and subnational anti-trafficking legislation. In some narrow instances women legislators are serving as agenda-setters through proposing and advocating for victim-centered legislation. But women who work for NGOs have also emerged as key actors advocating or opposing anti-trafficking legislation. These agenda-setters operate in both internal and external ways to move legislatures toward victim-centered and human rights–oriented policies.

Key Terms: Trafficking, Slavery, and Smuggling

Article 3 of the UN Anti-Trafficking Protocol defines trafficking as:

(a) "Trafficking in persons" shall mean the recruitment, transportation, transfer, harbouring, or receipt of persons, by means of the threat or use of force or other forms of coercion, of abduction, of fraud, of deception, of the abuse of power or of a position of vulnerability or of the giving or receiving of payments or benefits to achieve the consent of a person having control over another person, for the purpose of exploitation. Exploitation shall include, at a minimum, the exploitation of the prostitution of others or other forms of sexual exploitation, forced labour or services, slavery or practices similar to slavery, servitude or the removal of organs;

(b) The consent of a victim of trafficking in persons to the intended exploitation set forth in subparagraph (a) of this article shall be irrelevant where any of the means set forth in subparagraph (a) have been used;

(c) The recruitment, transportation, transfer, harbouring or receipt of a child for the purpose of exploitation shall be considered "trafficking in persons" even if this does not involve any of the means set forth in subparagraph (a) of this article.

According to this definition, neither the absence of victim consent nor transportation across national borders are essential features of sex trafficking. Providing one's consent implies that one understands the terms of the agreement—but when traffickers use fraud and deception to enslave victims into forced prostitution, the concept of consent is rendered meaningless. Likewise, state boundaries need not be crossed to accomplish trafficking, since the wrong of trafficking is not a question of the violation of state sovereignty through the disregard of a border. Rather, the wrong is expressly a violation of the rights of the individual who is trafficked.

Like the definition of trafficking adopted in the UN Anti-Trafficking Protocol, the US State Department's definition (per the US Trafficking Victim Protection Act) emphasizes fraud in the process of trafficking. The State Department's definition has become important because the US government mandates that the State Department produce an annual Trafficking in Persons (TIP) report evaluating how well each country in the world is preventing trafficking, protecting victims, and punishing traffickers. The State Department defines trafficking as "the recruitment, harboring, transportation, provision, or obtaining of a person for labor or service, through the use of force, fraud, or coercion for the purpose of subjection to involuntary servitude, peonage, debt bondage, or slavery" (US State Department 2018). Traffickers promise young women and girls legitimate jobs and employment contracts that show they will be employed in a variety of service jobs such as housekeepers, childcare workers, dancers, hostesses, or waitresses. Upon arrival at their destination, victims' identity documents are frequently taken away and victims are presented with large invoices for the services of transportation and support. The victims find themselves in debt to their traffickers, with no access to their immigration papers and enslaved into forced prostitution to try to get out of the situation. This is the quintessential scenario that the US Trafficking Victim Protection Act and the UN Anti-Trafficking Protocol address by emphasizing the use of fraud in the trafficking process. Such victims fall neatly into the category of sex-trafficking victim.

However, migration and employment patterns, situations, pressures, and decisions are complex systems. There are many scenarios wherein the State

Department's definition of trafficking obscures important factors that also contribute to the overall problem of sex trafficking. In many of the cases we describe, the women and girls who become sex-trafficking victims are not duped or defrauded entirely. In some cases girls are sold to bride traffickers by their families. While such decisions seem appalling from afar, they are difficult ones and may involve weighing the needs of the rest of the family against the sacrifice of a daughter. While these families often have a relatively good idea about the fate that awaits their daughters, they are constrained by circumstance rather than by deception or fraud. Often the dearth of economic opportunities, especially for women and girls in the Global South, means they are willing to take what they know to be risky jobs or perilous situations to gamble on a better future. Destiny, the young Nigerian woman described earlier, is a good example. Although she knew that once she arrived in Spain part of her job would involve sex work, she did not expect the conditions surrounding that work or the complete lack of agency or self-determination that it involved. Once in Spain she had no way to say "No" and no way to easily get out of the situation.

It is this lack of agency that has led many scholars to equate trafficking and modern slavery (Bales 2004; Cameron and Newman 2008; Scarpa 2008; Parrot and Cummings 2008; Bales and Soodalter 2009; Landman 2018). Whereas the era of the transatlantic slave trade involved formal legal ownership of slaves, modern slaves are not legally owned by their slaveholders (Bales 2004). But the experiences of sex-trafficking victims today bear many of the hallmarks of the transatlantic slave trade, including violence, forced labor without pay, and physical confinement, leaving many scholars to use the terms "slave" and "trafficking victim" interchangeably.

We use numerous terms to describe sex-trafficking victims, including "sex slave." When we write about "victims" we are writing about people who cannot say no, who lack autonomy. They are sex slaves. Landman (2018) highlights the nexus between loss of agency and uncompensated labor as the defining features of slavery, emphasizing how the international law of human rights tends to situate slavery within a criminal justice rather than an economic, social, and cultural frame (147–48). Landman's analysis draws on the Bellagio-Harvard Guidelines on the Legal Parameters of Slavery (2012), which emphasize the defining features of modern slavery as "control extended over a person tantamount to possession . . . control that will significantly deprive a person of his or her individual liberty for a period of time which is, for that person, indeterminate" (Members of the Research Network on the Legal Parameters of Slavery 2012, guideline 3). This emphasis on the extended and indefinite loss of agency also features prominently in the ways victims of slavery describe their experiences (Nicholson, Dang, and Trodd 2018).

In contrast, voluntary commercial sex workers have at least some agency in their labor conditions: they can make some decisions about services and pay and may even be able walk away from the industry if the conditions do not serve their interests. As Enloe (2014) explains, the critical difference between a sex-trafficking victim/slave and a sex worker is that sex-trafficking victims lack autonomy and have had their dignity "violated by those that have devised [their] enslavement and by those who gain satisfaction or profits from [their] enslavement" (90). Trafficking is often conflated with smuggling. Whereas trafficking is a process including recruitment, transportation, and ultimately forced labor, smuggling is more narrowly understood as the process whereby migrants hire smugglers to transport them across a border. In some cases those who initially advertise themselves as smugglers are in reality traffickers, enslaving the people who hired them.

We conceive of trafficking as a process. Sometimes that process involves fraud and deception surrounding the conditions of an employment contract. Women and girls are promised legitimate jobs for adequate pay, but when they arrive at a destination, whether within their own country or abroad, they find that they have become slaves. Traffickers often lock victims in hotels or apartments while threating the safety of their families or threatening them with arrest for immigration violations or prostitution (or both) to ensure their cooperation. Even if they are not physically forced to work as sex slaves, many find that they are saddled with outrageous debts to their captors for costs associated with their travel and living expenses. In other instances their families may have taken out a loan with grossly inflated interest to be paid back through the forced labor of the woman or girl. In either of these last two scenarios, victims are not only sex-trafficking victims but also victims of debt bondage. These large and growing debts can create a psychological constraint, making victims feel like they must continue to work. In this sense there is little difference between trafficking for labor and trafficking for sex: in both cases victims are recruited, transported, relieved of their identity documents, and forced to work through a variety of coercive practices, often going unpaid but facing growing and more exorbitant debts that they cannot realistically pay off.

Methodology and Plan of the Book

In chapter 1 we develop our approach to analyzing sex trafficking, focusing on how the deprivation of women's economic rights along with other intersectional aspects of their identity combine to make them vulnerable to traffickers. We contrast our approach to trafficking with others in the political science and international relations literature to draw attention to the ways patterns of gendered vulnerabilities contribute to sex-trafficking outcomes around the world. To give readers a better sense about global trafficking trends, chapter 2 highlights the most current data available from both the International Labour Organization (ILO) and the United Nations Office on Drugs and Crime (UNODC). We also use quantitative analysis to provide empirical support to show that in places where women's economic rights are not protected, women are at greater risk of becoming sex-trafficking victims. Our empirical analysis tests the roots of trafficking across all countries in the world using time-series data from the Human Trafficking Indicators (HTI) data set, discussed in depth later, covering the years 2000–2011. The HTI data set ends in 2011 and, as we show in subsequent chapters, is essential in getting at the questions that we wanted to answer primarily because it distinguishes between trafficking for sex and other types of labor.

Our quantitative analysis suggests that poor, populous countries with weak protections for women's economic rights are particularly susceptible to becoming major source countries for sex-trafficking victims. Our case studies in India, Thailand, Russia, Nigeria, and Brazil, to varying degrees, are each indicative of these patterns: large, poor populations where protections for women's economic rights are weak. We sought geographic diversity to ensure there is no locally specific and unique variable to explain our findings. We also selected cases to show variation on national approaches to trafficking. In some instances, national approaches to combating trafficking are oriented more toward criminal justice (Thailand, Nigeria, and Brazil), while India is better than the rest at protecting and promoting victims' human rights. In yet other instances, growing authoritarianism has hobbled national efforts to either support victims or prosecute traffickers (Russia). We further explicate our case selection and overall methodology in chapter 2.

In chapter 3 we examine the unfortunate but robust bride-trafficking routes across India. We highlight the ways a rigid caste system intersects with systems of gender dominance to make Dalit women and girls especially vulnerable to sex traffickers. We also show that India suffers from an enforcement problem, with relatively strong anti-trafficking legislation that goes unenforced in practice.

Chapter 4 is an examination of sex-trafficking patterns in Thailand, which has often been called the "hub" of sex tourism and trafficking in the world. The chapter highlights the ways Buddhist ideology and a history of government discrimination against ethnic Hill Tribe minorities has rendered a particular segment of the Thai population vulnerable to becoming sex-trafficking victims.

In chapter 5 we study how sex trafficking in Russia is a way to show that Vladimir Putin's strategic deployment of hypermasculine, anti-woman ideology has been used to expand his power and hobble the efforts of civil society to support trafficking victims. These forces have been particularly brutal for trafficking victims from surrounding countries, who are acutely vulnerable to sex traffickers in the wake of collapsing social welfare systems.

Chapter 6 focuses on Nigeria, showing that impoverished rural women and those living in refugee and internally displaced person camps are especially vulnerable to sex traffickers.

In chapter 7 we evaluate sex-trafficking patterns in Brazil. We find that dramatic income inequality and poor legal protections for Brazil's large Afro-Brazilian population have made them disproportionately vulnerable to sex traffickers.

Our cases cover the period beginning in the year 2000 and reach into 2020. We conducted interviews with victim-service organizations in each of the cases and secured access to previously unpublished data on some aspects of the identities of trafficking victims collected by those organizations. We combine this data with data published by the governments themselves, the US State Department, and other NGOs and intergovernmental organizations to get a sense of how trafficking works in these countries. In each case we highlight two victim-support organizations to show the innovative ways that local organizations around the world are indeed supporting victims' human rights by providing trauma-informed care.

Notes

1. A derogatory Hindi term meaning "purchased."
2. The full text of this speech is available at: http://www.americanrhetoric.com /speeches/hillaryclintonbeijingspeech.htm. Last accessed July 2018.
3. This account of women as both victims and perpetrators of sex trafficking bears resemblance to Sjoberg's (2009) analysis of female terrorists.

ONE

A Gendered Approach to Sex Trafficking

Our study of sex trafficking focuses on the intersections of gender, power, and politics. Feminist scholars of international relations have long argued that using a gendered lens to view global politics can yield important insights about power and hierarchy (Shepard 2015; Runyan and Peterson 2013; Tickner 2001; Sjoberg 2009, 2011; True 2012). Lenses essentially fix the way that we make sense of large amounts of information. We use subconscious lenses to guide what information we pay attention to and what information is dismissed (Runyan and Peterson 2013, 41). In the study of international relations, feminist scholars have shown that a traditional state-centric lens focusing on state power and survival can overlook important explanations for events. In explaining the durability of postconflict policies, MacKenzie (2012) demonstrates that when the experiences of female soldiers in Sierra Leone were ignored, the ensuing policies duplicated the exploitative policies that preceded the conflict. Similarly, while most view the stereotypical terrorist as hypermasculine and religiously inspired, this perspective on terrorists has consistently led scholars to neglect the long history of female terrorists (Gentry and Sjoberg 2015).

Two camps have emerged within feminist studies in international relations. The first shows the many ways that the gendered nature of the political-economic authority structure that extends from "the household to the global realm" can be used to explain a variety of outcomes (True 2012, 30). This branch, the feminist global political economy, or FGPE, focuses on the social, cultural, and economic bases of power that generate material inequality. For True (2012) this necessitates that we examine how power can be wielded even in the absence of threats of force or violence. For example, she explains that a woman with skills that make her valuable in the home as a wife and mother but render her dependent on a male breadwinner make her subject to both psychological and economic violence, even in the absence of physical violence. If her skills and abilities are not valued in the public sphere, she may find herself trapped in her role in the home. Her dependence on a husband and the knowledge that she has few options create, in True's opinion, other forms of violence against her (30).

The second feminist approach in international relations is grounded in security studies. Feminist security studies, or FSS, bring attention to all aspects of war and conflict that speak not just to the security of states but also to "the security of individuals and groups; it is about violence in all forms, including structural violence and violence we are committing against our natural environment" (Tickner 2011, 577). For example, D'Costa (2006) addresses the effects of war on marginalized populations in Bangladesh, detailing the forgotten experiences of victims of mass rape. We reconcile these approaches with reference to Stern (2017) and Elias and Rai (2015)—though some scholars who write within these fields see them as opposed and distinct, we do not. As the concept of violence that had previously been the domain of the FSS scholars has expanded into FGPE, we think that these approaches complement rather than rival one another.

The study of sex trafficking is, at its core, primarily a study of various forms of violence against women and girls. Economic violence can present at many stages of the trafficking process: in the form of material inequality that renders women and girls willing to undertake risky job prospects, and in the form of debt bondage that enslaves women with ever-growing debts to traffickers for grossly inflated travel costs and living expenses. Trafficking entails psychological violence against its victims when the safety of their families is used to secure their obedience. The realization that one has become, in no uncertain terms, a modern slave cuts to the heart of one's sense of identity and psychological well-being. Even after being freed from captivity, the prospect of revictimization through the process of working with police to prosecute traffickers or the uncertainty of the reception that may await the victim upon her return home can lead to further psychological harm. Finally, the various forms of physical violence that sex-trafficking victims experience—rape, confinement, commodification of the body, and routine beatings—all merge together to make the study of trafficking a study of the various forms of violence against women and girls.

The gendered lens used by feminist scholars of IR to explain outcomes reveal underlying power dynamics that can be applied to our global study of sex trafficking. Enloe (2014, 33–34) suggests,

Too often gender incurious commenters attribute women's roles in international affairs to tradition, cultural preferences, and timeless norms, as if each of these existed outside the realms where power is wielded, as if they were beyond the reach of decisions and efforts to enforce those decisions. What sacrifices a woman as a mother should make, what priorities a woman as a wife should embrace, what sexualized approaches in public a woman should consider innocent or flattering, what victim identity a refugee woman should adopt, what boundaries in friendships with other women a woman should police, what dutiful daughter model a girl should admire—in reality, all of these are shaped by the exercise of power by people who believe that their own local and international interests depend on women and girls internalizing these particular feminized expectations. If women internalize these expectations, they will not see the politics behind them. Political commentators who do not question these internalizations will accept the camouflaged operations of power as if there were not power at work at all. That is dangerous.

Drawing on a considerable body of trafficking scholarship that spans the fields of political science, social work, feminist and gender studies, sociology, criminology, and economics, we argue that an analysis of global sex trafficking must acknowledge the collective wisdom of feminist scholars because doing so will reveal patterns of embedded hierarchy that have the effect of objectifying and commodifying the bodies, indeed the very existence, of women and girls. Feminist scholars distinguish between sex and gender, with sex generally referring to the anatomical difference between men's and women's bodies (Runyan and Peterson 2013, 3). If sex connotes the biological or anatomical difference, gender is the much more complex process associated with learned behaviors and idealized expectations connected to one's sex. As Carver's (1996) book title so aptly says it, *Gender Is Not a Synonym for Women*. The important point is that gender is a social construction, with norms and expectations set by power holders, that has important consequences for the powerless.

The social construction of gender varies from society to society. We draw on Crawford (2017), who observes that "gender intersects with other systems of social dominance, such as caste, tribe, and ethnicity to produce populations of vulnerable women and girls" (111). Crawford argues that in order to understand who is vulnerable to becoming a trafficking victim it is critical to ask "about the gender context of trafficking in a particular society: What are the cultural beliefs about women? How are their opportunities curtailed? How are they discriminated against or oppressed? In addition, we should ask about the intersections of other systems of power and oppression in that society, whether they are caste, tribe, immigrant status, racial group, or minority ethnic identity" (111). A feminist analysis of trafficking necessities that we think about how multiple elements of a person's identity can contribute to their vulnerability.

For example, is a female orphan in rural Siberia in southern Russia more likely to fall victim to a sex trafficker than a Hispanic college student in Los Angeles? Is an ethnic Ibo woman in Abuja, Nigeria, more likely to be recruited by sex traffickers than a teenager from a wealthy family in Bangkok? What is it about the distinct elements of individual identities and the cultural norms and practices with which they intersect that make some populations more vulnerable to traffickers than others? Interrogating women's experiences within their societies can help solve this puzzle. Importantly, our work looks across various societies and cultures to identify commonalities and reveal a more complex understanding of the causes of sex trafficking.

Existing research on the causes of trafficking show that poor treatment of women in society does not serve as a robust push factor for victims of trafficking (Cho 2015). That is, just because women are mistreated in their society does not mean that they are more vulnerable to traffickers. The treatment of women interacts in a complex way with the large variety of trafficking push factors. For instance, in some conservative societies women are expected to remain home and have children, paradoxically making them less likely to fall victim to traffickers (Cho 2015). Yet some of the existing work on the cause of trafficking relies on trafficking data from the UNODC, which blends together statistics on trafficking for sex and trafficking for labor. This disregard for the type of trafficking may obscure the importance of gender in explaining sex-trafficking patterns.

We make two interconnected arguments in this work about the identity of trafficking victims and the provision of victim support. First, understanding how women and girls are treated in their country of residence helps to explain the prevalence of sex trafficking. *In countries where women's human rights are not protected, we expect to see higher rates of sex trafficking occur than in countries where these rights are protected.* Second, the formal political power of women shapes the approach to combating human trafficking. Thus, *the more integrated women are in the legislative process, as both legislators and NGO advocates, the more likely we expect to see a rights-based approach rather than a criminal justice approach to trafficking.* Understanding the level of equality for women in both a cultural and political power context is critical for understanding how states attempt to respond to human trafficking.

Women's Rights and the Prevalence of Sex Trafficking

Where women's rights are dismissed or repressed due to prevailing religious or other cultural practices, such social patterns exacerbate trafficking outcomes and lead to higher rates of sex trafficking compared to places where their rights are respected by law. Respect for women's rights is but one of many factors that contribute to trafficking outcomes. Trafficking is the result of a complex set of social, cultural, and economic factors that differ from case to case. We are particularly interested in understanding how the societal diminution of women and girls intersects with other factors to exacerbate trafficking outcomes. We draw on Bales (2004), who argues that modern slaves are those considered "disposable" by their own societies. Though his work applies more broadly to people enslaved across a variety of exploitative industries, this insight holds when considering the pre-exploitation status of sex-trafficking victims. To identify who may fall into this category we examine systems of social dominance and exclusion. It is our contention that simply testing the significance of the variables "gender" or "religion" miss important complexities that link vulnerability with other aspects of identity. Our case studies allow us to critically examine the social construction of gender to understand how it intersects with other elements of identity to make certain segments of a population more likely to become sex-trafficking victims. We look at caste status, immigration status, religion, age, and race to understand how these elements of identity, in conjunction with gender, make certain people vulnerable to sex traffickers. By examining how these other variables intersect with gender and systems of social dominance in each country, we can begin to develop a method for understanding who is more likely to become a sex-trafficking victim and therefore develop effective amelioration approaches.

But if patterns of sex trafficking can be explained, at least in part, by considering the degree to which cultural practices relegate the lives of women and girls to a second-class status, as we contend here, then such norms, or a move away from those norms, should also be written into laws and policies designed to advance women's rights. To operationalize our first argument we examine the nexus between legal protections for marginalized populations and the prevalence of sex trafficking among them. Where women's human rights are not protected in law and practice, we expect to find higher rates of sex trafficking.

Yet human rights can mean many different things. In this work we separate economic rights from political rights. Economic rights include the right to earn a fair wage for labor as well as the right to own property, to maintain that ownership regardless of marital status, to have equitable distribution upon dissolution of marriage, and to enjoy the rights of inheritance. Political rights include basic rights like the right to vote but also participatory rights like the right to run for office. We expect that where women's economic rights are not protected, there will be a higher probability that they will be trafficked for sex compared to places where women's economic rights are protected. Where women face discrimination in hiring, pay, and promotion, and may be subject to sexual harassment in the workplace, we surmise that they will be more likely to refrain from entering the formal labor market. Such discrimination will also render these women less financially independent, making them more susceptible to traffickers.

Beyond the discrimination women face in the workplace, which we think contributes to their vulnerability, we leverage a feminist frame across the case studies with a focus on examining how patriarchy and embedded gender hierarchies further exacerbate existing victim vulnerabilities. This allows us to examine the ways in which structural conditions malign women and girls, making them more vulnerable to being trafficked by manipulative traffickers but also, in many instances, by members of their own families. We also engage both the FSS and the FGPE literature to trace out the forms of violence women and girls experience throughout the trafficking process. At the intersection between FSS and FGPE is a focus on violence—violence that can be material, rendering women dependent on husbands due to poor economic prospects. It may also be families willing to sell daughters to traffickers to provide for the rest of the family. Or this violence can be physical—manifesting in the process of trafficking itself, with deprivation of liberty, demands for sex, and psychological abuse. Across our cases we highlight both the role of patriarchy, gender hierarchies, and various forms of violence that lead to and are bound up in the trafficking process.

This work builds on the considerable body of trafficking research that comes from many and varied disciplines, much of which links gender to trafficking. What we offer here, which we believe to be novel, is both the scope and methods employed. We use a mixed-methods strategy that begins with a quantitative analysis. Our quantitative consideration accounts for all countries in the world and provides support for the link between respect for women's economic rights and a lower probability that a country will be a source for trafficking victims. These findings are the foundation for our complementary case studies from around the world. Our qualitative case studies connect the quantitative results to the cultural conditions and other factors that intersect with gender to make some women and girls more susceptible to traffickers.

The Political Power of Women and Combating Trafficking

The second component of our analysis focuses on the genesis, approach, and impact of anti-trafficking legislation. Assessing the level of political rights afforded women, like the right to vote or run for office, is not sufficient when considering how, or even whether, countries choose to approach anti-trafficking legislation. Instead, the political power of women provides a more appropriate lens through which to assess the amelioration of trafficking efforts. We evaluate whether anti-trafficking legislation promotes or inhibits the human rights of sex-trafficking victims, which we assess through the lens of the political power of women.

Between the establishment of the Palermo Protocol in 2000 and 2016, approximately 158 governments adopted national anti-trafficking legislation (UNODC 2016, 48). Yet not all national approaches are equivalent, even when governments adopt the language contained in the Palermo Protocol. The differences are particularly apparent with respect to victim protection. We develop a new methodology for assessing whether a national approach to combating trafficking is more victim-centered or criminal justice–oriented because we are interested in understanding how well governments identify and protect sex-trafficking victims. Over time governments have had to make difficult choices using scarce resources to combat trafficking. Should they prioritize investigating, prosecuting, and convicting traffickers or, alternatively, should resources be devoted to funding victim shelters and providing post-trauma therapy and living or travel expenses?

At its core, the emphasis that a government ultimately chooses to adopt when it comes to the implementation of national anti-trafficking laws is severely constrained by a number of factors, including resources, population size, and prevailing respect for the rule of law. This work seeks to create space for the role of female legislators, female NGO workers, and trafficking survivors as critical players that can also contribute to the orientation and implementation of national anti-trafficking legislation.

The criminal justice approach to trafficking is one prong of the three-prong approach to combating trafficking contained in the Palermo Protocol. Preventing victimization and protecting and assisting victims constitute the other two prongs of the approach. Punishing traffickers is important for obtaining justice for victims and building trust within communities of victims. Roe-Sepowitz and Jabola-Carolus (2020) find that where there are no convictions of traffickers, victims are reluctant to come forward to aid authorities in the prosecution of traffickers. This makes a good deal of sense given that there may be inherent risks to the victim in cooperating with authorities; if authorities have no record of successfully convicting traffickers, then such cooperation may not be worth the risks to the victim. In this way authorities with a consistent track record of investigation, prosecution, and conviction of traffickers can more effectively build trust with survivors and increase the likelihood that future survivors will cooperate in the prosecution of their traffickers.

The criminal justice model is also important for deterring future traffickers. When traffickers see others convicted and sentenced, they may be less inclined to engage in trafficking themselves. In this way the criminal justice approach to trafficking is a critical piece in any comprehensive national approach in the fight against trafficking, as a record of convictions can serve as both a tool for building trust with victims and for deterring future traffickers. Across our case studies we look for three distinct indicators to determine whether a national approach is the prioritization of criminal justice. These indicators include sharply rising numbers of investigation, prosecution, and conviction rates of traffickers. Evidence for this approach can also come when governments direct resources to police rather than to victim-service organizations and shelters.

Alternatively, a government can choose to prioritize a rights-based approach to trafficking, which engenders prioritizing victim safety and rehabilitation over the prosecution of traffickers (see table 1.1).

A rights-based model is also important in any comprehensive national approach to combating trafficking. A rights-based model prioritizes the human rights and human dignity of trafficking victims by ensuring the provision of short-term residency permits, post-trauma therapy, medical care, and other types of assistance that can help victims heal. How victims are treated when authorities make initial contact is also important for understanding whether a government is emphasizing a rights-based model or a criminal justice model. We find that many laws adopt the language of victim protection but implementation of these provisions varies considerably both between countries and even within them. To overcome issues associated with uneven implementation of national laws we look for national-level data on the following to determine whether a government has primarily adopted a rights-based approach to combating trafficking.

First, following a series of interviews with police, NGOs, and local politicians in Portland, Oregon, for a different trafficking project, we learned from the Portland Police Division (PPD) that in 2009 a critical shift in the police approach to trafficking occurred that contributed to a new county-wide victim-centered approach.[1] The data from this dramatic shift informs our first indicator for a rights-based model in this project. Initially directed toward child trafficking, in 2009 the PPD decided that the Sex Crimes Unit, rather than the Vice Unit, should be called for any suspected instances of child trafficking. The law enforcement training that followed transformed the way that police approached both child and adult trafficking victims. As Ohlsen (2015) explains, "PPD publicly stated that children who were being trafficked were victims, not criminals" (7). This new approach constituted a change in the way that police interacted with suspected prostitutes of all ages. Rather than primarily pursuing a prosecution approach, police directed suspected victims to services and support. This shift in approach coincided with a dramatic decrease in the rate of prostitution arrests in the county—from more than 150 women arrested for prostitution in 2011 to fewer than 50 by 2013 (12).

As we learned in Portland, decreasing rates of prostitution convictions may be an indicator that authorities in general and police in particular have adopted a rights-based approach to sex trafficking. Police are often confronted with a decision about whether to make an arrest for prostitution whenever they come upon a potential sex-trafficking victim. Where we see prostitution arrests decreasing, we may have evidence that police are critically evaluating whether the people they encounter are trafficking victims rather than assuming that they are self-employed prostitutes. To be sure, many factors inform

Table 1.1. Human Rights–Based vs. Criminal Justice–Based Approach
to Trafficking

Human Rights–Based Approach	Criminal Justice–Based Approach
Decreasing rates of prostitution arrests and/or convictions	Increasing rates of trafficker prosecutions and/or convictions
Special trafficking visas provided to victims	Rising trafficker conviction rates
Consistent funding for victim shelters	Increasing funding for fighting trafficking

prostitution arrests rates, particularly at the national level. So we employ this metric as one of three potential indicators that authorities have adopted a rights-based model.

While many countries in the world have created special visas for trafficking victims, merely having a law on the books that prescribes that victims should be given temporary or permanent asylum is not by itself indicative of a rights-based approach to trafficking. If governments are providing this opportunity to victims, in practice victims should be successfully obtaining these visas. Conversely, if few special visas are issued, the law amounts to little more than cheap talk. Finally, funding patterns for victim services and support networks help speak directly to whether governments are truly concerned about assisting sex-trafficking victims. Where state and local government funding for victim-support agencies is nonexistent or so inconsistent as to cause disruptions in the provision of support to victims (shelter closings, program suspensions), the evidence runs counter to the human rights–based approach to trafficking.

For the sake of analytical clarity we employ these indicators to help us identify the hallmarks of rights-based and criminal justice–based models across cases, though in reality these two approaches do not usually operate in isolation from one another (Goodey 2004). For example, during the prosecution process, victims may be provided with housing, medical support, and short-term residency permits that are not conditional on cooperation with prosecutors. But, as other scholars have noted, there are tensions at work between these two approaches. Goodey (2004) shows that witness protection is particularly problematic, noting that in Italy witness protection programs for sex-trafficking victims are modeled after witness protection programs designed to protect organized crime informants (37). Yet there are important distinctions between organized crime informants and sex-trafficking victims—the former are criminal informants capable of providing authorities with key information that can be used to convict while the latter are, as Goodey describes them, "the commodity in the sex trafficking process" (37). Victims may be able to assist prosecutors, but they are unlikely to be able to provide sufficient information to ensure a conviction. Goodey concludes that we should question whether sex-trafficking victims should be compelled to testify against traffickers at all, given the dangers and the low probability of conviction. In some of our cases we find that cooperating with authorities is a precondition for obtaining a short-term visa for victims and, given these dynamics, there is an inherent tension between simultaneously protecting the human rights of victims and prosecuting traffickers by compelling the testimony of victims.

Additionally, victim identification, even among well-intentioned police, can be complicated. Nichols and Heil (2015) show that in the absence of specialized training, police may simply not realize that they have encountered a trafficking victim. In their study of trafficking in the US Midwest, they find that police may presume that trafficking victims are exclusively foreigners, thereby excluding domestic victims (10–11). Domestic victims can make police efforts to identify victims more complicated since they use hidden venues and move victims between states frequently.

These examples highlight some of the tensions associated with pursuing both a criminal justice and a rights-based model to combat trafficking simultaneously. Yet across the cases that we examine in this work, we find that many governments are pursuing both to greater or lesser degrees. We use the metrics in table 1.1 to help clarify where the greater emphasis lies in the national approach.

We also follow emerging literature that recognizes that female representation in the legislative process matters for compliance with international laws combating trafficking and offering victim protection (Bartilow 2012; Schonhofer 2017; Wooditch 2012). In his study of state compliance with the UN Anti-Trafficking Protocol, Bartilow (2012) shows that as the percentage of female representation in the legislature and cabinet increase, so too does the rate of state compliance with the international laws combating trafficking. His work also shows that where there is a greater proportion of male legislators, if women's parliamentary caucuses are involved in the legislative deliberations and those caucuses are influenced by the women's movement, then again, compliance with international anti-trafficking laws goes up. As Bartilow so aptly explains, "Since men tend to be consumers of the commercial sex trade[,] some feminist scholars argue that male legislators, relative to their female counterparts, are less likely to be sensitive to issues that concern women, which proxies their attitudes towards anti-trafficking legislation. And as a result, male legislators are less likely to support legislation that would ensure compliance with international rules against human trafficking" (6). Bartilow's findings are also consistent with Cho, Dreher, and Neumayer (2014), who show that compliance with the UN Anti-Trafficking Protocol is higher among countries with low levels of corruption and those that respect and protect the rights of women.

In her examination of factors contributing to policies that support trafficking victim protection among the thirty-three member states of the OECD, Schonhofer (2017) also shows that the share of female parliamentarians and left-wing/social democratic parties in a cabinet is positively associated with better protection of trafficking victims. Taken together, these works suggest that the degree to which women are integrated into the legislative process plays a critical role in explaining whether anti-trafficking policies on the ground will be more oriented toward criminal justice or human rights.

An important microfoundation to consider for our analysis concerns the conditions that make women, rather than men, more likely to advocate for victim-centered legislation. What might make women more willing to advocate for policies that provide for temporary housing, economic support, and rehabilitation services for victims? In our global analysis of sex trafficking we have found a few clues as to why women seem more apt to promote victim-centered legislation. In the field of political science, assumptions are made about politicians rationally seeking reelection (G. Black 1972). Those who hold office engage in activities that help them remain in office—which can mean advocating for legislation that is popular among a majority of their constituents or pandering to special interests in the hopes of attracting campaign donations. In the subfield of international relations, scholars generally make assumptions about governments seeking to maximize their power at the expense of others (Mearsheimer 2014). This sort of analysis can also be applied to better understanding why we expect women to advocate for victim-centered legislation.

We begin with the empirical observation that sex-trafficking victims are disproportionately female. In chapter 2 we review what we consider to be the most reliable global data, which show that approximately 99 percent of those victims accessing services as sex-trafficking victims are female (Walk Free Foundation 2017, 22). Children make up 21 percent of the total population of sex-trafficking victims (Walk Free Foundation 2017, 23). We reason that when women have an opportunity to impact the contours of anti-trafficking legislation, they have an interest in providing relief to victims. As a general rule we think it is not too much of a stretch to consider the female legislator considering sponsoring sex-trafficking legislation or the female NGO worker advocating for such legislation: both are rational actors with a set of interests that connect to their identity as female. Compared to the relatively low rate of male victims accessing relief services around the globe, we believe this means that women are looking out for their own interests and that their preferences will be translated into policy that is victim-centered.

Additionally, for many sex-trafficking victims who escape and are rehabilitated, the process can be powerful—transforming their life's purpose into helping other victims. Indeed, these are the women we encountered in our

Table 1.2. Summary of Arguments

Argument 1 (Cultural Power of Women): *In countries where women's human rights are not protected, higher rates of sex trafficking will occur, compared to countries where women's human rights are protected.*

Argument 2 (Legislative Power of Women): *The more integrated women are in the legislative process, as both legislators and as NGO advocates, the more likely a rights-based approach rather than a criminal justice approach will be taken toward trafficking.*

interviews with anti-trafficking organizations. In chapter 2 we explore the tension between policies that protect victims and policies that lead to the conviction of traffickers. In short, policymakers are confronted with a stark choice: in order to pass legislation that prioritizes the conviction and punishment of traffickers, they need the assistance of victims. But traffickers frequently threaten victims and their families, inhibiting the likelihood that victims will cooperate with authorities. Laws designed to punish traffickers must therefore coerce cooperation from reluctant victims. In other words, anti-trafficking legislation is generally either victim-centered or prosecution-oriented. We hypothesize that when women are more deeply integrated in the process of legislating (as both legislators and community advocates), the orientation of the resulting legislation will be more attuned to victim rights.

A Survey of the Causes of Trafficking from Existing Literature

Sex trafficking has gained enormous attention in the media and the popular press. Yet it has been subject to considerably less academic scrutiny—likely due to many of the empirical challenges associated with obtaining reliable statistics. Though political scientists, criminologists, and economists have made progress in advancing our understanding of the causes and consequences of trafficking, a considerable portion of this work does not distinguish between trafficking for sex, labor, organ harvesting, or other purposes.

Trafficking literature, like migration literature generally, distinguishes push factors (which "push" people out of their homes) from pull factors (which "pull" people into a different circumstances). These push-and-pull factors can help explain why potential victims are motivated to leave their homes, and may also help to explain why trafficking organizations choose to target some locales over others. Trafficking victims resemble migrants in the sense that factors that encourage out-migration also tend to encourage trafficking or allow trafficking to flourish (Cho 2015; Rao and Presenti 2012; Akee et al. 2010). Poverty in a source country is a push factor, as it encourages people to leave in search of better opportunities abroad (Akee et al. 2010; Cho 2015). Low GDP (gross domestic product) in a source country and a relatively higher GDP in a host country (which serves as a pull factor) increase the probability of trafficking to the relatively wealthier country (Akee et al. 2010; Cho, Dreher, and Neumayer 2013; Cho 2015). In other words, people who live in poorer countries tend to seek better economic opportunities in wealthier countries, making them susceptible to traffickers who offer to help them on their journey. Yet more recent work suggests that richer countries have greater capacity and more resources to combat slavery and therefore are more effective at dampening the prevalence of slavery within their borders (Landman and Silverman 2019). Countries with transitional economies have a much larger and statistically more significant problem with trafficking than other types of countries (Cho 2015; Akee et al. 2010). In her seminal work, Cho (2015) finds that countries in the midst of economic transition have a 26 percent higher rate of human trafficking than countries not in economic transition (8). Such economic transitions can create sufficient uncertainties surrounding labor conditions to the point that people may rationally seek out work abroad and find themselves caught in the web of traffickers.

With respect to push-pull factors for traffickers, corruption has been identified as a robust pull factor. Traffickers seek out countries with higher rates of corruption likely because they expect to more easily bribe law enforcement and other government officials (Cho 2015; Akee et al. 2014; Jakobsson and Kotsadam 2013; Bales 2007). It might also be that transnational organized crime networks thrive in places with high levels of corruption and a weak rule of law. For organized crime networks already running a thriving business in an illicit commodity (drugs and arms), the shift to trafficking in people can be lucrative and of course human traffickers may easily add additional types of contraband into their networks (Smith and Miller-de la Cuesta 2011). A weak rule of law and a high crime rate both serve as a trafficking push factor, encouraging people to leave in search of safety and better living conditions (Cho 2015). But a high crime rate also serves as a trafficking pull factor (Cho 2015, 10).

Interstate conflict in a source country (a push factor) serves as a statistically significant predictor of labor trafficking (Peksen, Blanton, and Blanton 2017). While interstate conflict may create a larger pool of vulnerable people willing to make a risky migration decision, these dynamics do not hold during civil wars (Peksen, Blanton, and Blanton 2017; Akee et al. 2010). When people are displaced from their homes but remain in their own countries, they are referred to as internally displaced people, or IDPs—their presence, like the presence of refugees in source countries, has the effect of increasing the rate of trafficking (Akee et al. 2010). Linguistically divided countries also create a significant pull factor for trafficking (Heller et al. 2016; Cho 2015; Akee et al. 2010). When the United Nations sends peacekeepers to quell hostilities, an often unanticipated

Table 1.3. Victim Trafficking Push-Pull Factors

Push	Pull
Poverty	Economically developed
Crime	Crime
Perception of corruption	Perception of corruption
Weak rule of law	Legalized prostitution (trafficking organization pull factor)
Interstate conflict	UN Peacekeeping Mission (trafficking organization pull factor)
Transitional economy	Transitional economy
	Linguistically divided
	State capacity

and tragic consequence is an increase in sex trafficking into the crisis zone (Smith and Smith 2011).

Governments may have some ability to influence the likelihood of trafficking within and across their borders through their trade and sex work policies. Trafficking has been referred to as the "dark side of globalization"[2] because policies that decrease government regulation of the economy and render borders more porous for trade may simultaneously increase the likelihood of labor and child trafficking (Peksen, Blanton, and Blanton 2017). Peksen et al. (2017, 683) argue that a business-friendly regulatory environment can serve as a pull factor for trafficking organizations because it "increases the probability that regimes will have significant labor trafficking, as adherence to these policies creates a permissive environment for such blatant violation of economic and personal integrity rights." There has been some disagreement in the literature about the effects of globalization on trafficking; some authors note that economic freedom is correlated with lower levels of human trafficking, which suggests that countries that are economically free are more likely to pass policies to combat trafficking (Heller et al. 2016). Similarly, where state capacity is high there is a lower probability of both sex and labor trafficking (Blanton, Blanton, and Peksen 2018).

The strength of anti-trafficking legislation (Cho and Vadlamannati 2012) and prohibitions against prostitution (Cho, Dreher, and Neumayer 2013; Jakobsson and Kotsadam 2011) can dampen the likelihood of sex trafficking, although some countries engage in cheap talk (Smith and Smith-Cannoy 2012). Where prostitution has been made legal, the process of legalization expands the demand for sex workers and traffickers to step in to satiate the demand (Cho, Dreher, and Neumayer 2013, 71), though again, more recent work has challenged earlier findings about the role of legalized prostitution on trafficking flows (Heller et al. 2016; Hernandez and Rudolph 2015).

Explanations of Trafficking Policy and Compliance

The work in this volume touches on the literature that pertains to the general thrust of anti-trafficking policy. We highlight some prevailing explanations for the contours of global anti-trafficking policy and seek answers to certain questions. For example: Are governments more inclined to pass legislation that punishes traffickers or protects victims? What can the literature tell us about why some countries are better at some aspects of anti-trafficking policy than others? When evaluating national approaches to curbing trafficking, we follow the system adopted by the US State Department in the annual Trafficking in Persons Reports. As mandated by the passage of the 2000 US Trafficking in Persons Act, the State Department evaluates each country in the world annually to determine how well they are preventing trafficking, prosecuting traffickers, and protecting victims.

To assess prevention, the State Department evaluates whether laws have been passed to outlaw trafficking and if those laws provide penalties stringent enough to deter would-be traffickers. For example, in 2018 the State Department chastised the Republic of the Congo for failing to pass sufficiently stringent national trafficking legislation (US Department of State 2018). Regarding prosecution, the State Department looks at the rate of investigations, prosecutions, and convictions, and frequently prods governments to improve their data-collection methods to facilitate better assessment of the prosecution pillar. To assess how well an individual country protects victims, the State Department examines the victim resources made available in both law and practice. This typically means assessing whether victims are entitled to financial support or special visas, whether the government runs a trafficking victim hotline, and whether shelters are adequately funded.

These assessments are based on an eleven-point scale that includes how vigorously a state prosecutes and investigates traffickers, whether they share trafficking data, whether public officials accused of trafficking are punished, whether victims are protected, and whether improvements have been made since the prior year. For governments that receive the lowest tier rating on the three-tier system (with tier 1 being those that meet the Trafficking Victims' Protection Act [TVPA] standards, to tier 3 being those that do not meet those standards and are not making efforts to do so), the United States may apply economic sanctions. While it is true that countries may petition for a waiver from sanctions and that waivers are liberally granted, there is no guarantee that future US administrations will continue this practice.

This *prevention—prosecution—protection* framework and the tier-ranking system are used among trafficking scholars to distinguish between elements of national anti-trafficking laws. We know that where women are engaged in the legislative process, the protection pillar is rated higher (Schonhofer 2017). And we know that with improved social, legal, and political equality between men and women, rates of trafficking prosecutions increase (Wooditch 2012). Globally, the governments of the world are more apt to pass anti-trafficking legislation (prevention) and prosecute traffickers (prosecution) than protect victims (protection) (Cho, Dreher, and Neumayer 2014). One explanation for the focus on criminal justice rather than on victim protection at the global level suggests that governments strategically use prosecution and prevention rather than protection because policies that provide generous support to victims may serve as a pull factor for migration (Blanton, Blanton, and Peksen 2018).

The Trafficking in Persons Reports and other forms of external pressure have also been used to explain why some governments are better than others at passing and implementing anti-trafficking legislation. The TIP Reports have been criticized for, among other defects, presenting subjective rankings as empirical fact, as well as for the political manipulation that may underpin those facts (Szep and Spetalnick 2015; Bernat and Zhilina 2011).

Yet, in spite of these criticisms, the TIP Reports have been very important for explaining why some governments comply with the TVPA and others do not. Scholars have shown that when countries score poorly on TIP Reports, the grade can serve as a catalyst for implementing and enforcing anti-trafficking legislation (Cho, Dreher, and Neumayer 2014; Simmons and Lloyd 2010). The TIP Reports are but one external pressure mechanism that trafficking scholars have identified that can improve the prospects for state compliance with the UN Protocol to Prevent, Suppress and Punish Trafficking in Persons. Or it may be that states are not coerced by a more powerful actor to comply with the Anti-Trafficking Protocol but rather choose to improve their trafficking policies as a way to achieve some other policy objective. Schonhofer (2017) suggests that strategic commitment to anti-trafficking may boost a government's reputation when it aspires to join the European Union or NATO, for example (157).[3]

Other domestic-level variables may also be important for understanding which trafficking policies are adopted. Domestic audience demand for amelioration policies might come from any NGO hosts or constituent clusters. Some religion-based groups are active in the fight against human trafficking. States with some level of a free press may see that coverage of human trafficking leads to an increase in the salience of the issue, which hence leads to a higher rate of compliance with the global anti-trafficking treaty. Indeed, even issues like dependence on tourism as a share of a regional or local GDP or internet access may impact the levels of push and pull factors. Although there are no doubt many variables that may contribute to the local and national calculation as to how—or whether—to combat human trafficking, we seek parsimony. We demonstrate that the quickest and most direct path to engaging those enmeshed in human trafficking—the victims rather than the criminals—is the enhancement of cultural equality and political equality for women.

While at this point it is almost trite to repeat Hillary Clinton's now famous—but at the time controversial—assertion at the United Nations in 1995, that women's rights are human rights, in the realm of human trafficking and its victims, progress still needs to be made (Clinton 1996). We cannot expect a comprehensive and functioning human trafficking amelioration regime so long as women are culturally and politically second-class citizens.

Notes

1. We interviewed the following people: Dennis Morrow, executive director of Janus Youth Programs, December 12, 2014; Detective Keith Bickford, Multnomah County Sheriff's Office, October 9, 2014; Commissioner Dianne McKeel, Multnomah County Board of Commissioners, District #4, September 22, 2015; and Erin Ellis, executive director of Sexual Assault Resource Center, Portland, Oregon, September 1, 2015. We also conducted additional interviews with police, local politicians, and NGOs in Los Angeles during the same period.
2. Cho, Dreyer, and Neumayer (2014). See also Heller et al. (2016).
3. See also Avdeyeva (2012).

A Global Perspective on Human Trafficking and Quantitative Analysis of Causes

A shadow economy of contraband and illicit networks reaches around the world and penetrates virtually every aspect of the global economy. Those who traffic in people for the purpose of sexual exploitation share much in common with those who work underground and outside of the legal channels of commerce. Whether they smuggle, manufacture, or distribute weapons, drugs, or illegal or counterfeit goods, these illicit networks operate in a black-market economy beyond the reach of regulated or legitimate commerce. Accordingly, as has been noted often, reliable and accurate data on the volume of contraband and illicit commercial behavior, perhaps especially regarding human trafficking and modern slavery, can be difficult to compile (Landman 2020; Smith-Cannoy 2018; Weitzer 2014; Guinn 2008). One of the most obvious challenges to acquiring accurate and comprehensive data on human trafficking is the absence of a reliable bureaucratic agency, whether global or national, to which those engaged in trafficking report their activities or profits and from which data could be collected or extrapolated. There are no revenue, tax, or inventory reports on human trafficking. Because of our inability to reliably, consistently, and accurately assess the actual volume of trafficking for sex, either globally or at the national level, we have no choice but to look to secondary indicators that allow us to draw some conclusions about and parameters of trafficking activity. For instance, we can know the rate and type of utilization of social services available to victims of trafficking. We can assess the amount and type of resources directed toward amelioration of trafficking efforts, whether from a law enforcement standpoint or from a social services standpoint. We can catalog the annual criminal investigations, prosecutions, and convictions in a given country. These are imperfect measures for a variety of reasons and, like those working more broadly on measuring the prevalence of slavery across a variety of industries, some rightly question the accuracy and value of these surrogate measures (Landman 2020). It is not clear whether victims of trafficking who lack legal immigration status or the proper documents in a foreign country might be able to seek out and utilize social services and not risk deportation or arrest.

Victims of trafficking are controlled through a variety of strategies, including threats of harm to their families, retention of legitimate travel documents, or straightforward threats of violence. These threats serve to keep victims in compliance as well as reduce the chance they would seek help through access to state or nonprofit services. Accordingly, even well-maintained records of the provision of victim services likely represent a dramatic underreport of the true scope and magnitude of the number of victims. Records of criminal investigations and trafficker prosecutions are likewise certainly underestimates and a weak surrogate for the actual magnitude of trafficking. Different governments have different resolves, resources, concerns, and capacities about trafficking (Laczko and Gramegna 2003). Still, despite the inherent challenges in collecting data for the assessment of human trafficking, we can make some broad conclusions and identify trends about the causes of trafficking. Specifically, the reliable data that *is* available suggests that victims of trafficking are likely to originate from relatively poorer countries and are, in general, trafficked and then exploited in wealthier countries (Cho 2015). Thus the initial engagement and recruitment of victims and the subsequent transport or trafficking of victims more often than not occurs in less economically developed countries with fewer investigatory and enforcement resources. The scarcity of enforcement infrastructure means the data represents but a small piece of extant trafficking bounded by the limits of the country's investigation and prosecution capacity.

In addition to the myriad challenges inherent in gathering empirical data about illegal activity, governments of the countries with the largest trafficking issues face a difficult political logic with respect to reporting about trafficking. There are a host of incentives to underreport the magnitude of human trafficking into and across their territories. Moreover, those same incentives push these governments to underreport but overstate their efforts at combating human trafficking. That is, they must simultaneously seem to present human trafficking as a minor problem caused by others and be effective at amelioration. As discussed in chapter 1, the annual US State Department assessments of global trafficking are built upon the analytical pillars of prevention, punishment, and protection. This framework is used by the State Department to assign scores and sort governments into categories within a tiered ranking system. Tier 1 consists of those countries that meet the Trafficking Victims Protection Act's minimum standards and tier 3 consists of those countries that not only do not meet the minimum standards but also are not making efforts to meet the minimums. Per the Trafficking Victims Protection Act, countries categorized as tier 3 can be sanctioned by the United States for their neglect of the problem. In addition to external political incentives to underreport and exaggerate their efforts at combating the problem, there is widespread corruption and self-dealing by both political and law enforcement authorities who actually profit from human trafficking. For example, Kara (2009) demonstrates that those engaged in human trafficking in Italy and in India could easily predict the volume of bribery necessary to operate effectively, such that the bribe amounts to be paid by traffickers are routinely factored into traffickers' overhead calculations.

Thus, any assessment or analysis of statistics about trafficking must be considered in light of various limitations and challenges. Given that caveat, some conclusions can be drawn from current data from two authoritative sources. Our "authoritative sources" are those whose data are sourced from credible organizations actually working to combat human trafficking in the field. Still, the data produced from even these sources are bounded by the same limitations mentioned. Rather than viewing these accounts as precise measurements, this information should be used to provide a general conceptualization about global patterns of sex trafficking while recognizing there is an inherent undercount of the phenomenon and the victims.

In 2016 the ILO, in cooperation with the Walk Free Foundation and the International Organization for Migration, created a comprehensive overview of the global human-trafficking picture. The report arrived at an estimation that the modern slave population exceeds 40.3 million people (ILO 2017, 10). This staggering number encompasses not only people enslaved by economic actors across all economic categories, including sex work, but also those enslaved through forced marriages who are unable to procure divorces or any other form of freedom. Analysis of the split between the two categories reveals that 62 percent (24.9 million people) are enslaved by those in the economic sectors of agriculture/farms, factories/production, and commercial sex trade (9). Another 38 percent (15.4 million people) are enslaved in forced marriage (10). Here it is important to acknowledge a substantial overlap between sectors of these categories because women and girls sold under the umbrella of an "arranged marriage" are often actually trafficked for sex (see fig. 2.1).

The ILO report reveals a persistent reality: women and girls make up a disproportionate share of forced labor. Roughly 70 percent of enslaved victims are women and girls. That is, over 28.9 million victims are women and girls (10). This group of victims consists of those enslaved as forced labor in domestic servitude, manufacturing, and, of course, the commercial sex trade. Juveniles are particularly vulnerable to sex trafficking and are the most common victims of forced marriage. The ILO report reveals that 21 percent of those trafficked and enslaved for exploitation in the commercial sexual trade are children (23). Indeed, women and girls comprise roughly 99 percent of all victims of forced sexual exploitation (22). In contrast, men are more commonly enslaved through

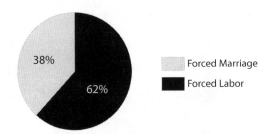

Figure 2.1. Modern Slavery in the World

Source: ILO, "Global Estimates of Modern Slavery: Forced Labour and Forced Marriage" (Geneva, 2017), http://www.ilo.org/global/publications/books/WCMS_575479/lang—en/index. htm, last accessed April 2019.

state-imposed forced labor in the construction and manufacturing sectors and through conscription (23).

The UNODC routinely collects information from governments and produces the annual Global Report on Trafficking in Persons (TIP). An examination of the UNODC data reveals at least some aspects of trafficking patterns over time. The reports cover four broad categories of data about trafficking: 1) trafficking for forced labor or services, slavery, and similar practices; 2) trafficking for sexual exploitation; 3) trafficking for organ removal; and 4) trafficking for other forms of exploitation. The last category, "other forms," includes activities such as forced begging, forced marriage, and child soldier conscription. Between 2007 and 2018 a greater share of detected victims were trafficked for sexual exploitation than for any other purpose (see fig. 2.2).

The fluctuations over time in the percentage of victims in forced labor has ranged from a low of 18 percent of the total population in 2006 to a high of 40 percent of the total population in 2011 (UNODC 2020, 16; 2016, 6). More men were detected as victims over the broad time frame. For example, in 2004 only 13 percent of detected victims were male, but by 2016 more than 23 percent of detected victims were male (UNODC 2020, 16). A considerable percentage of male victims (38 percent) were trafficked for forced labor, with merely 5 percent trafficked for sexual exploitation (UNODC 2020, 36), which suggests that while sexual exploitation is still about a system for exploiting women and girls—with women being the largest share of detected trafficking victims and children the second most commonly detected group—the detection and reporting of male victims is increasing (UNODC 2020, 36).

In addition to revealing who is trafficked, the data about prosecutions and convictions in the UNODC reports reveal important information about the identity of the traffickers. More than 60 percent of those convicted of trafficking offenses are male (UNODC 2020, 39). This majority of male perpetrators

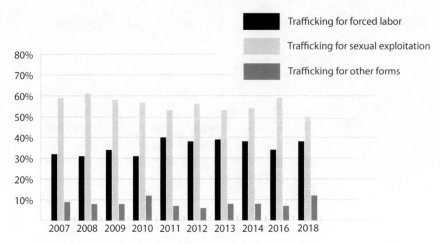

Figure 2.2. UNODC's Trends in the Forms of Exploitation among Detected Trafficking Victims, 2007–18*

*No data for 2015. Trafficking in organ removal omitted because it is such a small percentage of the total percentage of detected trafficking victims.

Source: UNODC (2018), Global Report on Trafficking in Persons, 24, https://www.unodc.org /documents/data-and-analysis/glotip/2018/GLOTiP_2018_BOOK_web_small.pdf, last accessed December 2020. Data for 2018 comes from UNODC Global Report on Trafficking published in 2020, https://www.unodc.org/documents/data-and-analysis/tip/2021/GLOTiP_2020_15jan _web.pdf.

holds true regardless of the stage of the trafficking prevention process. That is, whether at the investigation, prosecution, or conviction stage, almost two of three suspects are male. The report also reveals that a significant percentage of those engaged in trafficking are women, with a geographic variation in the prosecutorial patterns. For instance, in East Asia and the Pacific more than 50 percent of those convicted are women (UNODC 2020, 39). In Eastern Europe and central Asia these dynamics are even more pronounced, with women making up more than 80 percent of the total population of people convicted for trafficking offenses (UNODC 2020, 39). In Italy, Nigerian women "host" other Nigerian women who have come to Italy. The new arrivals are persuaded that their host is trying to secure their freedom from the traffickers and generally looking out for their best interests. In reality these women hosts are the traffickers. Occasionally husband-and-wife teams are used to lure juveniles and younger women, where the woman in the team can comfort and reassure any suspicious victim (UNODC 2016, 36). In Thailand, female trafficking victims in Bangkok are dressed in expensive clothing and made to appear very successful and wealthy so they will return to their villages to recruit for similar easy and lucrative "jobs" (Kara 2009). Thus, women play important roles in trafficking and are especially important in lower-tier activities, like recruitment, while male traffickers tend to participate in organizational work (UNODC 2016, 35).

As might be expected, types of trafficking differ by geographic region. Traffickers respond to markets for demand. Where domestic labor is desired, women and girls are trafficked for domestic labor. Where tourism or some other push factor increases the demand for sex workers, traffickers respond. For example, in 2018 sex trafficking was the most prevalent form of trafficking (64 percent of all detected victims) in East Asia and the Pacific. In contrast, labor trafficking was far more common (66 percent of all detected victims) in central Asia and Eastern Europe (UNODC 2020, 35). In sub-Saharan Africa, Central America, and the Caribbean, trafficking of children as domestic servants is very common. In the Caribbean, the centuries-old colonial *restavek*[1] system institutionalized a structure whereby the rural poor send their children to work for urban wealthy families. In concept the children work around the house in exchange for access to better schools and more opportunities for security and advancement, but in reality the children are slaves tasked with long days of difficult work, leaving no time or access to schools or advanced training. We summarize some of the generalizable conclusions from the reports in table 2.1.

Since the initial creation of the UN Anti-Trafficking Protocol in 2000, the international community has focused on human trafficking as a serious problem and has engaged in the amelioration of human trafficking in a variety of ways. The Anti-Trafficking Protocol encourages states to reduce and prevent human trafficking in part through both the adoption of laws against trafficking and genuine enforcement of those laws and punishment for traffickers. The Anti-Trafficking Protocol also urges the creation of protection regimes for victims of trafficking. The articulation of a prevention-punishment-protection structure has in practice splintered into two distinct state approaches to fighting trafficking. The first approach emphasizes the prevention and punishment aspects of the model and relies on the passage of anti-trafficking laws and enforcement of those laws focused on the national level. This prosecutorial, or criminal justice,

Table 2.1. Summary of Victim and Trafficker Data

- Victims exploited for commercial sex make up the largest share of detected global trafficking victims, but other forms of exploitation are persistent
- Women, followed by children, make up the largest share of detected sex-trafficking victims
- Male trafficking victims are more frequently exploited for labor rather than for sex
- While suspects investigated, prosecuted, and convicted of trafficking are predominantly male (60 percent), women also make up a substantial share of those convicted of trafficking (40 percent)

approach in state policy is assumed when sharply rising trafficker conviction rates are seen.

The victim-centered approach focuses on protecting victims of trafficking through passage of laws that guarantee victims' rights will be protected. That is, the social safety net needs of the victims are the primary concern. As will be shown, the criminal prosecution of human traffickers often requires that the rights and best interests of the victims are subordinated to obtain convictions. For instance, some countries allow foreign-trafficking victims to remain in the host country only to assist in the prosecution of their trafficker(s). But issuance of this type of specialized visa usually depends on victims' unfettered cooperation with authorities. When the trafficker is part of a network, as is usually the case, the process of cooperating with prosecutors by testifying and participating in the trafficker's trial can jeopardize the safety of the victim and the victim's family.

The trafficking literature assessment reveals that most countries have chosen to focus on prosecution of traffickers over protection of victims (Cho, Dreyer, and Neumayer 2014). Since the creation of the Anti-Trafficking Protocol, 158 governments have adopted anti-trafficking legislation (UNODC 2016, 48). And while Cho, Dreyer, and Neymayer (2014) show that states are much better at passing anti-trafficking legislation and prosecuting traffickers than they are at protecting victims, even global conviction rates have stagnated in recent years. Of 136 countries reporting trafficker conviction data for the years 2014–17, only 17 percent reported more than fifty annual trafficking convictions (UNODC 2018, 45) (see fig. 2.3).

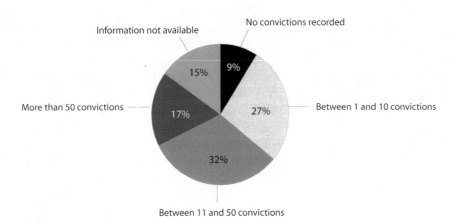

Figure 2.3. UNODC's Countries by Number of Trafficking Convictions, 2014–17

Source: UNODC (2018), Global Report on Trafficking in Persons, 45, https://www.unodc.org /documents/data-and-analysis/glotip/2018/GLOTiP_2018_BOOK_web_small.pdf, last accessed January 2021.

Quantitative Analysis of the Causes of Trafficking

Because existing global data sets suggest that women and girls make up the largest share of detected sex-trafficking victims, a quantitative analysis of the causes of sex trafficking is vital. Data used here are drawn from "Human Trafficking Indicators, 2000–2011: A New Dataset" (Frank 2013), which pulls from the annual US State Department TIP reports and distinguishes among four types of trafficking: forced prostitution, forced labor, child sexual exploitation, and child labor. The universe of cases includes all countries in the world and covers the years 2000 to 2011. We would have preferred that the data cover the entire span of our analysis (2000–2020), but this smaller data set is critically relevant for the current analysis because it is one of the few available that distinguishes between trafficking for sex and trafficking for labor. Blending these two forms of trafficking together as a single dependent variable obscures the significance of the variable of interest: gender. The HTI data set helps to reveal a critical link between protections for women's economic rights and the probability of sex trafficking.

Dependent Variable: Sex-Trafficking Victim Source Country

Previous work on the quantitative causes of trafficking provides some support for the link between women's vulnerability in society and trafficking outcomes (Bettio and Nandi 2010; Di Tommaso et al. 2009). Although some of these studies employ data from the UNODC or the ILO to measure trafficking, these quantitative data sets do not distinguish between sex trafficking and labor trafficking. Blending these metrics together is problematic if the goal is to isolate the effects of women's marginalization as a predictor of sex trafficking because women are disproportionately likely to be detected as victims in the commercial sex industry, while men are disproportionately likely to be detected as victims of labor trafficking. Because a key goal of this work is to determine whether support exists for the relationship between the deprivation of women's economic rights and their exploitation in the commercial sex industry, it is vital to use a dependent variable that distinguishes between the various types of trafficking.

Data are drawn from the Human Trafficking Indicators (HTI) for the years 2000–2011; this data set is unique because it breaks out the four types of trafficking: forced prostitution, forced labor, child sexual exploitation, and child labor. Importantly, the HTI data set also draws on the TIP Reports' distinction between trafficking source and transit and destination countries. We developed a dummy variable from the HTI data set that captures whether a country is considered a source country for forced prostitution in a given year. A score of 1 means that the country is a source; a score of 0 means that it is not. Because the explicit focus in this work is an examination of global patterns that account for female victimization in sex slavery and sex trafficking, this variable is a good indicator of the phenomenon.

Independent Variables: Women's Economic Rights and Women's Political Rights

We draw on Cingranelli, Richards, and Clay (2013) to define women's rights in two ways: women's economic rights and women's political rights. We use women's economic rights as a surrogate for cultural power. While not a perfect surrogate, it works because the cultural position and strength of women in a society is revealed by their economic rights (Apodaca 1998). The Cingranelli, Richards, and Clay (2013) data are especially helpful because they both establish whether laws are in place to ensure women's economic and political rights and they indicate how well these laws are enforced. They describe women's economic rights as the choice of profession, including whether a decision can be made without the need for a male family member's approval; the ability to work in "dangerous" occupations; and the right to work in the military or the police (7). Equality in the workplace as evidenced by equal pay, equality in hiring and promotion, and nondiscrimination by employers, as well as economic security through unemployment benefits and maternity leave, are also components of women's economic rights (7). These variables are scored on a four-point scale: 3 means all of these economic rights are enshrined in law and enforced in practice; 2 means some of these economic rights are enshrined in law and enforced in practice; 1 means some of these economic rights are enshrined in law but are not enforced in practice; and 0 means none of these economic rights are enshrined in law.

Women's political rights include the right to vote, to run for political office, to petition government officials, to join political parties, and to hold elected and appointed positions in government. Again, they are assessed on a four-point scale, with 3 indicating all rights are enshrined in law and enforced in practice, down to 0, indicating these rights are not enshrined in law. We also run models with one-year lags on each variable to provide additional evidence of causality, rather than simple contemporaneous correlation.

Other independent variables are primarily drawn from the findings in the broader trafficking literature (discussed in detail in chapter 1).[2] Other independent variables such as *polity* and *GDP* are ones typically included in large, global, quantitative studies. The *polity* variable measures regime authority, from very autocratic hereditary monarchy to very democratic consolidated democracy; it is scored on a twenty-one-point scale, with a low score of -10 indicating that a country is very autocratic and a high score of +10 indicating that a country is very democratic. The quantitative human rights literature supports a link between democracy and better human rights outcomes, from longer life expectancy (Pinzon-Rondon et al. 2015) and better health outcomes (Bollyky et al. 2019) to reductions in child labor (von Stein 2016). Scholars working on trafficking have also found a link between democracy and trafficking (Frank 2013). *Polity* is included in our analysis to determine whether there is a relationship between regime characteristics and the likelihood that a country will be a source for sex-trafficking victims.

We include *GDP PPP* (logged) in the analysis to capture whether poorer countries tend to be source countries for sex-trafficking victims. GDP captures vulnerability within a population, which can be a push factor for trafficking (Blanton, Blanton, and Peksen 2018; Rao and Presenti 2012; Akee et al. 2014); it may also be that wealthier countries have greater deployable resources to combat slavery and trafficking (Landman and Silverman 2019). We use a *population* (log transformed) variable to assess whether countries with larger populations are more likely to be source countries for sex-trafficking victims. The inclusion of this variable is intuitive in the sense that a large population may create more competition for jobs in the conventional labor market, making persons excluded from such opportunities more vulnerable to traffickers. Previous research on trafficking push factors also identifies some support for this relationship (Frank 2011; Rao and Presenti 2012).

Both *homicide rate* and *prosecution* of traffickers are included in the models to measure how prevailing crime rates and institutional efforts to punish traffickers impact the probability that a country will be a source for forced prostitution. *Homicide rate* is used as a proxy for crime rate. A high crime rate may reasonably encourage people to flee in search of safety and a better life, which in turn may make them more vulnerable to traffickers. Data on homicide rates comes from the UNODC; it captures rates of international homicide per 100,000 people. This variable is measured between 0 and 100. We include the *prosecution* variable to assess whether a country has adopted anti-trafficking legislation in line with the Palermo Protocol and whether that legislation is effectively enforced. Such efforts may serve to dampen trafficker recruitment efforts in what would otherwise be source countries. The prosecution variable is an ordinal measure that is scored from 1 to 5, with 5 indicating highest compliance with anti-trafficking prosecution efforts prescribed by the UN. This variable is drawn from the 3P Anti-Trafficking Policy Index (Cho 2015a).

We include a variable for *interstate war* because the literature has identified this variable as a trafficking push factor (Peksen, Blanton, and Blanton 2017). Though similar findings have not been similarly identified with intrastate war, an *intrastate war* variable is included because anecdotal evidence suggests that instances of forced prostitution, sexual slavery, and systematic rape are linked to both interstate and intrastate wars. Examples of such crimes during intrastate wars abound, including the recent International Criminal Court case of Bosco Ntaganda, a former rebel leader in the Democratic Republic of the Congo who was convicted of rape and sexual slavery as crimes against humanity (Amnesty International 2019). Both these variables come from the armed conflict data set of Uppsala Conflict Data Program/Peace Research Institute, Oslo (UCDP/PRIO) (Gleditsch et al. 2002; Pettersson and Oberg 2020) and are scored between 0 (no conflict) and 1 (conflict).

The trafficking literature shows strong support for the relationship between corruption and trafficking, with corruption as a statistically significant push factor for trafficking (Jonsson 2019; Cho 2015; Akee et al. 2014; Jackobson and Kotsadam 2011; Bales 2007). Recent research also shows that corruption is tied to lower levels of compliance with the Palermo Protocol (DiRienzo 2018). In countries with high levels of public corruption, traffickers can more easily bribe police and public officials to "look the other way." We use the World Bank's Worldwide Governance Indicators *control of corruption* variable. This variable measures "the extent to which public power is exercised for private gain, including both petty and grand forms of corruption, as well as 'capture' of the state by elites and private interests" (World Bank 2009). The *control of corruption* variable is measured from -2.5 (high levels of corruption) to +2.5 (low levels of corruption).

The *rule of law* variable comes from the Worldwide Governance Indicators and captures perceptions of the extent to which agents have confidence in and abide by the rules of society. It is measured on an ordinal scale, from -2.5 (low levels) to +2.5 (high levels). Because previous work has identified economic transitions as a significant trafficking push factor, we include a self-generated dummy variable to account for whether a country is a former Soviet Bloc member because it suggests a link between countries with transitional economies. For a complete list of variables used in the models, see appendix 2A at the end of this chapter.

Bivariate Correlations

In table 2.2 we report the first-order bivariate correlations between variables of interest, control variables, and dependent variables to determine whether a country is a source for sex trafficking. The first set of significant associations indicate a positive relationship between the source of human trafficking and the log of population ($r = .207$), homicide rates ($r = .248$), civil war ($r = .109$), and whether a country is a transitional economy ($r = .187$); all of these are significant at greater than .05, meaning that they are not likely the result of random chance. As levels of these variables increase so too does the likelihood that a country will be a source for sex-trafficking victims. With the exception

Table 2.2. Bivariate Correlations

	Source	Econ. rights	Econ. rights lag	Pol. rights	Pol. rights lag	Polity	GDP PPP (log)	Pop. (log)	Homicide rates	Prosecution	Int'l war	Civil war	Corruption	Rule of law
Econ. rights	-.319 (.000)	-												
Econ. rights lag	-.323 (.000)	.757 (.000)	-											
Pol. rights	-.011 (.653)	.277 (.000)	.284 (.000)	-										
Pol. rights lag	-.008 (.749)	.302 (.000)	.276 (.000)	.783 (.000)	-									
Polity	-.025 (.349)	.365 (.000)	.351 (.000)	.380 (.000)	.383 (.000)	-								
GDP PPP (log)	-.586 (.000)	.472 (.000)	.471 (.000)	.108 (.000)	.107 (.000)	.237 (.000)	-							
Pop. (log)	.207 (.000)	-.224 (.000)	-.222 (.000)	.129 (.000)	.123 (.000)	.016 (.500)	-.064 (.003)	-						
Homicide rates	.248 (.000)	-.076 (.002)	-.071 (.006)	.069 (.005)	.066 (.010)	.117 (.000)	-.146 (.000)	-.043 (.079)	-					
Prosecution	-.036 (.159)	.295 (.000)	.281 (.000)	.274 (.000)	.280 (.000)	.409 (.000)	.322 (.000)	.206 (.000)	-.134 (.000)	-				
Int'l war	-.033 (.202)	.053 (.020)	.090 (.000)	.002 (.915)	.004 (.884)	.041 (.077)	.062 (.007)	.126 (.000)	-.003 (.911)	.032 (.199)	-			
Civil war	.109 (.000)	-.181 (.000)	-.189 (.000)	-.088 (.000)	-.072 (.003)	-.085 (.000)	-.216 (.000)	.102 (.000)	-.021 (.426)	-.197 (.000)	-.019 (.415)	-		

	C1	C2	C3	C4	C5	C6	C7	C8	C9	C10	C11	C12	C13	C14
Control of corrupt.	-.515	.601	.589	.307	.302	.450	.692	-.217	-.216	.339	.054	-.226		
	.000	.000	.000	.000	.000	.000	.000	.000	.000	.000	.023	.000		
Rule of law	-.512	.591	.581	.229	.220	.502	.696	-.275	-.284	.389	.047	-.271	.941	
	.000	.000	.000	.000	.000	.000	.000	.000	.000	.000	.048	.000	.000	
Transit. econ.	.187	-.041	-.045	-.008	-.006	-.118	-.023	.051	-.018	.129	.012	-.067	-.179	-.158
	.000	.052	.046	.716	.788	.000	.288	.015	.463	.000	.584	.003	.000	.000

of a finding that links civil war to a higher probability that a country will be a source for sex-trafficking victims, these findings largely support broader findings in the trafficking literature.

Of greatest interest to us is the relationship between the two key independent variables, *women's economic rights* and *women's political rights*, and the dependent variable, whether a country is a source for sex-trafficking victims. We find a significant negative relationship between *women's economic rights* ($r = -.319$) and the likelihood that a country will be a source for sex-trafficking victims. As protections for women's economic rights increase, a lower probability that a country will be a source for sex-trafficking victims appears. This makes intuitive sense and helps to highlight one of the core arguments we advance in this book: gendered economic vulnerability contributes to increased sex-trafficking outcomes. The absence of support for the relationship between women's political rights and sex-trafficking outcomes provides some initial clues as to the gendered factors that influence sex trafficking—rather than political opportunities for women informing the likelihood of sex trafficking, initial findings indicate that economic opportunities better explain sex-trafficking outcomes.

The bivariate correlations also support some of the larger findings in the trafficking push factor literature—as the log of *GDP PPP* ($r = -.586$)—and the perception that as the *control of corruption* decreases ($r = -.515$), so too does the likelihood that a country will be a source for sex-trafficking victims. Our findings here regarding *rule of law* also largely confirm what we see in the trafficking push factor literature: as the *rule of law* increases ($r = .591$), the likelihood of sex trafficking decreases. These relationships between *women's economic rights*, the log of *GDP PPP*, *control of corruption*, and *rule of law* are all significant at the .05 level.

Multivariate Model

The multivariate model used is a logistic regression with random effects, to account for heteroscedasticity from the cross-sectional or panel structure of the data; with temporal splines, to account for the independence of observation assumption violations from time-series data, as suggested by Beck, Katz, and Tucker (1998). The outcome predicted by the model is a binary measure for whether a country is a source of human sex trafficking. The main predictors— that is, the key independent variables—tested in the model are women's economic rights and women's political rights within each country and year.

We performed a six-step model-building process. The first, the baseline model, includes only the key independent variables; the control variables are introduced in the second model. The third and fourth models follow the same procedure but introduce the lagged versions of the key independent variables.

In the final two models the same procedure is followed but includes temporal splines (see table 2.3).

Model 1

In model 1, the baseline model, the variable *women's economic rights* is correlated with a reduction in the likelihood of being a source country for human trafficking. That is, as a country increases its protections for women's economic rights, the country becomes less likely to be a source of human trafficking. A one-unit increase in women's economic rights leads to a decrease in odds of being a source country by approximately 58 percent (57.977). However, model 1 reveals no association between the variable *women's political rights* and the odds of being a source of human trafficking. The lack of support for women's political rights suggests that gendered economic vulnerabilities rather than a lack of political opportunities for women is linked to forced prostitution and sex trafficking. This finding helps to reinforce the work of feminist political economists such as Suchland (2015), who show that complex social dynamics interact with economies of violence to entrap women and girls.

Model 2 and Model 3

In model 2, control variables are added to the baseline model. In model 3 the lagged values of the independent variables of interest—women's economic rights and women's political rights—are added to the baseline. While neither model 2 nor model 3 indicates a significant relationship between either of the women's rights variables, model 2 shows a strong relationship between GDP PPP and the probability that a country will be a source for trafficking victims. Countries with higher GDP per capita are significantly less likely to be a source of human trafficking than are countries with lower GDP per capita. A one-unit increase in logged GDP per capita decreases the odds of becoming a source country for trafficking by 1,111 percent. One unit of logged GDP is a very large number because GDP per capita ranges from 377 to 145,723.8. The logged value of GDP per capita ranges from 5.9 to 11.9. Thus a one-unit increase, from 6 to 7 logged GDP per capita, is akin to an increase of from 403 to 1,096 GDP per capita not logged. While model 1 tells a story about women's economic deprivation contributing to trafficking, model 2 indicates that poverty is a good predictor of whether a country will be a source for sex-trafficking victims. Together these models point to economic vulnerability and poverty to explain how countries become sources for sex trafficking victims.

The variable *population (logged)* shows that countries with larger populations are more likely than countries with smaller populations to be sources of human trafficking. A one-unit increase in population logged increases the odds of becoming a source country by 61 percent. The *homicide rate* is suggestive

Table 2.3. Factors Contributing to a Country Becoming a Source for Human Trafficking, 2000–2011

Variables	1	2	3	4	5	6
Women's economic rights	0.633*	0.818				
	(0.158)	(0.219)				
Women's economic rights lag			0.813	0.860	0.526*	0.605
			(0.213)	(0.234)	(0.177)	(0.252)
Women's political rights	1.422	0.908				
	(0.530)	(0.344)				
Women's political rights lag			1.412	1.291	0.692	0.724
			(0.505)	(0.481)	(0.320)	(0.415)
Polity		1.046		1.035		1.310***
		(0.057)		(0.057)		(0.130)
GDP PPP (log)		0.090***		0.088***		0.002***
		(0.031)		(0.031)		(0.002)
Population (log)		1.607***		1.610**		2.810***
		(0.360)		(0.366)		(1.109)
Homicide rate		1.079**		1.076**		1.088*
		(0.034)		(0.034)		(0.056)
Prosecution		2.073***		1.963***		1.765*
		(0.409)		(0.390)		(0.570)
Year spline					3.698***	3.786**
					(1.662)	(2.225)
Year spline 2					0.166	0.340
					(0.204)	(0.517)
Year spline 3					50.960	10.143
					(124.113)	(30.342)

Panel variance	41.161***	7.274***	44.240***	7.543***	126.144***	29.603***
	(9.687)	(2.144)	(10.456)	(2.240)	(26.484)	(9.025)
Constant	90.714***	1,318,730.715***	78.028***	926,994.748***	0.000***	0.000**
	(80.990)	(6,275,194.699)	(67.790)	(4,476,617.203)	(0.000)	(0.000)
Observations	1,549	1,090	1,542	1,087	1,542	1,087
Countries	176	147	176	147	176	147

* p<0.10
** p<0.05
*** p<0.01
Note: Odds ratios are reported with standard errors in parentheses.

as well: as the homicide rate rises within a country, the country becomes more likely to be a source of human trafficking, with a one-unit increase in the homicide rate increasing the odds of becoming a source country by 8 percent. While this is consistent with Cho's (2015) findings, which show that a high crime rate serves as a robust trafficking push factor, our results expand that finding to show that this relationship also applies specifically to sex trafficking. Where crime is more prevalent there is a greater probability of sex trafficking.

Finally, the variable *prosecution*, which measures both whether a country has passed domestic laws consistent with the Palermo Protocol and how vigorously those laws are enforced, reveals that human trafficking source countries are more likely both to have passed legislation and to have used it to prosecute and convict traffickers. A one-unit increase in *prosecution* increases the odds of becoming a source country by 208 percent. This finding is somewhat surprising because intuitively it would seem more plausible that increased trafficking prosecutions should function as a deterrent to would-be traffickers and reduce the probability that a country would emerge as a source for trafficking victims. It may be that when a country has a serious problem with trafficking, as officials begin prosecuting traffickers the effects of prosecutions take time. This finding also suggests there are good reasons to select a case study that exhibits a high degree of trafficking prosecutions to better understand this relationship.

Model 4

In model 4 we include the lagged values of the independent variables of interest, *women's economic rights* and *women's political rights*, and the control variables. We find no support for the relationship between the lagged women's rights variables with the likelihood of being a source of human trafficking. This is consistent with findings in the empirical literature on trafficking push and pull factors, which do not establish a statistically significant relationship between gender-related factors, such as female labor force participation or female literacy and trafficking (Cho 2015; Jac-Kucharski 2012; Adepoju 2005).

As we found in the other models, poverty is a statistically significant predictor of sex trafficking. Once we logged *GDP PPP*, the data revealed that countries with higher GDP per capita are much less likely to be a source of human trafficking than are countries with lower GDP per capita. A one-unit increase in *GDP (logged)* per capita decreases the odds of becoming a source country by 1,136 percent. This finding is largely consistent with other empirical studies on both push and pull factors associated with trafficking (Blanton, Blanton, and Peksen 2018; Rao and Presenti 2012; Akee et al. 2014). Likewise, *population (logged)* reveals that countries with larger populations are more likely than countries with smaller populations to be sources of human trafficking. A one-unit increase in population logged increases the odds of becoming a source country by 61 percent. Like in model 2, the variable *homicide rate* demonstrates that as homicide rates rise within a country, that country becomes more likely to be a source of human trafficking. A one-unit increase in the homicide rate increases the odds of becoming a source country by 8 percent. Also similar to model 2, *prosecution* is correlated with human trafficking, as source countries have higher compliance with anti-trafficking prosecution. A one-unit increase in the prosecution rate increases the odds of becoming a source country by 196 percent.

Model 5

In model 5 we include lagged values of both *women's economic rights* and *women's political rights* plus temporal splines and find that high levels of women's economic rights during the previous year leads to a decreased likelihood of a country being a source of human trafficking within the current year. After controlling for autocorrelation in the data with temporal splines, we find a one-unit increase in lagged women's economic rights leads to a decrease in odds of being a source country by approximately 190 percent. However, we find no association with odds of being a source of human trafficking with respect to women's political rights.

This is significant because when we use a dependent variable that isolates sex trafficking from labor trafficking, a relationship between higher protections for women's economic rights and lower likelihood that a country will be a source for sex-trafficking victims becomes more apparent. In this model the relationship is both significant and in the predicted direction, with fewer protections for women's economic rights correlated with a significantly higher probability that the country is a source for sex-trafficking victims. This result also runs counter to other empirical studies that find no relationship between measures of women's discrimination and trafficking—but some of those findings may be due to the blending of statistics on trafficking for sex and trafficking for labor within the dependent variable (Cho 2015; Jac-Kucharski 2012; Adepoju 2005).

Model 6

In model 6 we include the control variables and the lagged values of the two variables of interest: *women's economic rights* and *women's political rights*. Again, we do not find support for the relationship between discrimination against women and the probability that a country will be a source for sex trafficking. The *polity* variable suggests that democratic countries are more likely than autocratic countries to be sources of human trafficking: a one-unit increase in *polity* score leads to an increase in odds of becoming a source country by 31 percent. This could be attributed to several different characteristics of authoritarian regimes. For instance, the manipulation of data, high levels of corruption, and a focus on social control could all contribute to this statistical outcome. Yet the literature on compliance with the Palermo Protocol suggests, perhaps intuitively, that democracies are more likely to comply with the treaty in their domestic anti-trafficking policies (Cho and Vadlamannati 2012; Neumayer 2005). Set against the findings in the literature on compliance with the Palermo Protocol, our finding in model 6, linking higher levels of democracy to a higher probability that a country will be a source for sex trafficking, suggests there are distinct factors that inform trafficking patterns on the one hand and compliance on the other.

As found in the other models, we find in model 6 that countries with higher GDP per capita are significantly less likely to be a source of human trafficking than are countries with lower GDP per capita. A one-unit increase in logged GDP per capita decreases the odds of becoming a source country by an astounding 50,000 percent. *Population (logged)* reveals that countries with larger populations are more likely than countries with smaller populations to be sources of human trafficking. A one-unit increase in *population (logged)* increases the odds of becoming a source country by 281 percent. Additionally, as homicide rates rise within a country, that country becomes more likely to be a source of human trafficking. A one-unit increase in the *homicide rate* increases the odds of becoming a source country by 9 percent, indicating this variable may simply be a surrogate for general levels of criminal activity.

The variable *prosecution* reveals that human trafficking source countries have higher compliance with anti-trafficking prosecution such that a one-unit increase in *prosecution* increases the odds of becoming a source country by 177 percent. The directionality is likely the opposite, however, because if there is no human trafficking, there would be no need for prosecution. Our analysis here indicates that any understanding of what drives a country to be a source for human trafficking is intertwined with economics. Recall that the variable *GDP PPP (logged)* reveals a relationship of enormous magnitude between GDP per capital and the likelihood that a country will be a source of human trafficking.

Interpretation of Findings and Case Studies

Our empirical analysis uncovers some support for the relationship between a lack of women's economic rights and a higher probability of sex trafficking, but these findings are not robust across our models, so we do not overstate their importance. The support that we do find for the relationship between the deprivation of women's economic rights and the probability that a country will be a source for sex-trafficking victims in the multivariate analysis can be found in models 1 and 5. These results suggest that where women possess equal access to protections in the formal labor market, they are less inclined to pursue opportunities in the informal labor market. Where governments pass and enforce laws that prohibit sexual harassment in the workplace, provide for equal pay, and more generally enforce provisions that create equality in the workplace, women may be encouraged to apply for jobs and feel less pressured to seek alternative ways of generating income (such as sex work). These economic protections for women in the workplace may therefore serve as a buffer, redirecting women away from less dangerous forms of work. Importantly, when groups of women and girls—such as noncitizens and marginalized minorities—are shut out of the formal labor market, they may be at greater risk of falling victim to traffickers.

To account for these mixed empirical results, we chose case studies that exhibit low scores on the women's economic rights variable in the hope that further exploration might reveal the reasons behind these mixed findings. Each of the countries we examine received a low score of 1 or 0 on the women's economic rights variable in the most recent year that it was available in our data set, 2011. Recall that the variable is an ordinal measure on a scale of 0 (no legal protections for women's economic rights) to 3 (existing legal protections that are generally enforced in practice).

The absence of evidence for the link between women's political rights and sex trafficking suggests that trafficking is largely an economic story, not a political one. In trying to parse out what factors contribute to the probability that a country will become a source for sex-trafficking victims, the array of political opportunities women possess is not correlated with whether a country will emerge as a source for sex-trafficking victims. Though we did not test factors contributing to compliance with the Palermo Protocol in our quantitative analysis, recent research has uncovered a link between women's political participation as an intermediate variable that reduces levels of corruption, which in turn reduces the likelihood of trafficking (DiRienzo 2018). So, while women's political participation may not directly impact the probability of trafficking, there are reasons to expect that it shapes whether and how countries comply with the Palermo Protocol.

Beyond the mixed results uncovered for the women's economic rights variable, we use our other empirical findings to help guide case selection. Across all models, a large population, a high rate of poverty, and a high homicide rate (the latter an indicator of crime) are robust predictors of the likelihood that a country will become a source for sex-trafficking victims. Our case study countries are among the most populous in their regions because a global analysis

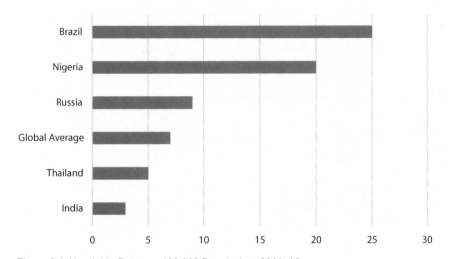

Figure 2.4. Homicide Rate per 100,000 Population, 2011–12

Source: UNODC (2013), Global Study on Homicide, https://www.unodc.org/documents/gsh /pdfs/2014_GLOBAL_HOMICIDE_BOOK_web.pdf, last accessed April 2021.

should allow for interregional comparison. India is the second most populous country in the world after China, but in South Asia it is the most populous. Similarly, Brazil and Nigeria are the most populous countries in their regions. As a transcontinental country, Russia could be classified as in either Europe or Asia. Russia is the most populous country in Europe but in a pan-Asian context it comes in behind China, India, Indonesia, and Pakistan. In Southeast Asia, Thailand is the second most populous country after Indonesia, and its history as a sex-trafficking hub makes it an especially important case to explore some of these relationships. Similarly, all these countries except Russia are situated among the bottom half of the world when the logged GDP PPP is calculated, suggesting that their populations are more impoverished and therefore potentially more vulnerable to traffickers relative to the rest of the world.

Since we are not developing predictions around the relationship between crime and the likelihood of sex trafficking, we selected cases that exhibit variation on the number of homicides per 100,000 people in the population. Again, using 2011 as a reference point, figure 2.4 situates our case study countries in ascending order of homicides, from fewest (India) to most (Brazil). This variation provides good metrics for comparison across our cases.

Our empirical findings show that populous, relatively poor countries with high crime rates and weak protections for women's economic rights are most likely to emerge as sources for sex-trafficking victims. Since we are interested in exploring both the factors contributing to trafficking and the ways governments have approached traffickers and victims, we expect that case studies in India, Thailand, Russia, Nigeria, and Brazil will provide for rich cross-case comparison. We now turn to an investigation of India, where a large, marginalized population of women and girls are trafficked for sex as brides, forced prostitutes, and temple slaves.

Appendix 2A: Women's Economic and Political Rights Variables

Women's economic rights coding (from Cingranelli, Richards, and Clay [2014]):

(0) No economic rights for women exist under law and systematic discrimination based on sex may be built into the law. The government tolerates a high level of discrimination against women.

(1) Some economic rights for women exist under law. However, in practice the government DOES NOT enforce or only weakly enforces the laws. The government tolerates a moderate level of discrimination against women.

(2) Some economic rights for women exist under law. The government DOES enforce these laws effectively. However, the government still tolerates a low level of discrimination against women.

(3) All or nearly all of women's economic rights are guaranteed by law. The government fully and vigorously enforces these laws and does not tolerate discrimination against women.

Women's political rights coding (from Cingranelli, Richards, and Clay [2014]):

(0) Women's political rights are not guaranteed by law, and some laws completely restrict the participation of women in the political process.

(1) Political equality is guaranteed by law. However, in practice significant limitations exist. Women hold less than 5 percent of seats in the national legislature or other high-ranking government positions.

(2) Political equality is guaranteed by law. Women hold more than 5 percent but less than 30 percent of seats in the national legislature or other high-ranking government positions.

(3) Political equality is guaranteed by law and is enforced in practice. Women hold more than 30 percent of seats in the national legislature or other high-ranking government positions.

Appendix 2B. Variables Used in the Model

Name	Description	Source	Years Covered	Number of Observations	Minimum Value	Maximum Value	Mean	Standard Deviation
DV: Source country for sex trafficking	Measured annually; drawn from data in US TIP report; receives a score of 1 in a given year when the TIP report identifies it as a source country for forced prostitution in that year	Frank (2013)	2000–2011	1,573	0.00	1.00	0.73	0.44
Women's economic rights	Captures whether laws exist to protect women's economic rights and whether those laws are enforced	Cingranelli, Richards, and Clay (2013)	1981–2011	2,194	0.00	3.00	1.35	0.76
Women's economic rights lag	Captures score for women's economic rights, lagged by one year	Cingranelli, Richards, and Clay (2013)	1981–2011	2,004	0.00	3.00	1.35	0.75
Women's political rights	Captures whether laws exist to protect women's political rights and whether those laws are enforced	Cingranelli, Richards, and Clay (2013)	1981–2011	2,193	0.00	3.00	1.96	0.58
Women's political rights lag	Captures score for women's political rights, lagged by one year	Cingranelli, Richards, and Clay (2013)	1981–2011	2,003	0.00	3.00	1.95	0.58
Polity	Captures range of regime authority on 21-point scale: -10 (hereditary monarchy) to +10 (consolidated democracy)	Marshall, Gurr, and Jaggers (2019)	2000–2013	1,873	-10.00	10.00	3.59	6.50
GDP PPP (log)	Captures economic growth measured as purchasing power parity, logarithmically transformed	World Bank (2011)	1960–2017	2,196	5.93	11.89	8.89	1.24

Population (log)	Captures country population, logarithmically transformed	World Bank (2011)	1960–2017	2,284	9.15	21.02	15.47	2.18
Homicide rate	Captures rate of intentional homicide victims per 100,000 population	UNODC	2000–2011	1,676	0.00	85.06	8.08	11.74
Prosecution	Captures country's legislative measures to make trafficking a crime and whether those laws are effectively enforced	Cho (2015a)	2000–2015	1,743	1.00	5.00	3.52	1.26
Interstate conflict	Dummy variable; measures interstate conflict (based on variable 3.12 conflict type in PRIO data set)	Gleditsch et al. (2002); Pettersson and Oberg (2020)	1946–2019	1,946	0.00	1.00	0.01	0.09
Intrastate conflict	Dummy variable measuring whether the country experienced an intrastate conflict (based on variable 3.12 conflict type in PRIO Dataset)	Gleditsch et al. (2002); Pettersson and Oberg (2020)	1946–2019	1,946	0.00	1.00	0.04	0.20
Control of corruption	Captures perceptions of the extent to which public power is exercised for private gain	Worldwide Governance Indicators*	1996–2016	2,060	-1.87	2.47	-0.05	1.00
Rule of law	Captures perceptions of the extent to which agents have confidence in and abide by the rules of society	Worldwide Governance Indicators	1996–2016	2,095	-2.61	2.014	-0.058	0.997
Transitional economy	Dummy variable that captures whether a country was a former Soviet republic transitioning to a market economy	Self-generated	2000–2011	2,296	0.00	1.00	0.078	0.269

* The conceptual definitions were drawn from the World Bank's WGI Methodology and Analytical Issues 2010: http://info.worldbank.org/governance/wgi/, last accessed April 2021.

Notes

1. This translates from Creole as "stay with."
2. See "Explanations of Trafficking Policy and Compliance" in chapter 1.

THREE

India

Sex trafficking in India is a complicated, diverse industry that has thrived on centuries of intense social stratification that relegates those at the bottom to religiously sanctioned abuse, culturally embedded gender discrimination, and grinding poverty (Toast Advisory 2019). Victims may be sold by family members as "brides," devoted to gods in temples, or kidnapped and forced to work in a brothel, bar, or other place of "entertainment." There are a multitude of ways that sex-trafficking victims find themselves enslaved in India. But one overwhelming commonality can be noted here: victims tend to be Dalit women and girls, who are considered so low in the social hierarchy that they do not warrant a position among the four main castes. Their existence outside the social system hierarchy in a society that is rigidly guided by specific cultural principles of societal order makes Dalits acutely vulnerable to traffickers. Dalit women face a sort of double discrimination—they are relegated to the bottom of the caste system as a consequence of their caste affiliation and to the bottom of the gender hierarchy as a consequence of their status as women (Selvi 2020). India provides a vivid illustration of the consequences of not protecting the economic rights of women and girls.

We make two arguments here: first, that poor enforcement of existing laws designed to protect the economic rights of women in India have had a particularly nefarious effect on the rights of Dalit women and girls. This exclusion from the rights regime makes the Dalit female population especially vulnerable to becoming sex-trafficking victims in India. Second, as expected, the low rates of female representation in government have rendered the national approach to trafficking more criminal justice–oriented than victim centered. Recently, however, in the midst of a public reckoning about India's rape culture, individual women have emerged as critical actors in proposing new legislation that, if passed in both houses of Parliament, will push the country's anti-trafficking legislation more toward a victim-centered approach. Throughout the chapter we highlight both the role of patriarchy and embedded gender hierarchies in India as well as the various forms of violence against women experienced throughout the trafficking process as a way to leverage the feminist frame.

Background on Trafficking in India

The British colonization of India contributed to the emergence of one of the largest red-light districts in Asia, Kamathipura in Mumbai. In 2013 an estimated twenty thousand sex workers were on the streets of Kamathipura (*BBC News* 2013). During the eighteenth and nineteenth centuries the British used Mumbai, known as a "comfort zone," as a place to rest and relax and satisfy their carnal desires (Shared Hope International 2010; *BBC News* 2013). Although the red-light district initially developed as a locale for British colonizers to patronize prostitutes, once the colonial era ended in 1947, Kamathipura remained a hub for trafficking (Burke 2014). For sex workers in India, little has changed between the colonial era and today. Then poor rural girls were recruited to work in brothels (*BBC News* 2013); today rural women, girls, or their families are promised legitimate, well-paying work in the city only to find themselves enslaved by sex traffickers throughout the major red-light districts across India—Sonagachi in Kolkata, Budhwar Peth in Pune, and Meerguni in Allahabad.

In 2018 the Walk Free Foundation awarded India the dubious distinction of having the highest absolute number of people in slavery, with an estimate of an astounding 7.9 million slaves (Walk Free Foundation 2018b). Though our focus here is on sex trafficking and the sex slavery that ensues, slaves in India can be found working as bonded laborers in a multitude of industries, including agriculture, brick kilns, rice mills, mines, jewelry and embroidery factories, among many others. As Bales (2007) puts it, "almost any handmade good in India might be produced by a bonded laborer" (198). A bonded laborer secures a loan using their labor as collateral; if the debt is not paid, the victim must work to pay off the debt. Additional fees and debts are added in the course of working off the original loan. These debts can be and often are inherited from a relative, contributing to the enslavement of multiple generations within the same family (Bales 2007). Workers in the service industry in hotels and restaurants may also be bonded laborers, which is important to acknowledge in a study of sex trafficking and sex slavery because victims, who might otherwise appear to be prostitutes, may in fact be bonded laborers.

Factors Contributing to Sex Trafficking in India

We begin by evaluating our first argument regarding the factors that make certain populations of women and girls more vulnerable to becoming sex-trafficking victims: that the deprivation of women's economic rights intersects with caste status and poverty to make Dalit women and girls especially vulnerable to sex traffickers. That is, any country that deprives women of basic economic rights reveals itself as a culture that diminishes the value of women.

We also show that Dalits are at a distinct disadvantage because many of their human rights, which exist on paper, are not enforced or protected in practice. Dalit women and girls, who are both at the bottom of the social caste–based hierarchy and subjugated as a consequence of their gender, become acutely vulnerable to traffickers. Throughout we contrast our argument against other explanations of sex trafficking found in the literature—including crime, corruption, and legalized prostitution—to show that those factors are less effective in explaining outcomes in India.

Caste Status and Poverty

The caste system and widespread poverty, which affect women in particularly acute ways, are important for understanding the dynamics of sex trafficking in India. Despite having the fourth-largest economy in the world, more than 21.2 percent of India's population, or 262.8 million Indians, live below the poverty line and earn less than US$1.90 per day (World Bank 2017b). India's economy has been growing in recent years and India has transformed itself into a major exporter of agriculture. However, despite this dramatic economic growth, wide income inequality exists across many dimensions of Indian society. Within India the median household income varies considerably between states. Goa, Sikkim, and Delhi have the highest median incomes, with families bringing in between US$25,044 and US$19,543 annually in 2019–20, and the central states of Bihar, Uttar Pradesh, and Jharkhand have the lowest median household incomes, with families in Bihar earning approximately US$2,300 annually in 2019–20 (Government of India 2021). This regional variation in employment opportunities creates tremendous economic pressure for people living in poorer regions, which results in poor families frequently selling their daughters to bride traffickers, sometimes knowingly and other times because they are promised their daughters will be brides or will have legitimate employment.

The caste system, a centuries-old system of social and cultural stratification, further exacerbates differences between the economic groups and particularly renders Dalit women and girls highly vulnerable to sex traffickers. The caste system divides people based on their karma (work) and dharma (duty). The four varna (classes) consisted of Brahmins (priests), Kshatriya (fighters and rulers), Vaisya (farmers and cattle keepers), and Shudra (artisans such as blacksmiths, weavers, and potters) (Ghuman 2016, 10). A fifth group, the Candala (untouchables), exists completely outside of this system and are tasked with the most menial jobs in society. Within each caste are thousands of subcastes. The Hindu scriptures outline the obligations and duties incumbent upon each caste as well as the penalties associated with transgressing those rules, which gives this rigid social system religious sanction and cultural persistence (Ghuman 2016, 11).

The caste system in India diverges from a class system (with an elite, middle, and working class) because there is no possibility for social mobility between castes. One's position in the system is a permanent consequence of birth and is linked directly to behavior in past lives. For untouchables, or Dalits, as they have referred to themselves since a movement in the 1930s to expand their rights, the consequences of caste on rights enjoyment have been devastating. The upper castes consider Dalits impure and avoid any form of physical contact. The Dalit Freedom Network, a Dalit NGO, illustrates the extent to which other castes will go to avoid contact with Dalits: "In 70 percent of India's rural villages, members of other castes will not eat or drink with a Dalit. When a Dalit person asks for a drink, he or she is given a clay cup—which is to be crushed on the floor after use. Why? So no other person risks being polluted by it" (Dalit Freedom Network 2016).

The caste system amounts to an apartheid structure in India, as Dalits have separate housing and schools and are denied access to land (Human Rights Watch 2014). Manual scavengers work in dry latrines clearing human waste. Manual scavenging is part of a centuries-old feudal and caste-based custom that prescribes that this dirty and dangerous work is undertaken by those in scheduled castes and scheduled tribes (Human Rights Watch 2014a). Dalits are also exploited to clear sewer blockages, which is particularly dangerous work. Compared to other castes, the lowest median household income across India belongs to rural Dalits, who earn just RP18,000 per year (Desai et al. 2010, 14).

Guddi's story helps to illustrate how vulnerable those who exist outside the social system can be to traffickers (*BBC News* 2013). When she was eleven and living in West Bengal, which has become a major source for trafficking victims in India, a neighbor encouraged Guddi's parents to send her to Mumbai to work as a housemaid. West Bengal is notoriously poor and drought-prone, which makes survival challenging for many who live there. In Guddi's case the prospect of better-paying work in Mumbai was not a luxury. The family hoped that she would be able to send money home for food and the survival of the rest of the family. She was sent to a brothel in Kamathipura, Mumbai. Guddi's story is a common one: a family in severe economic distress sent their daughter off to what they thought would be decent work to improve the family's circumstances. Traffickers take advantage of the vulnerable, as they did in the case of Guddi and her family.

Across many surveys and studies of sex-trafficking victims in India, poverty is cited as the single most significant reason individuals become victims (Pandey 2018; Uddin 2017; HAQ 2016). The national survey of sex-trafficking victims completed for the Indian National Human Rights Commission by Sankar and Nair in 2004 suggests that the bulk of victims come from impoverished homes. The study classifies "impoverished" as less than RP2,000/month per family (approximately US$26.84 at 2021 conversion rates). Of the sex-trafficking victims surveyed, 47.5 percent came from impoverished homes: 25 percent were from families that earned more than this amount, and 27.7 percent could not speculate about their family's income (Sankar and Nair 2004, 100). The link between poverty and victimhood is even stronger among victims in the state of Maharashtra. In Maharashtra 95 percent of sex workers who were surveyed came from a home where the father earned less than RP3,500/month (approximately US$47.00 in 2021 conversion rates) (Vahini 2005, 23). Vahini's study identifies economic marginalization as the primary reason women find themselves in commercial sex trafficking.

Cultural Expectations Regarding Women's Role in Society

Scholars of feminist political economy highlight the ways in which gender hierarchies contribute to material violence against women (True 2012). India's rigid gender and social hierarchies display evidence of this link between patriarchy and material violence against women. Cultural expectations surrounding female babies, marriage, and child-rearing also tend to undermine women's access to education, which renders them more dependent on men or able to take only unskilled labor positions. Female feticide, which has increased dramatically since the introduction of ultrasound technology, has contributed to uneven birthrates (Trivedi and Juran 2015). States in northwest India have very low rates of female births (Trivedi and Juran 2015). Female children, if they are born at all, are often perceived to be a costly burden for their families due to the costs of marriage dowries that must be paid to the families of their potential husbands. With a high demand for brides in areas of the country lacking a more balanced male-to-female ratio, a thriving bride trafficking market has developed. Girls are often chosen to enter into the sex trade at a very young age and are expected, by their families and society, to become an important source of revenue for the family (Dalla et al. 2020).

The perception that girls are a costly burden to the family emanates from and is born of patriarchy and gendered stereotypes about the superiority of men and male children within Indian society. These embedded power dynamics contribute to gendered violence against women and girls. The prevalence of female feticide is particularly the sort of physical violence that feminist security scholars highlight, which quite literally deprives female fetuses of the right to life. But when families choose to sell their daughters to traffickers, they expose them to yet more forms of physical violence—deprivation of liberty and confinement, rape, and sexual violence. Deploying a feminist framework in India helps to reveal the link between embedded gender hierarchies and the gendered violence that female trafficking victims experience. Not surprisingly, the gendered underpinning of the societal value structure permeates all aspects of human trafficking in India. Even amelioration efforts are structured around patriarchal understandings of the vulnerability of women without men and the avoidance of responsibility by men for their bad acts toward women (Chetry and Pande 2019).

Deprivation of Women's Economic Rights

Prevailing cultural norms that serve to subjugate women and girls also contribute to both physical and material violence against them. When the economic rights of women and girls are neither protected by law nor enforced in practice, women and girls are at greater risk of becoming sex-trafficking victims precisely because they lack the means to support themselves economically. Recall that the roster of economic rights—equality in the workplace in hiring and promotion, equal pay, and nondiscrimination by employers—functions as a surrogate for the cultural status of women in general. Both the Indian Constitution and the Indian penal code are relatively progressive in their support for gender equality in the workplace. However, enforcement of this progressive approach to gender equality is lacking in India and the lack of enforcement of these provisions has particularly deleterious consequences for Dalit women and girls across India.

Article 14 of the Indian Constitution provides for equality before the law, while Article 15 prohibits discrimination on the basis of sex. The Equal Remuneration Act of 1976 also provides for gender equity in pay (Government of India 1976). However, in spite of these provisions, it has been very difficult for Indian women to obtain equal rights in the workplace. As India's economy experiences rapid growth, women have been disappearing from the formal labor market. By 2010 India's female labor force participation was just 29 percent, a decline of approximately 15 percent from the prior decade (ILO 2018). Women tend to work in the informal economy and are left out of the more lucrative manufacturing sector. For those women who do obtain jobs in the formal sector, they earn on average 24 percent less than their male counterparts (ILO 2018).

In a far-reaching survey conducted across seventeen states in India in 2018 by the Confederation of Indian Industries Indian Women's Network, female respondents paint a startling picture of workplace discrimination.[1] More than 42 percent of the female respondents felt they had suffered from managerial bias, while 33 percent believed there were different standards for male and female employees. Until 2013 there were no national laws prohibiting sexual harassment in the workplace. Even the passage of a new anti-harassment law in 2013 failed to improve the situation since it makes the employers solely responsible for addressing sexual harassment in their workplaces.

Poor enforcement of existing laws designed to create gender parity in the workplace acts as a disincentive for Indian women who might seek employment in the formal labor market. And while there are a variety of other reasons that Indian women are disappearing from the formal labor market, their retreat means they have fewer opportunities to support themselves financially.

Deprivation of Dalit Rights

The poor enforcement of gender parity laws has served to make already marginalized populations especially vulnerable to traffickers in India. Although there are a series of laws that protect the rights of all Dalits, in practice those laws are not consistently enforced and Dalits are targeted for a variety of crimes by people in upper castes (Selvi 2020). Dalits who attempt to report crimes committed against them are often subject to retribution, rendering this population vulnerable to traffickers. Rape and sexual violence are used by members of upper castes as weapons of political terror to silence and further malign Dalit women and girls. As Selvi (2020, 12) explains:

> Countless challenges are part of the daily lives of Dalit women. They battle for their livelihood as daily wage labourers in the fields of landlords, usually from the dominant caste. Gender-based discrimination manifests in multiple ways in the lives of these women. The economic exploitation of Dalit women is a common phenomenon; they are paid less than their male counterparts, even when working for the same landlord. Dalit women are assigned subordinate roles at their workplace. Dalit women are also subjected to sexual violence by the landlord; this is typical of the power-dynamic that persists due to caste-discrimination. The severity of the sexual violence against them and the pernicious disrespect they face makes their economic exploitation pale in significance.

Though many laws have been passed in India that ought to protect the rights of Dalits, the varied forms of structural, economic, and sexual violence experienced routinely by Dalit women in India cannot be understated. In 1949, following independence from Great Britain, a new Indian Constitution was passed. Article 17 of the constitution formally abolished the concept of untouchability. The passage of this article was followed by the Untouchability Offenses Act of 1955, which served to outlaw discrimination against Dalits in places of worship, eating establishments, and hospitals, among many other areas. The purpose of this law is to prevent discrimination against Dalits throughout their daily lives and facilitate equal social and economic rights between Dalits and other castes (Government of India 1955). Similarly, the 1989 Scheduled Castes and Scheduled Tribes (Prevention of Atrocities) Act was passed in an effort to better protect the human rights of Dalits. The 1989 law is a far-reaching effort to prevent atrocities committed against specific castes and tribes. The law also creates special courts to try those accused of such crimes and provides rehabilitation support to victims (Government of India 1989).

The robust laws passed to prevent discrimination against Dalits are complemented by similarly far-reaching laws designed to stamp out sex trafficking. We discuss anti-trafficking laws at length in subsequent sections of this chapter, but here it is important to remember that the trafficking literature points to strong anti-trafficking laws and a strong rule of law as being important mechanisms for preventing sex trafficking (Cho and Vadlamannati 2012), and our study of India calls the sufficiency of these laws into question. The Indian government has passed progressive laws designed to protect scheduled castes and tribes and to prevent sex trafficking, but by every measure sex trafficking of Dalit women and girls continues to be a pervasive problem.

Despite the passage of these laws, discrimination and outright violence against and trafficking of Dalits are common. Physical violence is particularly severe for Dalits who are perceived to oppose the demands of the upper castes. This violence takes the form of beatings, rape, and death. In a single year (2001–2), more than 58,000 cases of violence against scheduled castes and scheduled tribes were reported (Human Rights Watch 2007).[2] Yet the conviction rate for cases of atrocities committed against Dalits in 2006 was just 5.3 percent (*Times of India* 2016). When Dalits report crimes committed against them to authorities, they face a double threat. First, authorities are generally disinclined to investigate and prosecute when the victim is Dalit. Indeed, a major effort that Dalit human rights groups undertake is accompanying Dalit victims to police stations to persuade the often upper caste officers to file the report (Selvi 2020, 16). If they do prosecute, the conviction rate for those accused of committing crimes against Dalits is startlingly low. The second threat comes in the form of retaliatory violence from members of upper castes. The retribution through violence that Dalits experience for reporting crimes or agitating for their rights is well known and well documented (Naurla 1999; Human Rights Watch 2007).

In 2007 the UN Committee on the Elimination of Racial Discrimination evaluated the Indian government's efforts to investigate, prosecute, and convict those accused of crimes committed against Dalits. The committee's report observed: "The Committee notes with concern allegations that the police frequently fail to properly register and investigate complaints about acts of violence and discrimination against members of scheduled castes and scheduled tribes, the high percentage of acquittals and the low conviction rate in cases registered under the Scheduled Castes and Scheduled Tribes (Prevention of Atrocities) Act (1989), and the alarming backlog of atrocities cases pending in the courts (art. 6)" (CERD 2007). Thus those who commit crimes against Dalits frequently do so with impunity. This calls into question one of the prevailing explanations for sex trafficking in the literature, namely that a lack of respect for the rule of law within a country beset by crime contributes to trafficking (Cho 2015). In India, police investigate and prosecute a wide variety of crimes, but when it comes to crimes committed against Dalits they have a much lower propensity to prosecute, a dynamic that emboldens criminals who wish to commit crimes against this population.

Deprivation of economic rights are a critical factor in explaining ongoing patterns of discrimination against Dalits. Human Rights Watch (2007, 16) argues:

> The denial of the right to work and free choice of employment lies at the very heart of the caste system. Dalits are forced to work in "polluting" and degrading occupations such as manual scavenging and are subject to exploitative labor arrangements such as bonded labor, migratory labor, and forced prostitution . . . —Dalits are also discriminated against in hiring and in the payment of wages by private employers. Dalits' attempts to enforce their rights are met with retaliatory violence and social and economic boycotts.

Dalits experience routine discrimination, repression, and violence across India. The enormity of the problem comes into focus as this group—approximately 201.4 million people in India are Dalit—represents a large and vulnerable pool of victims for traffickers to exploit.[3]

Forms of Sex Trafficking in India

Sex trafficking in India manifests through several specific channels. Here we briefly discuss how the different types of common trafficking occur.

"Bride" Trafficking

"Brides" are trafficked primarily to states in the northwest of India—the provinces of Punjab, Rajasthan, western Uttar Pradesh, and particularly Haryana. In 2019 UNICEF estimated that one in three child brides in the world lives in India (UNICEF 2019). Haryana, the state with one of the highest average individual incomes in India, is a major destination point for brides trafficked from the much poorer states of West Bengal, Bihar, and Assam (UNODC 2013). Part of the demand for trafficked brides is a consequence of female feticide, which leads to a highly imbalanced male-to-female birth ratio. The prevalence of female feticide in India has, according to a 2019 report from the Population Research Institute, contributed to the elimination of 16 million girls in India through female feticide since 1990 (Abbamonte 2019). When large segments of the male population in these northern states were unable to find wives, a thriving trade in girls and women emerged. But female feticide alone cannot fully explain the phenomenon because many of the source states in India also have highly imbalanced male-to-female birth ratios (Khan 2013).[4] Khan (2013) suggests that the high rate of bride trafficking into Haryana is also connected to the types of professions widely practiced in the region—the police, army, and transport truck drivers frequently driving to other regions for work make connections for traffickers possible. Trafficked brides in the Jatland region of Haryana are called *molki*, meaning "purchased"; in some regions in Haryana and Rajasthan they are called *paro*, meaning "stolen" (Khan 2013, 45). Molki and paro are both derogatory terms, and any girls who become molki and paro are not treated like wives in the traditional sense. Rather, they are thought of and treated like slaves. Their families are often paid a small amount, in one case only US$40, and told (frequently by a relative) that they will help the daughter "settle" and find a husband elsewhere (Trivedi and Juran 2015). Rural families with many daughters are often relieved to send their daughters away because a proper marriage requires a dowry, which in 2015 was, on average, approximately double the cost of the median annual income of a middle-class Indian family (Trivedi and Juran 2015). Once they arrive in the home of their new family, they are considered something akin to a household slave and "sex toy."[5] They are confined to the home and may be used for the sexual gratification of all male members of the family (Glerstorfer 2014). They are expected to cook, clean, run the household, and care for the children and elderly.

If they do escape, they cannot return to their homes because they are no longer considered part of their nuclear family and will usually be turned away. But they also are never accepted as a part of their new community (Dalla and Kreimer 2017). They are seen as outsiders and viewed as property. If they are recaptured, they are likely to endure beatings or be sold once again. Because molki and paro are property for the families who acquire them, they are frequently resold, to another family or a brothel, to generate income for the family. The average molki or paro will be resold between two and five times over the course of their lives (Raza 2014).

The varied forms of violence that molki and paro experience are captured by Roshini's story. Roshini was just thirteen years old when her parents sold her to a trafficker to get money to feed their other children (BBC 2014). Her family lives in Jharkhand, a state in eastern India. During the time that she was "married" she gave birth to nine children, but when her husband died, she and her children were thrown out of their home. Like many paro and molki, she now lives in a shack trying to eke out a living to feed her children. Her brother-in-law visits her frequently and threatens her because he expects her to "marry" him. Roshini's story is indicative of many whom we have come across, with parents selling their youngest daughters to feed the rest of the family. A feminist frame allows us to highlight the ways in which marginalized women from Dalit communities are more likely to be trafficked as molki and paro as compared to other groups in India. This framework also reveals the many forms of gender-based violence these women and girls experience as part of the trafficking process, starting with material dependence on a family willing to sell them to traffickers, followed by material dependence on a new "husband's" family (Guha 2018). As Roshini's story illustrates, these women and girls are also highly vulnerable to sexual slavery and violence.

In our interview with Soumya Pratheek, the senior program assistant for Aapne Aap World Wide, we learned that certain scheduled tribes have embraced forced prostitution of molki and paro following the birth of the first child. The daughter-in-law is not sold to traffickers; her new "family members" themselves act as her pimps.[6] In a 2010 study conducted by the NGO Drishti Stree Adhyayan Prabodhan Kendra in Haryana, of the 10,000 brides surveyed, 9,000 were purchased and imported from other regions of India (UNODC 2013, 94).

Brothel-Based Prostitution and Red-Light Districts

Women and girls are also trafficked for the purpose of commercial sexual exploitation in brothels, bars, and other places of "entertainment." Though historically these victims have been found primarily in brothels, modernization is expanding the venues by which women and children are sold for sex in India. Johns visit spas, beer gardens, massage parlors, and dance bars to seek out sex on demand (UNODC 2013, 11). These victims tend to come from poor rural communities within India as well as from neighboring Nepal and Bangladesh, and globally from former Soviet Bloc countries. Domestically, the primary source states for these victims are the same as the source states for bride-trafficking victims: West Bengal, Andhra Pradesh, Karnataka, Maharashtra, and Odisha (UNODC 2013). Tribal girls from Chhattisgarh, in eastern India, are particularly vulnerable because they live in very rural areas and their tribes have limited contact with the outside world. They tend to be trafficked to major cities for forced prostitution: "According to a former Chief Minister of Chhattisgarh, 20,000 girls belonging to Chhattisgarh's tribal region have been sold to traffickers in the last eight years in cities like Delhi, Mumbai, Bangalore and Chennai" (UNODC 2013, 76).

One of the major red-light districts in India, Delhi's GB Road, has approximately ninety-two brothels where more than 4,000 women and girls are engaged in sex work (UNODC 2013, 80). Victims found on GB Road come from various Indian states (Jharkhand, Madhya Pradesh, Uttar Pradesh, Uttarakhand, Haryana, Assam, Tamil Nadu, Karnataka, Maharashtra, Rajasthan, and Bihar)

(UNODC 2013, 80). Foreign victims on GB Road come from neighboring Nepal and Bangladesh or from Common Wealth of Independent State (CIS) countries, including Ukraine, Georgia, Kazakhstan, Uzbekistan, Azerbaijan, Chechnya, and Kyrgyzstan (UNODC 2013, 11). The border with Nepal has relatively few checkpoints, which allows for easy crossing as a means of bringing Nepalese women and girls into West Bengal (Sen 2005). Missing children from Delhi are often kidnapped by the Bedia, Nat, and Kanjar tribes, held until they reach puberty, and then sold to brothels in Mumbai (UNODC 2013, 80).

Historically, sex-trafficking victims found in Kamathipura in Maharashtra tended to come from regions that are poor and drought-prone, which enhances food insecurity. Dalits, who face tremendous discrimination, find it particularly hard to survive in the regions surrounding Kamathipura and thus become acutely susceptible to traffickers who promise legitimate work or simply buy or kidnap women and girls (UNODC 2013, 118). In a study interviewing 580 sex workers in Delhi brothels, nearly one in four (24 percent) were trafficking victims (Sarkar et al. 2008). The vast majority of the victims interviewed for that study were Indian (84 percent), but victims from Nepal and Bangladesh were also identified.

Foreign victims who are found within India come from marginalized minority communities such as the Rohingyas (US Department of State 2013, 195). The Rohingyas are a Muslim minority group from Burma who have been severely oppressed by the military junta there following the passage of a 1982 citizenship law denying them Burmese citizenship. Since that time the Rohingyas have settled in refugee camps in Thailand and Bangladesh and have sought to travel to Malaysia. They have faced widespread persecution throughout the region and their most basic human rights remain imperiled (Human Rights Watch 2021).

Devadasis

Within India there are many paths that lead women and girls (and in some cases boys) to become sex-trafficking victims. For example, temple slavery is particularly prevalent in southern India—in Karnataka, Tamil Nadu, and Andhra Pradesh states—but can also be found in Maharashtra.[7] Temple slaves, or *devadasis*, are handed over to temples in their childhood or infancy to be dedicated to Hindu gods (M. Black 2007). Once there, they may perform a variety of functions for the religious personnel, including sexual favors (Sankar and Nair 2004, 195). Dedicating one's daughter to a temple has a long history in India, but it has today become a way of essentially selling a daughter into prostitution while hiding behind a cloak of religious legitimacy.

HuligeAmma, a Dalit woman in her midforties, was just twelve when her parents devoted her to the Hindu goddess Yellamma (Paul 2015). From that point forward she lived at the temple and served as the concubine of a wealthy man, a temple priest, and a village elder until they tired of her, at which point her official role was to serve the sexual "needs" of the town's men as a devadasi

(Sarkar 2014). Going without food or pay, she was forced to perform sexual acts for any and all men who visited the temple. HuligeAmma was impregnated by five different men, none of whom assisted her with the costs of child-rearing (Paul 2015). Although this ritualized system of temple slavery was outlawed in 1988, the practice perseveres. Estimates suggest that there are more than 17,000 devadasis in Andhra Pradesh and 23,000 in Karnataka, with these women and girls coming almost exclusively from the lowest socioeconomic castes in India (M. Black 2007). In a 2007 survey of devadasis, 93 percent were from scheduled castes (Dalits) and 7 percent were from scheduled tribes (Black 2007). HuligeAmma's story has a happier ending than most: following her escape from the temple, she spent years with one of her daughters working in an iron ore mine, until she sought the assistance of Sakhi Trust in 2009. The NGO helped her get all her children into school and trained her to become a seamstress, a skill she uses both to support herself and share with other Dalit women and girls to help them become self-reliant.

Attention to the intersectional aspects of identity are critical in revealing the embedded power hierarchies that render Dalit girls prone to sexual slavery. Dalit girls are in a double bind—at the bottom of the Indian social hierarchy as a consequence of their Dalit status and at the bottom of the gender hierarchy because they are female. Families who worry about the high cost of a dowry may choose to dedicate their daughters to temple slavery. Once dedicated to a temple, girls are exposed to significant physical, emotional, and sexual violence, violence that includes deprivation of liberty and the freedom to make the most basic life decisions about where one eats and sleeps, to severe, life-altering sexual violence that leads to multiple pregnancies. Without the means to support themselves or their children, the range of opportunities and possibilities for these girls narrows significantly, leaving many resigned to living as temple slaves or bonded laborers.

Recruitment Strategies

Traffickers in India employ many and varied recruitment strategies. In many of the cases we encountered, traffickers simply approached poor children and promised good jobs in far-off places. For example, in Bhoot, a small rural village in the eastern state of Jharkhand where the Indian government has been locked in a battle with Maoist insurgents, girls have become acutely susceptible to traffickers (Kumar 2013). When women and girls go missing, family members assume that they have been picked up by state security forces or abducted by Maoist rebels. State authorities, on the other hand, estimate that approximately 100,000 girls are trafficked out of Jharkhand every year (Kumar 2013).

Slightly more than half of the respondents to the Indian National Human Rights Commission survey (51.8 percent) explained that they had been forced, deceived, or lured by traffickers (Sankar and Nair 2004, 102). For the other half of the respondents, the decision to enter the sex trade was not the result of deception on the part of the traffickers but rather a complex set of personal circumstances that made them feel as though they had few choices; 13 percent said that poverty gave them no other options so they "knowingly" became victims to survive. Consistent with the information already presented, 22 percent of those surveyed said that marriage-related problems were responsible for their victimhood, while 7.3 percent said that it was related to community customs (Sankar and Nair 2004, 102). An earlier and widely cited study of prostitution in India suggests that after economic distress, which among respondents accounts for 43.7 percent of the motivation for becoming a prostitute, desertion by a spouse (24.5 percent of cases) and deception by another person (11.9 percent of cases) were the most significant reasons women entered the commercial sex trade in India (Mukherjee and Das 1996, 42). A final set of statistics from respondents paints a startling picture about recruitment tactics used by traffickers. Victims knew their traffickers in 52.5 percent of cases and in an additional 34.8 percent the traffickers were part of the victims' families. In only 11.1 percent of cases were the traffickers unknown to the victims (Sankar and Nair 2004, 104; Sarkar et al. 2008). These dynamics link back to India's strong cultural preferences for sons and the widely held belief that daughters are a drain on the family. Traffickers create opportunities for families to relieve themselves of the obligation to pay a potential husband's family a costly dowry and at the same time shed the cost of supporting an unmarried woman or girl.

Taken together, these statistics suggest that many victims are deceived by those who recruit them and that recruiters are most frequently people the victim knows, including members of their own families. When husbands desert their wives, those women sink quickly into desperate poverty and become easy prey for traffickers. Traffickers come along and promise either good jobs to victims (68.1 percent of cases) or marriage (16.8 percent of cases) (Sankar and Nair 2004, 105). Poverty, economic marginalization, and caste affiliation make victims particularly susceptible to traffickers. Further, the cultural devaluation of women in India creates the unfortunate situation that, more often than not, the victims are deceived or recruited by people they know or their family members.

Combating Trafficking in India: Criminal Justice or Victim-Centered?

We now turn to the question of whether the human trafficking amelioration regime in India is victim-centered or prosecutorial. Recall that for anti-trafficking policy to be identified as victim-centered, governments must provide consistent funding to victim shelters, reduce the number of arrests of victims living under the guise of prostitution, and provide special visas to foreign trafficking victims. Alternatively, sharp spikes in the rate of trafficker convictions provide support to the idea that the country has developed a more criminal justice or prosecution-oriented approach.

Two caveats are relevant for understanding law and policy in India. Under federal law, prostitution is legal, so there are no arrests for prostitution, but it is a crime to solicit a client for sex in a public place or to engage in hotel-based prostitution.[8] While the Indian Crime Records Bureau collects and reports data on the rate of trafficker investigations dating back to 2006, the data are not disaggregated between investigations of traffickers and investigations of solicitation. Therefore we can assess whether the Indian government is more interested in investigating trafficking-related crimes but cannot draw conclusions about who is more likely to be arrested—traffickers or victims. In assessing the approach taken to curbing trafficking in India, we rely on funding patterns for shelters and the provision of special visas. Additionally, since 2005 the federal government has created special anti–human trafficking police units, making it possible to examine the growth in the number of policing units over time—a larger police presence corresponds closely with a criminal justice approach to combating trafficking.

Between 1956 and 2013 trafficking in India was penalized under the Immoral Traffic (Prevention) Act (ITPA). Passed in 1956, the act "prohibits trafficking in persons, criminalizes sexual exploitation, and provides enhanced penalties for offences involving minors" (US Department of State 2003, 80). Yet Section 8 of the ITPA also allows for the arrest and prosecution of sex-trafficking victims and provides harsher penalties for soliciting for women than for men (Indian Government 1956).[9] The result is that the prevailing law in India treats sex-trafficking victims as though they are criminals. The data on arrest and prosecution rates of sex workers in the 2002–3 Indian National Human Rights Commission survey reinforces that assessment. The majority of the women interviewed (57.9 percent) had been arrested by the police for solicitation (Sankar and Nair 2004, 85).

The brutal gang rape of twenty-three-year-old Jyoti Singh on a moving bus in Delhi in 2012 sparked nationwide protests about violence against women and led to an important change in federal anti-trafficking laws. Following the rape, Ms. Singh died of her injuries in a Singapore hospital. As protests about her death and the status of women intensified, two former and one current Supreme Court justices wrote a report assessing the status of women in the country (Verma, Seth, and Subramanium 2013). The report included a damning section on sex trafficking of women and girls in India and argued that Parliament should pass new national anti-trafficking legislation. Following the publication of this report the Indian Parliament amended Section 370 of the Indian Penal Code to prohibit trafficking and provide punishment for traffickers that range from seven years to life. The new law does not criminalize prostitution of children under the age of eighteen (US Department of State 2015). We can evaluate the extent to which the Indian approach to trafficking relies on a criminal justice approach versus advancing the human rights of victims to determine whether that outcome can be explained with reference to the role of women in society. While the death of Joyti Singh was one catalyst for new anti-trafficking laws in India, her death and the subsequent protests have led to an approach that is more victim-centered.

Criminal Justice?

In 2005 the Ministry of Home Affairs, in conjunction with the UN Office on Drugs and Crime, began placing special anti–human trafficking units (AHTUs) embedded within police departments (US Department of State 2009). The purpose of the AHTUs is to strengthen awareness and training of law enforcement regarding human trafficking. Seminars and special programs are offered to officers to improve investigations and increase the likelihood of prosecutions against traffickers (UNODC 2013, 29). In the pilot program run jointly by the UN Office on Drugs and Crime and the Indian government, five Indian states were selected for a three-year trial run—Andhra Pradesh, Bihar, Goa, Maharashtra, and West Bengal (UNODC 2013). Following the success of the pilot program, the Indian Ministry of Home Affairs earmarked US$18 million for the creation of 297 AHTUs across India (US Department of State 2009).

Over time the Ministry of Home Affairs has consistently earmarked funds toward the creation of new AHTUs. Following the initial commitment of $18 million in 2008, the ministry approved the establishment of eighty-seven new AHTUs as a part of its Comprehensive Scheme for Strengthening Law Enforcement Response in India (Bernat and Zhilina 2011). In 2009 the federal government expanded the number of AHTUs from nine to thirty-eight throughout India (US Department of State 2010, 173). By 2013 the approximate number of AHTUs in India was three hundred (US Department of State 2013, 197).

There is wide variation in the effectiveness of these AHTUs. While in Andhra Pradesh the AHTUs did not meet once during the 2013 reporting period, the 2013 TIP Report praises the AHTUs in Mumbai and West Bengal for assisting with investigations (US Department of State 2013, 197). NGOs report that when police officers receive training as members of the AHTUs they are less inclined to arrest victims for solicitation, which suggests that the AHTUs foster an increased awareness of the need for victim protection (US Department of State 2009).

At the state level, approaches to combating trafficking have varied dramatically. For example, the state government in Maharashtra has been proactive in
developing legislation to combat human sex trafficking, but the treatment of
victims as a result of this legislation has been controversial. In 2000 a bill was
proposed in Maharashtra titled "The Protection of Maharashtra Commercial
Sex Workers Act." If it had passed it would have required prostitutes to register
and undergo regular medical screenings by the state. The most controversial
portion of the law was the proposed "branding" of prostitutes with tattoos for
identification and monitoring (Patkar and Patkar 2000, 15). In 2003 trafficking
and brothel-keeping became a crime in Maharashtra under a revised version
of the Maharashtra Control of Organized Crime Act. In practice it meant that
individuals accused of these crimes could not receive bail (US Department of
State 2003, 81). That same year, the performance standards for police were
revised in Andhra Pradesh—they were to be evaluated on how many traffickers
and brothel owners they arrested, not on how many sex workers they arrested
for solicitation (81).

Despite the growth in the number of AHTUs over time, there has not been
concurrent growth in the number of prosecutions and convictions for trafficking. Though the data are sparse, two points can be made. First, over time
there has been growth in the number of cases registered under the 1956 ITPA,
meaning more investigations into trafficking-related offenses. Figure 3.1 shows
the steady rise in the number of cases investigated under the 1956 law. However, investigations into solicitation are also included in these totals, meaning
that both traffickers and victims are combined, further obfuscating the picture.
This suggests that while the necessary legal mechanisms are in place to combat
trafficking and convict traffickers, India is still suffering from an enforcement
problem.

Second, though the data are very sparse, the higher rate of investigations
noted in figure 3.1 does not yield higher trafficker conviction rates. Rather
than reporting conviction rates, the Indian government reports acquittal rates
(see fig. 3.2). Across the three years for which we could find reliable data, the
acquittal rates hover somewhere between 77 percent and 65 percent, meaning
the majority of trafficking cases that make it to the courts result in acquittal.
Again, because the data on investigations are not disaggregated between traffickers and victims, we cannot draw conclusions about what these acquittal
rates mean for the protection of trafficking victims.

Victim-Centered?
In India the federal government distributes funds to state governments,
which play a considerable role in running the shelters for victims of trafficking. The federal government also distributes funds to NGOs, but the role of

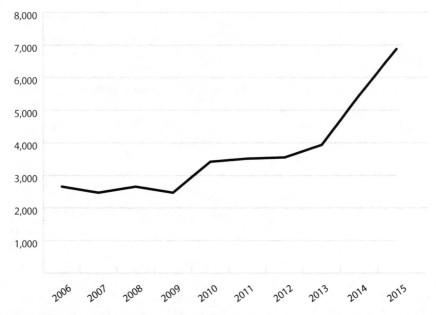

Figure 3.1. Cases of Trafficking Registered under the 1956 Immoral Trafficking Prevention Act

Source: Indian National Crime Reports trafficking section, Indian National Crime Bureau (2005–16), http://ncrb.gov.in/, last accessed January 2021.

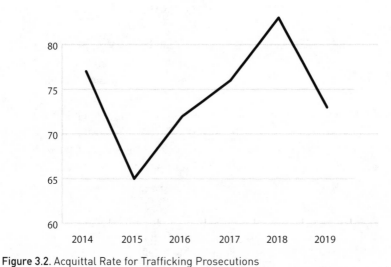

Figure 3.2. Acquittal Rate for Trafficking Prosecutions

Source: US State Department Trafficking in Persons Reports 2016, 2017, 2020, and 2021.

state governments in victim assistance makes the Indian approach distinct from that seen in other countries. Unfortunately, by most accounts the government's reach into these shelters has resulted in exceptionally poor shelter conditions for victims and inconsistent funding (US Department of State 2004, 214; 2013, 197).

The Department of Women and Child Development (DWCD), a federal institution in India, is responsible for distributing funds through two programs to assist trafficking victims. The Swadhar program is designed to distribute money from the central government to NGOs to build shelters (US Department of State 2006, 139). In 2008 the central government added a second program to distribute funds to assist sex-trafficking victims, the Ujjawala program (US Department of State 2009, 157). The Ujjawala program provides funding for fifty-three state-level projects to assist trafficking victims. Maharashtra was one of the first states to receive funding in 2008. State authorities in Andhra Pradesh developed a special fund that provides $200 to each victim out of the funding received through the Ujjawala program (157). By 2010 the DWCD had funded 134 projects under the Ujjawala program. These projects are spread across sixteen states and include the creation of 238 women's helplines (US Department of State 2011, 190).

In Maharashtra, NGOs have a considerable task as they co-run with state authorities all juvenile trafficking–victim shelters (US Department of State 2004, 215). The influence of NGOs has led to many improvements in the conditions at the shelters, including more staff, nurses, and physicians, better nutrition, and more recreation and vocational training. Nationally, NGOs play a very important role as well because the government funds 100 NGO-run hotlines for victim identification (US Department of State 2012, 185). NGOs are instrumental in lobbying state officials to release rehabilitation funds that should be disbursed to victims. Beginning in 2013, many of the Ujjawala and Swandhar homes were closed because cases of abuse were discovered within the homes (US Department of State 2013, 197).

Shelters face continued serious financial shortages, making it difficult for them to employ trained staff. Gaps in funding to shelters have also been blamed for the possibility that victims are vulnerable to being retrafficked, since victims being transferred from temporary detention to long-term shelter facilities are often not escorted by police or shelter staffs (US Department of State 2015). By 2016–17, the Indian government increased the budget for the Ujjawala program from $3.2 million to $5.5 million. A corresponding decrease in the budget for the Swadhar program, from $13.2 million to $11.8 million, seems to suggest that the government is not making a new commitment to funding shelters, but only just shifting the same money from one program to another (US Department of State 2017).

India does not provide visas to allow foreign trafficking victims to remain in the country. Instead, the government treats foreign victims as illegal migrants and deports them for violating the Foreigners' Act. Foreign sex-trafficking victims are treated slightly differently than foreign victims trafficked for other purposes because they are detained in government shelters until they are repatriated to their country of origin (US Department of State 2014). For some foreign sex-trafficking victims, especially those from Bangladesh, shelter detentions can stretch on for two to four years. While being detained in these shelters victims cannot work or leave the premises, so this policy is equivalent to incarceration of victims. A memorandum of understanding signed by Bangladesh and India in 2015 sought to repatriate victims as expeditiously as possible but made no reference to the possibility of Bangladeshi victims being permitted to stay in India.

Between July 2014 and March 2015 the Indian government also confiscated "T" visas marked from Indians returning home from the United States (Szep and Spetalnick 2015b). Under the terms of the US Trafficking Victims Protection Act, the T-visa must be provided to adult trafficking victims who can demonstrate that their arrival in the United States meets at least one of the following conditions: 1) that they were transported at some point against their will; 2) that they were the victim of coercion or fraud; or 3) that the goal of their traffickers was to force them into slavery of some form. The Indian government's decision to confiscate the passports of Indians who had been recognized as trafficking victims by the US government was a political decision in response to a conflict over the indictment of Devyani Khobragade, the Indian deputy consul general in New York, for visa fraud. Khobragade was charged in a Manhattan district court for making false statements in the visa application process for a woman she brought over from India to work in her household. The household worker was also allegedly paid less than minimum wage. Khobragade's arrest set off a diplomatic firestorm, with the Indian government vowing that "everything that can be done will be done" in response to what it called the "barbaric" act of arrest (Gowen 2013).

Taken together these data suggest numerous important things about the national anti-trafficking regime in India. First, great improvements have been made in federal legislation since 2013 and have shifted the government's focus toward convicting traffickers rather than arresting victims. The introduction and expansion of AHTUs across India has also created a dedicated police force capable of arresting traffickers and rescuing victims.

India's approach to combating trafficking thus falls somewhere along the middle of our proposed continuum—rising investigation and prosecution rates as well as a financial commitment to funding victim shelters evince considerable state efforts to pursue both a criminal justice and a human rights–based approach. Like in many other countries, however, challenges persist. A considerable number of prosecutions are accompanied by low levels of convictions, which undermine any deterrent effect such prosecutions might have on would-be traffickers. Similarly, while the Indian government has directed the DWCD to fund many victim shelters, the conditions in these shelters are still lacking. To be sure, the task of providing for such a large population of victims is fraught with challenges, so it may well be that India has not yet achieved the sort of victim-protection regime that is needed to secure victims' rights in meaningful ways or that such policies will be emplaced in the years to come. Although social workers have become the front line of defense for victims of human trafficking, they have few resources at their disposal and are but one link in the continuum of care that would be necessary to effectively combat sex trafficking (Sekhar and Kaushik 2017). However, an investigation into the forms of sex slavery and the identities of victims does shed light on the underlying cultural causes of these outcomes, namely, that bride trafficking, temple slavery, and brothel-based forced prostitution primarily affect women and girls from minority communities. The next question concerns the extent to which women have been involved in pushing the needle closer to the victim-centered approach in India.

The Role of Women

Since the rape and death of Joyti Singh in 2012, women in India have been protesting the rape culture that exists in India. Women and girls have been the targets of rape in public places, often by groups of men, at previously unseen rates. Rapes of girls reported to police have doubled between 2012 and 2016 (Biswas 2018). Efforts to protest and confront the rape crisis frequently intersect with the efforts of civil society groups advocating for the rights of sex workers and the rights of sex-trafficking victims. Though they have historically lacked high or even average rates of formal representation in the legislature and cabinet, women have been instrumental in proposing and advocating for new victim-centered anti-trafficking legislation in India in recent years.

Whether examining cabinet positions in the lower house (Lok Sabha) or upper house (Rajya Sabha) of Parliament, rates of female representation in India are very low. Between 2008 and 2017 female representation in Parliament never exceeded 12 percent (see fig. 3.3). For comparison, in 2017 the global average for female legislative representation was 21.3 percent (UN Women and Inter-Parliamentary Union 2017). Between 2015 and 2017 a larger proportion of cabinet positions went to women, which coincides with the introduction of

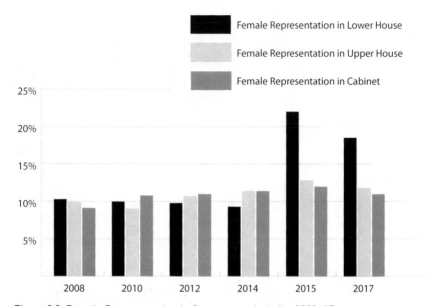

Figure 3.3. Female Representation in Government in India, 2008–17

Source: UN Women and Inter-Parliamentary Union, "Women in Politics," assessed annually between 2008 and 2017. For 2008–16 see Appendix 2B; for 2017 see http://www.unwomen.org /en/digital-library/publications/2017/4/women-in-politics-2017-map.

new victim-centered legislation in the Lok Sabha in 2018 (*Hindustan Times* 2018). However, the bill stalled out in the Lok Sabah, never making it to the Rajya Sabha when Narendra Modi's first term ended (Pandit 2020).

To get a sense of whether these are only regional effects, meaning that perhaps there are distinct regional norms surrounding the role of women in society that inhibit women from participating in government throughout South Asia, a review of data on rates of female representation in the lower house of Parliament in other South Asian countries during the same period of time is useful. Data is included for Bangladesh and Pakistan between 2008 and 2017 in figure 3.4. Even when compared to its regional peers, some of which arguably should be more conservative with respect to the role of women in society, India lags far behind in terms of female political representation.

Expectations based on the literature are that where female legislative representation is high, stronger national efforts to protect the rights of sex-trafficking victims will be seen. In India a dismally low rate of female legislative representation coincides with an anti-trafficking regime that is neither victim-centered nor prosecutorial. Throughout the period leading up to 2015, all available evidence suggests that the government was simply not advancing laws or policies capable of promoting victims' human rights. And while

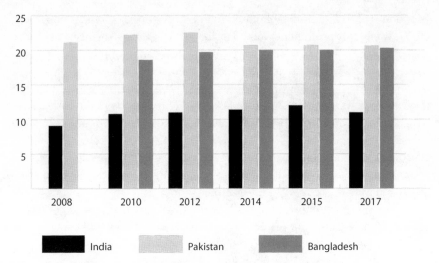

Figure 3.4. Female Representation in the Lower House in India, Pakistan, and Bangladesh, 2008–17*

*In 2008 the Bangladesh Parliament was dissolved.

Source: UN Women and Inter-Parliamentary Union, "Women in Politics," assessed annually between 2008 and 2017. For 2008–16 see Appendix 2B; for 2017 see http://www.unwomen.org /en/digital-library/publications/2017/4/women-in-politics-2017-map.

this does not shift dramatically with the increase in female cabinet positions in 2014, that year was a turning point. Under the Bharatiya Janata Party (BJP) government that came to power in 2014, women were put into seven of forty-five cabinet posts, or 15 percent.[10] Though this is not to suggest that the election of the BJP was the sole cause, nevertheless the push to transform India's anti-trafficking legislation coincided with the shift in female representation in the cabinet. Later we show that the female minister of Women and Children's Development, appointed in 2014, was instrumental in advocating for the new 2018 legislation. Although Modi's second term effectively killed this bill in the upper house, the fact of its introduction by one of the few female ministers in his cabinet provides some support for the argument that the role of women in promoting victims' rights is essential.

The Bharatiya Janata Party is a Hindu nationalist party that came to power in India in 2014. The policies of the BJP have historically been socially conservative, and by many accounts the party has struggled to handle the country's ongoing rape crisis. Indeed, in March 2017 the general secretary of the party's women's wing in the state of West Bengal, Juhi Chowdhury, was arrested for running a child-trafficking ring. Along with two other party members in West Bengal also indicted, Chowdhury is alleged to have run an international adoption ring, selling Indian children to families overseas (*South Asian Times* 2017). While this prominent woman in the party has allegedly been running a trafficking ring, the party has also simultaneously tapped the female minister of the Department of Women and Children, Maneka Gandhi, to introduce new anti-trafficking legislation. If passed in the Rajya Sabha, the bill will usher in minimum ten-year sentences for traffickers and provide for victim and witness confidentiality, time limitations on trials, and victim repatriation. The bill also proposes the establishment of a national anti-trafficking bureau, which would coordinate the national law enforcement response and help police overcome the challenges associated with interstate trafficking prosecutions within India (e.g., from Maharashtra to West Bengal).

In her speech supporting the bill, Gandhi explains that the bill is "victim centric," and continuing: "Yes, there are other laws but they only focus on the criminal aspect. This law will focus on the victim and rehabilitation. The purpose of this law is very clear that there will be zero tolerance toward any kind of trafficking crime" (Pandit 2018). Gandhi focused on victims in her speech supporting the bill:

> When 11-year-old Tara is trafficked from her village and sold into bonded labour, beaten and burnt by her owner, how do we save her? When she is sold to marriage to a 45-year-old man and raped every day for months, how do we save her? We have no institutions, no processes to do so. And today, if we are not choosing to pass this bill, we are choosing to deny Tara and all the millions like her [a] fundamental right to life and liberty. (*New Times of India* 2018)

The work of female politicians to call attention to trafficking victims in India has been buttressed by the efforts of several NGOs. NGOs have historically done the most of the work to rehabilitate victims, especially in lobbying for changes in national anti-trafficking legislation. In the course of our research in India we interviewed victim-service organizations that have become important voices in critiquing the newest anti-trafficking law. Both organizations are run almost exclusively by women.

Aapne Aap World Wide was established in 2002 by a group of twenty-two women (who themselves had lived and worked in Kamithpura, Mumbai's historic red-light district) in conjunction with a journalist and UN aid worker, Ruchira Gupta (AAWW 2018). The organization aims to empower women and girls who are sex-trafficking victims or are highly vulnerable to becoming victims. In self-empowerment groups of ten, women and girls work together to exercise their rights to safe space, legal protection, education, and livelihood (McKean 2016, 3). Over the course of its history, the AAWW has helped 124 self-empowerment groups to participate in micro-saving programs and open bank accounts and over half of its members, more than approximately 9,000 people, obtain official identification cards (McKean 2016, 2). Obtaining identification cards is a critical step for securing victims' legal rights, as victims often lack official documentation. In 2007 the AAWW also created the Kasturba Ghandi Bal Vidyalaya residential middle school for girls, which reserves twenty-five seats each year for girls at risk of prostitution (McKean 2016, 9).

The AAWW is a large organization that goes to tremendous lengths to empower women, assist victims, and prevent sex trafficking across India. It works hard to lobby for change at the local, state, national, and even international levels, such as at the United Nations. For example, AAWW members were intimately involved in the passage of the 2013 Criminal Law Amendments Act, and a group of its members testified at the UN Human Rights Council in Geneva with the UN High Commissioner for Human Rights (McKean 2016, 13). AAWW members also advocated for the successful creation of the UN Voluntary Trust for Victims of Trafficking in Persons, Especially Women and Children. Ruchira Gupta, the president of the AAWW, has been a vocal critic of the 2013 law, arguing that "the bill is extremely dangerous for victims and activists alike" (*Times of India* 2018). She takes aim at the extraordinary powers the bill gives to the National Anti-Trafficking Bureau.

Located in Andhra Pradesh, Prajwala is an NGO started in 1996 with the aim of preventing sexual exploitation and trafficking through education. Over time Prajwala has developed the innovative Rescue and Rehabilitation Program (RRP), designed to overcome ineffective police raids, which tend to lead to victim rather than trafficker or brothel-keeper arrests (Prajwala 2018). The RRP conducts rescue missions, provides crisis counseling, conducts investigations, and assists with the judicial process. In its history Prajwala has rescued 205 victims and its work has led directly to the arrest of 124 traffickers (Prajwala 2018). This organization runs two shelters for sex-trafficking victims that aid with psychological rehabilitation, Astha Nivas (children's home) and Asha Nikethan (adult home).

Like the AAWW, Prajwala has been involved in advocacy at both the state and national levels. Prajwala lobbied the Federal Department of Women and Child Welfare to better assist victims, leading this government entity to get involved in rescue work (Prajwala 2018). In 2003 Prajwala lobbied the government for change and the introduction of a draft law that would provide victims with housing, food, medical treatment, and voter ID cards. The organization was also one of the key groups contributing to the language inserted in the anti-rape bill passed in Parliament in 2013. At the state level, Prajwala lobbied Kerala to develop a comprehensive anti-trafficking legislation, titled Nirbhaya Scheme for Women and Children.

Conclusion

Across our investigation of sex trafficking in India we find that female and minority subjugation creates rigid and deeply embedded power dynamics, rendering women and girls from marginalized communities especially vulnerable to becoming trafficking victims. Our work reinforces the important insights of feminist international relations scholars from the subfields of both FGPE and FSS. Whether victims are sold as brides or dedicated to temple gods as a part of the devadasi system, they experience a range of violence and acute loss of their human rights. Moreover, these vulnerabilities are exacerbated by the lack of enforcement of laws designed to protect their economic rights. Women and girls in scheduled castes and scheduled tribes are more likely to be the victims of bride traffickers, sex traffickers, and brothel-based sex slavery.

The nature of assistance provided to victims of human trafficking, as well as the avenues provided for reintegration into society, are shaped around the political preferences of the policymakers and their constituents rather than the needs of the victims (Kaloga et al. 2019). Even the help itself provided is bounded by gendered societal and economic constraints (Kumar et al. 2020). In some instances women in the Indian Cabinet, such as Maneka Gandhi, have promoted victim-centered legislation, suggesting that there are moments of opportunity for female legislators to advance legislation that will support trafficking victims. Yet Indian women in positions of political power have also been convicted of engaging in trafficking themselves, revealing that the link between female representation and victim-centered legislation in our analysis is tenuous at best. However, the sheer volume of female-led NGOs working under challenging conditions to support victims and lobby for legislative change provides reasons for guarded optimism about the future of anti-trafficking legislation in India. It may yet be that the feminist pushback against Modi's nationalist agenda will usher in an era in which victims' rights are advanced as part of a larger feminist tide.

Notes

1. For a link to the findings of the survey see: https://economictimes.indiatimes.com /magazines/panache/women-face-bias-at-workplaces-in-india-gender-parity -a-problem-at-senior-levels-survey/articleshow/63732652.cms, last accessed November 2018.
2. The language of scheduled caste/Dalit is used interchangeably here. Scheduled castes are those listed in an appendix to the Indian Constitution. An additional category, the Backward Caste, is above the Dalits in the social hierarchy but they too face widespread discrimination and economic challenges. In 2001 members of the Backward Caste were estimated to make up 52 percent of the Indian population.

Scheduled tribes are deemed criminal because of the challenges they pose to local landlords (Hepburn and Simon 2013).

3. According to the 2011 Indian Census, this is the total number of individuals belonging to a scheduled caste.

4. For example, Khan (2013) suggests there is little difference in the child sex ratio and the overall sex ratio in Haryana and West Bengal, suggesting that female feticide is a common practice in both source and destination states.

5. In interviews Khan conducted with police, they referred to molki as "gifted sex toys" (Khan 2013, 46).

6. Author interview of Soumya Pratheek, senior program assistant of Aapne Aap Women Worldwide, July 16, 2013.

7. On the prevalence of devadasi devotion in India, see Black (2007).

8. State laws on prostitution vary across the country. For example, prostitution is a crime in Maharashtra.

9. Women can be sentenced for a maximum penalty of six months in jail for soliciting while men can be sentenced for a maximum penalty of three months.

10. For a list of council ministers in Modi's government see: *The Hindu*, "List of Council Ministers in Modi Cabinet," May 27, 2014, https://www.thehindu.com/news/national/list-of-council-of-ministers-in-modi-cabinet/article6052078.ece.

FOUR

Thailand

Thailand has a notorious global reputation as a hub for commercial sex and sex tourism. Tourists stream into Thailand to walk along the streets littered with neon lights in places like Bangkok's Nana Plaza or Walking Street in the coastal town of Pattaya. To the foreigner, Thailand has come to represent an "anything goes" vacation destination, where beautiful beaches abound and sex can cheaply and easily be purchased. The Thai Tourism Authority advertises Thailand as "the land of smiles," but behind this veneer of "smiles" lies a very serious, complex, and robust sex-trafficking problem. Women and children, both girls and boys, from surrounding countries and from marginalized communities within Thailand are frequently trafficked and enslaved in debt bondage in the commercial sex industry. Even for those who find themselves "working" in the commercial sex industry—that is, not technically enslaved by the typical mechanisms of coercion, such as the withholding of documents, physical restraint, threats, or debt bondage—prostitution creates an opportunity to alleviate a particular Thai cultural pressure to contribute to the well-being of one's family.

Sex trafficking has thrived in Thailand because it is a place where picturesque coastal scenery attracts tourists, where religion and notions of filial piety combine to create a large pool of potential victims, and where a long history of marginalization of ethnic Hill Tribe minorities and economic migrants creates an enormous pool of vulnerable people. Like in India, in Thailand embedded patriarchy and weak economic protections for women and girls contribute to patterns of material and physical violence against these populations. To repay the debt owed for raising them, families often pressure daughters to earn money. Early lessons girls receive about their relative importance both to their families and to their society helps to facilitate sex trafficking—families are more apt to send daughters to traffickers and, out of a sense of duty and obligation, daughters accept questionable "jobs." In this sense the patriarchy can imbue in Thai girls a sense of psychological inferiority that makes the trafficker's job that much easier.

Our assessment of Thai anti-trafficking laws and practices suggests an emphasis on criminal justice. Thai authorities have worked hard over the years to consistently increase both trafficker conviction rates and sentences associated with those convictions. Like India, however, limited resources have forced Thai authorities to make difficult choices, prioritizing convictions over victim support in many cases. Moreover, low levels of female legislative representation and a military coup in 2014 have coalesced to imperil women's rights and status in Thai society. Women and girls from marginalized groups experience especially acute deprivation of their human rights. These groups include economic migrants from surrounding countries, Rohingyas fleeing genocide in Myanmar, and ethnic minorities collectively referred to as the "Hill Tribe" communities.

Factors Contributing to Sex Trafficking in Thailand

The last Thai census identified 65.9 million people in Thailand, making this country the fourth largest, by population, in Southeast Asia (Thai National Statistical Office 2016).[1] In 2018 the Global Slavery Index estimated that 610,000 people were enslaved in Thailand (Global Slavery Index 2018a). This number is not specific to sex slavery and includes forced and bonded laborers in other industries such as agriculture, construction, and manufacturing. The Walk Free Foundation suggests that Thailand is twenty-third in the world for prevalence of slavery (Walk Free Foundation 2018c). We refrain here from offering estimates about the size of the sex-trafficking population in Thailand for the Greater Mekong subregion because the numbers that are available are notoriously unreliable (Feingold 2010). A number of factors contribute to a bustling sex-trafficking trade in Thailand. These include lower poverty relative to most regional neighbors, conflict and geographic location within the Golden Triangle, prevalence of tourism, religious practices, filial norms, and corruption, each of which has been previously documented. Yet to really understand who becomes a sex-trafficking victim in Thailand it is also imperative to examine economic rights for women and girls as a stand-in for their cultural position in Thailand.

Deprivation of Economic Rights of Women and Girls
Recall the expectation that where women and girls are devalued by society, scant attention is given to assisting victims of human trafficking. We assess the economic rights of women and girls as a surrogate for their cultural standing: where their economic rights are neither protected by law nor enforced in practice, these populations will be at greater risk of becoming sex-trafficking victims than in countries where their economic rights are protected. Whereas

in India the legal protections exist on paper but are not enforced in practice, in Thailand the laws providing for the protection of economic rights by gender are weak and seldom enforced. The Thai Constitution provides for gender equality in Section 27, which states gender discrimination is prohibited (Kingdom of Thailand 2017). While the Gender Equality Act B.E. 2558 (2015) aimed to protect women by establishing multiple committees to evaluate complaints of unfair gender discrimination, the act is undermined by some of its own provisions. Chapter 3, Section 17 of the act allows for discrimination against women "to eliminate the obstacles or to encourage the persons to exercise their rights and freedom as other persons, or for protection of the persons' safety and welfare, or for the compliance with religious principles, or for national security" (Kingdom of Thailand 2015). This broad religious and personal freedom exception allowance undermines the effect of the Gender Equality Act by expressly allowing virtually any form of discrimination. In chapter 1, Section 15 of the Labour Protection Act B.E. 2541 (1998), employers are required to treat male and female employees equally, except when the nature of the work dictates disparate treatment. The conditions under which disparate treatment can occur under chapter 3 of the Labour Protection Act include protections from generally hazardous work and additional protections for pregnant employees. Subsequent provisions designed to protect pregnant women from termination (Sections 41 and 43) and a more recent amendment to B.E. 2562 (2019) provide for equal pay. Again, though, these mandates of equality can be circumvented by religious or personal beliefs, so the actual equality regime is weak or little more than a showpiece without substance.

In 2012 the Thai government released Ministerial Regulation No. 14 on the Protection of Domestic Workers B.E. 2555 (2012) to replace the Revolutionary Council Announcement from 1972, which had governed labor protections in Thailand. Although the 2012 ministerial regulation provides certain entitlements to domestic workers whether or not there is an employment contract, the language used is vague. The enumerated protections include provisions for time off for public holidays and sick leave, child labor provisions, a prohibition against sexual harassment, and a requirement of equal pay for men and women (Anderson 2016). Additionally, there is no state enforcement mechanism, so the regulation is little more than a suggestion.

Although the constitution and these legislative measures create mechanisms that give formal gender equality to citizens in general and in the workplace in particular, the lack of enforcement structures have left the cultural legacy of discriminatory practices against women and girls in place. This broad devaluation of women has a significant impact on female migrant workers in various industries. The population of migrant workers in Thailand is large and comprises 10 percent of the labor force, including approximately 4.8 million migrants

(Harkins 2019). Due to their citizenship status, many female migrant workers are paid less than minimum wage and fear prosecution if they report labor violations (OHCHR 2017). Male migrant workers also out-earn their female counterparts across a variety of industries (Napier-Moore and Sheill 2016). Pregnant migrant workers are in especially tenuous circumstances because they may be fired without pay (Napier-Moore and Sheill 2016, 11), prompting some to try and conceal their pregnancies (Mendoza 2018). Female migrant workers account for a majority of people employed in domestic work, which increases their vulnerability to human rights abuses due to the private nature and cultural stigma associated with domestic work (Anderson 2016). Migrant domestic workers are generally compensated below minimum wage, they work very long hours, and they are usually on call during days off (Anderson 2016).

The lack of a mechanism for the enforcement of the legally established gender equity laws is in keeping with the generalized negative cultural attitudes toward women and girls, both in Thailand and more broadly throughout the region (ECPAT 2018, 26). This weak cultural status of women and girls means that any laws that speak to gender equality are either unenforceable in practice or weak even when they are enforced. Moreover, women and girls are taught that society has a high expectation that they contribute to the family income regardless of personal sacrifice, that their contributions are worth less than those of men and boys, and that they should always be submissive and obedient (ECPAT 2018, 26). In this way patriarchy and gender-based violence are both a cause of trafficking and a method that can be used to retain control over victims once enslaved (Burke, Amaya, and Dillon 2019).

Strong Economy vis-à-vis Regional Peers

Throughout the 1980s and 1990s Thailand's economy grew rapidly, at an average annual rate of 7.5 percent, which lifted the Thai economy from a low-income country to an upper-income country in short order (World Bank 2016). An important consequence of this rising growth has been a parallel decline in poverty—between 1986 and 2018 the poverty rate dropped from 65.2 percent to just 9.85 percent (World Bank 2018). When compared against the incomes of surrounding countries, it is clear that average annual individual income is much higher in Thailand and Malaysia than in other countries in the subregion (fig. 4.1). The strong Thai economy serves as a robust pull factor for trafficking, drawing those from relatively poorer areas within the Greater Mekong subregion to Thailand with the lure of lucrative legitimate employment.

Drug Trafficking in the Golden Triangle

Beyond the strong regional economy, another factor contributing to sex trafficking, particularly in northern Thailand, is the prevalence of drug cultivation

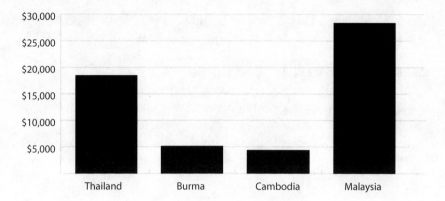

Figure 4.1. GDP per Capita, 2019

Source: CIA World Fact Book, https://www.cia.gov/the-world-factbook/, last accessed July 2021.

and smuggling in the Golden Triangle. Whether trafficking drugs or people, the routes, porous borders, and proximity to commercial hubs in the north function as a trafficking pull factor. Since the 1880s, when the British introduced poppy cultivation into the Golden Triangle—Burma, Thailand, and Laos—opium, and eventually heroin production, became common in the region, particularly in the Shan and other border states of Burma (Lijun 2006). Historically, colonizing powers in the region established clear borders between these three countries, but at the end of the colonial era border regions became lawless and more akin to frontier territories (Sauterey 2008). Since 2006 poppy cultivation in both Laos and Burma has grown exponentially, making this region a major source for both opium and heroin (UN News Centre 2014). The dominance of drug smugglers, lack of government control of the border territories, and proximity to the capital city of Chiang Mai, a commercial sex hub in northern Thailand, together create an easy opening for traffickers (Lintner 2003; Shelley 2010, 158). In essence, any contraband network can lay the groundwork for a lower transaction cost for additional contraband networks (Smith and Miller-de la Cuesta 2011).

Within Thailand, the central government has historically emphasized economic development in Bangkok and the coastal towns, which left the north relatively poor and underdeveloped (Bales 2005). Those living in rural areas have not benefited from the rapid economic growth that characterizes individual incomes in urban areas (World Bank 2016). Uneven development has especially left out the minorities of the Hill Tribes, including the Hmong, which are clustered in the highlands in the north and in deep remote areas of the southwest. When large groups of geographically concentrated people are disadvantaged economically, they become easy targets for traffickers. Yet economic deprivation alone does not account for the severe trafficking problems in Thailand. Cultural factors also play a major role.

Religious Practices and Filial Norms

The dominant religion in Thailand, Theravada Buddhism, has at least two major tenets that contribute to the cultural acceptance of prostitution and sex slavery and further the cultural devaluation of women (Bales 2004; Vejar and Quach 2013). The first is that according to Buddhist scriptures, women are inferior to men, with no hope of attaining spiritual enlightenment or Buddhahood (Appleton 2011).[2] Bales (2004) explains that Buddhist writings warn that women are impure and corrupting. These same scriptures sanction prostitution and polygamy in a series of rules for monks to follow. The second tenet is what Vejar and Quach (2013) call a "sense of karmic reckoning" (107). One's fate is preordained, a direct consequence of sins committed in present or past lives. Acceptance of one's fate, no matter how abysmal, is understood as necessary for the soul to progress to higher stages of enlightenment. When combined, these two religious tenets help to explain how sexual slavery has found a ready home in Thailand: women are inferior, disposable, and best served, at least spiritually, when they obediently accede to their fate, regardless of how miserable or demeaning it is.

Filial norms further compound these dynamics, making women as well as children feel acutely responsible for their family's well-being. Bales (2004) explains that Thai children, especially girls, owe "a profound debt" to their parents for being born, fed, and generally cared for. They are expected to contribute to the well-being of the family as a means to repay this debt (39). From this perspective it is natural and sometimes necessary for daughters to be sold in the interest of the family. The extent to which these family obligations, felt by both Thai girls and boys, contribute to prostitution and sex slavery cannot be understated. Montgomery (2008) conducted a field study of 65 children between the ages of six and fourteen, living and working on the edges of a large tourist area in Thailand. Approximately 35 of the 65 children in this village engaged in sex work, exclusively for Western customers, with their parents' full knowledge and support. After trying to find other work, they turned to sex work:

> Prostitution paid them considerably more than these jobs and they perceived it as less physically demanding. More importantly, however, they used prostitution as a way of fulfilling what they understood to be their filial duties. The children felt that, by earning money for their parents and keeping the family together, they were acting in socially sanctioned roles as dutiful daughters and sons and that prostituting themselves with the "right"

intentions meant that there was no moral opprobrium attached to what they did. (Montgomery 2008, 908)

Tourism-Based Economy

Combining Thailand's cultural and religious practices, which diminish the role of women, with its notorious reputation and long history as a hub for commercial sex means that it will be difficult to alter the reality of Thailand as a land of robust prostitution, sex slavery, and sex trafficking. The history of sex tourism in Thailand dates to the beginning of the US war with Vietnam. American troops used Thailand as a place to rest and relax, which generated a previously unseen demand for sex workers (Rennell 2004). The bar and brothel infrastructure quickly emerged to meet this demand (Montgomery 2001). The commercial sex industry in Thailand was, at its birth, designed to cater to Westerners—Thai women working in the industry were encouraged to learn English, while Western music played inside the clubs (Montgomery 2001). Over time, live sex shows in the main commercial sex centers, including the three red-light districts in Bangkok—Patpong, Soi Cowboy, and Nana Plaza—have become ever more extreme in an effort to draw in tourists. Child sex tourism continues to be a problem in Thailand, although recent reports suggest that the practice has become more clandestine, found in karaoke bars, massage parlors, hotels, and private residences but no longer overtly visible elsewhere (US Department of State 2014).

Thailand's reputation as a hub for commercial sex is so well known that it was incorporated into Longman's dictionary entry on Thailand in 1993, describing Bangkok as a place with Buddhist temples and "a lot of prostitutes" (*The Independent* 1993). The Thai government responded by banning the dictionary and pulling it from the shelves there. Though it is difficult if not impossible to directly link sex trafficking to a tourism-based economy—there are many countries that are heavily dependent on tourism but are not particularly known as commercial sex hubs—Thailand has the unique distinction of being synonymous with commercial sex as a tourism draw. "Thailand, Not Sex-land" was a slogan created by Thai protestors and held on placards at the Bangkok airport in the 1990s in their efforts to challenge lax government policies surrounding prostitution and sex tourism (Montgomery 2011).

The Thai economy is heavily reliant on revenue from tourism, an industry that brings in billions of dollars each year. Tourism revenues have increased steadily since 2005, accounting for nearly 10.4 percent of Thailand's GDP in 2019 (World Travel and Tourism Council 2021). Of the 184 countries assessed by the World Travel and Tourism Council, Thailand ranks fourteenth in the world in importance of tourism to total contribution to GDP between 2005 and 2021 (World Travel and Tourism Council 2021). Scholars have argued that the pressure to appease both domestic and international tourists largely explains why the Thai government has done so little to fight sex trafficking and prostitution (Hepburn and Simon 2013; Montgomery 2008).

Corruption

The economic incentives associated with trafficking have compelled some social workers as well as members of the Thai military, navy, police, and provincial councils to use their authority to run trafficking rings (Thai Government 2015, 109–10).[3] Earning salaries equivalent to minimum-wage workers, the need for police in Thailand to supplement their incomes is particularly acute (Rusling 2015). Thailand has faced tremendous international criticism regarding official complicity and involvement in human trafficking in a variety of industries, not just with respect to sex work. In May 2015 the discovery of a mass grave in the Thai jungle on the border with Malaysia containing the remains of 36 people led to a widespread investigation. Maj. Gen. Paween Pongsirin, a senior Thai police officer, was tasked with investigating how those deaths occurred. The investigation led to trafficking charges being filed against 90 people, including members of the Thai army, navy, local and national politicians, and the police (Ramzy 2015). A lieutenant general in the Thai Army, Manas Kongpan, was among the accused. Following the indictments, Paween fled Thailand and sought asylum in Australia, citing the mortal danger he faced in Thailand following his investigation (Ramzy 2015).

Forms of Sex Trafficking and Identities of Victims in Thailand

Unlike other countries examined in this book, there are relatively few distinct forms of sex trafficking in Thailand. Most sex trafficking in Thailand takes place in brothels, hotels, karaoke bars, massage parlors, and private residences (US Department of State 2019). Labor trafficking and slavery in the fishing industry is also an area of acute concern in Thailand, with men and boys from Thailand, Cambodia, Laos, Burma, and Vietnam ensnared by traffickers and forced into slavery on fishing boats and in fisheries. Between 2016 and 2018, Human Rights Watch interviewed 138 former and current fishers; 90 of those fishers were employed in forced-labor situations (Human Rights Watch 2018). While there are other types of forced labor beyond sex work, our focus is on sex trafficking. Because there is little variation in the forms of sex trafficking in Thailand, the focus here is to show how certain populations of victims are more vulnerable to traffickers than others.

Our research in Thailand revealed five categories of victims: 1) women and girls from Thailand; 2) children from Thailand and the Greater Mekong subregion; 3) ethnic minorities from the Hill Tribes in the north; 4) economic migrants from the Greater Mekong subregion; and 5) the Rohingyas, a Muslim stateless people escaping genocide in Myanmar.[4]

Women and Girls from Thailand: "Girls for Dessert"

In 2017 a seventeen-year-old Thai girl fled to Bangkok from her home in the sleepy northern coastal town of Mae Hong Son. She was a victim ensnared in a child-sex-trafficking ring, run not by local gangs or criminal traffickers but by the Mae Hong Son police.[5] This scandal is part of a much larger social tradition whereby lower-level municipal officials roll out the red carpet for visiting senior officials. Senior officials are treated to fine food and drink and presented with a choice of girls for "dessert." Initially abducted from her parents at the age of fourteen, the girl was one of many teenage girls forced to engage in sex acts with government officials. It was only because her mother appealed to the media to help her find her daughter in Bangkok that news of this child-sex-trafficking ring was made public and the prosecutions began (*New Straits Times* 2017). To date, more than eight former police officers in Mae Hong Son have been convicted, with penalties ranging from 8 to 320 years in prison (*The Nation Thailand* 2018).

Thai women and girls in the sex industry make up a large number, though not a majority, of trafficking victims who are assisted in government shelters. There are at least two reasons for this: Thai women and girls are victimized at high rates, and the Thai government has focused its anti-trafficking efforts on women and girls in the sex industry. So, while the numbers reported here suggest that a large share of victims assisted in government shelters in Thailand are indeed Thai nationals, this situation is also related to government efforts to provide direct aid and support to this population and often at the expense of serving other groups of trafficking victims, particularly labor-trafficking victims in the fishing industry.

According to the Thai Ministry of Foreign Affairs (2014a), between 2012 and 2014 Thai women and girls tended to be about as likely as foreign victims to be assisted in trafficking shelters. In 2012, 106 Thai sex-trafficking victims were assisted in Thai shelters, of the 216 victims total from Thailand and neighboring countries who were assisted in Thai shelters (30). In 2013 a total of 364 sex-trafficking victims were assisted in Thai shelters, 210 of whom were Thai (30).

More recently, these dynamics have changed, evincing growth in the number of foreign victims and a reduction in the number of Thai victims (see fig. 4.2). Beginning in 2015 the number of foreign victims assisted in Thai trafficking shelters outstripped the number of Thai victims assisted, with 126 Thai victims and 345 foreign victims (US Department of State 2016).

Thai women and girls can be found in the sex industry in the Patpong Market in Bangkok (southern Thailand) and in the cities of Chiang Mai and Chiang

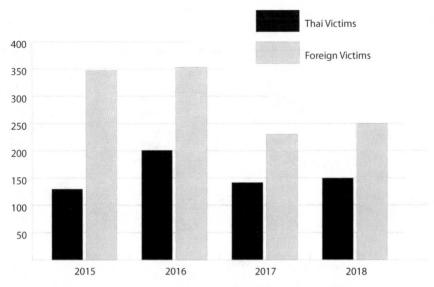

Figure 4.2. Comparison of National vs. Foreign Victims Assisted in Thai Shelters
Source: US State Department Trafficking in Persons Reports 2016–19.

Rai (northern Thailand). Like in India, there are different ways Thai victims find themselves enslaved in the sex industry. Many of the sex workers who operate in bars are not necessarily trafficking or slavery victims. After conducting a series of interviews with women in the Patpong night market, Siddharth Kara (2010) learned that many of these individuals had not been coerced or deceived by traffickers but were instead pressured by their families to earn money to send home. Pressure to be a good daughter means that the youngest unmarried daughter must find a way to financially support the family (Kara 2010, 155; Berger and van de Glind 1999, 8). Once employed in the bars and clubs, the women had to earn a certain amount to give to the club each month or be fired (Kara 2010, 155). In this way prevailing cultural expectations around the role of women and girls in Thai society can serve as a sex-trafficking push factor.

Thai sex-trafficking victims are also sent abroad—frequently to Bahrain, where they are trapped in debt bondage. In Bahrain, Thai women are recruited to work as masseuses or receptionists in bars, then forced into sex slavery (*Bangkok Post* 2016a). In 2017 the death of a young Thai woman in Bahrain brought into focus the dangers associated with sex trafficking. Katnipa Boon-tien, a twenty-one-year-old single mother, was recruited along with two friends to work in Bahrain. The young women were told by the recruiter that they would work in bars as receptionists and earn thousands of baht. However, once they arrived they were detained for three days and forced to work against their will. Boontien's story gained national attention in Thailand because she managed to send a few texts to her mother that indicated she was afraid for her life. She wrote: "Mother, I think I may not be safe now, I may not be able to return home" (*Bangkok Post* 2017b). Though some details remain unclear, we do know that Boontien died as she tried to escape, falling from a building in the capital, Manama.

Patterns of sex trafficking of nationals in Thailand and India bear some similar characteristics. In both countries deeply ingrained gender hierarchies subjugate women and girls. Whether families feel pressure to save money for costly doweries (India) or daughters feel a sense of obligation to contribute to the family (Thailand), the consequences are similar. Feeling that they are a costly burden to the family, daughters can become easy targets for traffickers, who exploit these feelings. Whereas in India nationals are often sold as brides, in Thailand daughters may themselves opt into the commercial sex industry. The prevailing power dynamics in both countries contribute to significant forms of violence against women and girls once they are ensnared in the trafficking process.

Children from Thailand and the Greater Mekong Subregion

Both male and female children are trafficked for sex in Thailand. Children exploited as sex slaves come from neighboring Burma and Laos, as well as internally from Thailand and the northern Hill Tribes.[6] In one of the few studies to focus exclusively on boys and young men in the commercial sex industry in Thailand, Davis, Glotfely, and Miles (2017) found that a large proportion of those interviewed (one in four) were forced to engage in sex acts, and of those interviewed who worked specifically in bars, 72 percent reported being forced to engage in sex acts. A large proportion of these boys and young men reported that they were sending the money they earned home, to provide for younger siblings or ill parents (ECPAT 2011, 14). The children of foreign migrants and ethnic minorities, as well as stateless children, are the most vulnerable to sex trafficking in Thailand (ECPAT 2015, 2016). Homeless children who live on the streets are also at high risk of being trafficked for sex because they tend to be poor and lack adult support (ECPAT 2018, 24).

Other Thai children found in the sex industry may be runaways, escaping abusive conditions at home. Once being forced to live on the streets, older street children introduce them to sex work as a means of survival. This was the situation with nine-year-old Poon, a boy who left home to escape an abusive mother.[7] After fleeing he lived on the streets of the red-light district in Chiang Mai. The older street boys sold him to both tourists and locals for a year (Keenapan 2012). In February 2011 Thai police raided a karaoke bar in Chiang Mai where Hill Tribe girls between the ages of thirteen and fifteen were bought and sold for sexual services (*The Nation* 2013). These children tend to be trafficked from their rural homes in northern Thailand to cities where they are sexually exploited (ECPAT 2011, 10).

Children of migrants are also at great risk of being trafficked and enslaved for sex work. The International Organization for Migration (IOM) estimates that in 2018 the total number of migrant children in Thailand coming from Laos, Cambodia, Vietnam, and Myanmar rose to between 300,000 and 400,000 (*Bangkok Post* 2019). Before 2008, children born to undocumented migrant workers in Thailand were not granted birth registration, rendering them stateless (ECPAT 2011). Though their stateless status technically should not inhibit their ability to enroll in school, following the passage of the Thai 2005 Education for All Act, these children still face many obstacles to getting an education. For example, the costs of uniforms, textbooks, and the lack of classes offering instruction in native languages makes the practical realization of this right to education very limited (IRIN 2009). Additionally, there is great anti-migrant sentiment within Thailand, which means that teachers often refuse to bring migrant children into their classrooms (IRIN 2009). Those who are able to attend school frequently do not receive the official education certificates that verify their education (IRIN 2009).

Underage sex-trafficking victims are also trafficked into Thailand from neighboring Laos. In 2011 police raided a karaoke bar in Prachin Buri from which 30 Laotian teenage girls were rescued after being trafficked into the commercial sex industry (Fernquist 2012). In December 2013 Thai police rescued 31 Laotian women and girls, who had been trafficked and forced into prostitution, from a brothel in Chonburi Province (Thai Government 2015).

A group that is almost entirely excluded from government data on trafficking victims are the "ladyboys" or "kathoey," who are mostly transgender women, though the label is also applied to effeminate men (Aldous and Sereemongkonpol 2008). As members of the LGBTQ+ community, kathoeys experience widespread discrimination in employment, education, healthcare, and housing (Davis and Miles 2018, 1). In some ways the traditions of kathoey in Thailand resemble those of geishas in Japan: they are often respected for their beauty and artistic abilities as dancers, musicians, and performers.[8] This type of performance work means actors can frequently be found working in Thai cabarets and bars, which makes them vulnerable to traffickers. In 2018 Celest McGee, who founded Dton Naam, an organization that assists boys and transgender women, explained that there were approximately 10,000 ladyboys working in the sex industry in Thailand (Chandran 2018). They can face extraordinary levels of violence and abuse at the hands of those paying for sex and there is little interest from the authorities to protect them from that abuse.

The bulk of victim-support systems throughout the world are not well equipped to support the often distinct needs of nonconforming populations (see chap. 7 regarding Brazil). For example, Tomasiewicz (2018) shows that transgender sex-trafficking victims in shelters have special needs for items that allow them to continue to "pass," like cosmetics and weaves. For cisgender victims, these items may be considered extras, but Tomasiewicz shows that for transgender victims these items should be understood as violence-prevention objects (10). Victim-support services are primarily designed to support female sex-trafficking victims, a fact borne of the patriarchal Western-dominated rescue narrative that portrays innocent and weak young girls as the tragic victims caught in the crosshairs of evil male traffickers (Baker 2013). The prevalence of gender nonconforming victims in the sex trade, like kathoey in Thailand, demands a rethinking regarding both the identity of sex-trafficking victims and the ways in which victim-support services are structured.

Ethnic Minorities from the Thai Northern Hill Tribes

The term "Hill Tribe" refers to a diverse group of ethnic and religious minorities who live in the northern part of Thailand. This includes Akhas, Hmongs, Iu-Miens, Lahus, and Lisus, all of whom the Thai government has categorized as "foreign transgressors" (Morton and Baird 2019, 11). The Thai government has historically denied Hill Tribe populations access to Thai citizenship, and although a recent change in citizenship laws allows individuals from the Hill Tribes to seek citizenship, the process is burdensome and seldom used. A 1992 law mandating the integration of Hill Tribe children into Thai public schools has never been enforced, so these children have few opportunities for education or employment (Thai Freedom House 2014). Lack of citizenship status also inhibits access to state welfare services, medical care, the ability to vote, the ability to travel freely outside the province in which they live, and the right to own land (UNESCO 2016). This lack of citizenship and employment opportunities contributes to poverty among the Hill Tribe peoples and makes them particularly susceptible to becoming trafficking victims. Thai Freedom House, an NGO working to support the interests of the northern Hill Tribe people, suggests that one in three sex-trafficking victims in Chiang Mai is from a northern Hill Tribe (Thai Freedom House 2014). One study conducted by Mahidol University in Thailand suggests that Hill Tribe children are trafficked to Bangkok and Pattaya and forced into sex slavery (Pimonsaengsuriya 2008).

Women and girls trafficked into Chiang Mai and Chiang Rai and enslaved in the sex industry are burdened with the challenge of repaying the cost of their purchase. Room and board and money sent home to family are subtracted from the money they earn, and financial penalties for infractions can be taken out of their earnings. Taken together these costs make the likelihood that these girls and women will succeed in obtaining their freedom exceptionally low. Kara (2010) illustrates this with the story of Panadda, a fifteen-year-old from the

Akha Hill Tribe in northern Thailand. She was purchased initially for $200 and resold to a brothel in Chiang Mai for $875. Her initial debt was therefore $875, but $250 per month for room and board was deducted from her earnings, plus $12.50 per month was sent to her parents. She explained that she only made enough money to chip away at this debt after sleeping with fifty men per month (Kara 2010, 159–60).

Panadda's story reveals another form of gender-based violence that feminist scholars warn about: precarious labor in a system of structured economic violence. As Suchland (2015) explains, precarious laborers work in "either formal or informal labor markets in order to make a living" (5). This labor "remains precarious because the people are vulnerable to exploitation, lack of rights and are undervalued" (5). Panadda's experience—her lack of opportunities in skilled wage positions and her inability to chip away at her growing debt—resembles the conditions of bonded laborers in India and can be situated within a larger economic system that has accelerated patterns of precarious labor. An initial debt continues to grow despite considerable efforts to work toward paying it off. The game is rigged against victims, forcing them into a never-ending cycle of slavery.

Foreigners from the Greater Mekong Subregion

Sex-trafficking victims in Thailand tend to come from Laos and Burma.[9] However, the number of Thai sex-trafficking victims assisted in shelters suggests the population of Thai nationals trafficked domestically is quite large, relative to foreign victims (Thai Ministry of Foreign Affairs 2014a, 30–31). Figure 4.3 shows the number of Thai and foreign trafficking victims assisted in Thai shelters in 2012 and in 2013. In both years the largest number of foreign victims assisted in shelters came from Laos. However, the challenge with relying too heavily on the nationality of those assisted in shelters is that many victims in Thailand are detained as irregular migrants or repatriated before receiving any help. Approximately 17,000 Laotians are deported back to Laos annually without receiving any formal bureaucratic hearing; many among this group are likely trafficking victims (US Department of State 2015). The stated numbers therefore represent very rough estimations of actual populations and should only be understood as suggestive of the actual relative size of these populations.

Thailand and Laos share a border that was drawn arbitrarily by colonizing powers, with large numbers of Laotians on both sides. A shared sociocultural identity among people on both sides of the border, a relatively strong Thai economy, and political instability in Laos motivates individuals to emigrate. Traffickers active on the Laos-Thailand border intercept economic migrants who are leaving Laos to find work in Thailand (US Department of State 2015).

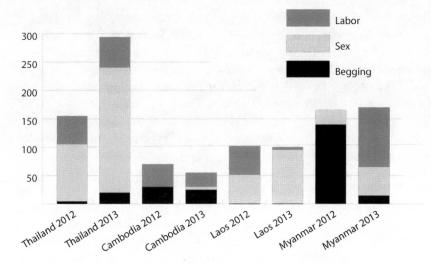

Figure 4.3. Nationality of Victims Assisted in Thai Shelters by Type of Exploitation, 2012–13

Source: Thai Ministry of Foreign Affairs (2014a), "Thai Report to US State Department," June 2014, 30, on file with authors.

Relatives and acquaintances may also recruit young Laotian women and girls (often between the ages of twelve and eighteen) with promises of legitimate work in Thailand. Regardless of the method of recruitment, the desperation to eke out a living makes these young victims easy prey to traffickers. Once they arrive in Thailand, their travel documents are confiscated and they are forced to work in bars and brothels. Vahn, a Laotian girl from a village in southern Laos, was fifteen when her stepsister persuaded her to travel to central Thailand to work on a farm and send money back to her family (Kimmons 2014).[10] Instead, Vahn was sent to a brothel in Thailand and told that she must earn money to repay the traffickers for her travel costs and living expenses. The brothel owners sold her virginity. For a year she worked as a sex slave in Thailand, trying to escape twice before being confined to a locked room when she was not working (Kimmons 2014). The further tragedy of Vahn's story is that despite eventually being permitted to return home to Laos with her stepsister, once there she was once again duped into returning to Thailand.

Burmese women and girls are also trafficked for sexual exploitation into Thailand, though they are also often trafficked north to China, where they may choose to or are forced to marry Chinese men (UNIAP 2010). The IOM estimates that through mid-2016, as many as 3 million Burmese have left their homes, emigrating most frequently to Thailand and Malaysia (Walk Free

Foundation 2018c). According to the 2015 Burmese census, 70 percent of those who have emigrated out of Burma reside in Thailand, while 15 percent reside in Malaysia (Myanmar Government 2015). In a small study of 128 Laotian nationals deported from Thailand in 2013, a primary vulnerability factor for feeling cheated or being deceived by the type of work they engaged in while in Thailand was whether the victim used a broker to get to the Laos-Thailand border. Though only 15 percent of respondents had used such a broker, these individuals felt far worse about their working experiences in Thailand than those who had not used such a broker (UN-ACT 2015, xiv).

The Rohingyas

The Rohingyas are a Muslim ethnic minority who have historically resided in western Burma. Burmese authorities have long considered the Rohingyas irregular migrants of Bengali descent and persecuted them as foreigners. The Burmese state and Buddhist nationalists have carried out a slow process of ethnic cleansing and genocide against the Rohingyas. In 1982 the government passed the Burmese citizenship law denying the Rohingyas citizenship, rendering them stateless. In June 2012 the government's campaign against the Rohingyas gained momentum. Rohingya villages were burned while men, women, and children were subject to summary execution and sexual violence. The extreme violence used against them led to between 300,000 and 540,000 Rohingyas fleeing from Burma to neighboring Bangladesh and Malaysia (Human Rights Watch 2020a). When the government initiated a second campaign against the Rohingyas in August 2017, another 740,000 Rohingyas were forced to flee (Human Rights Watch 2020a). The 600,000 Rohingyas who remain in western Burma live in extremely perilous conditions—confined to camps, unable to travel, without adequate food, medical care, or education, and with no ability to earn a living (Human Rights Watch 2020a).

Rohingyas making their way to Malaysia through Thailand are frequently picked up by the Thai Royal Police or immigration officials, them removed from immigration detention facilities under cover of night and sold to human traffickers waiting in ferries on the water, eventually being held in jungle camps on the Thailand-Malaysia border (Smith-Cannoy 2019; Marshall and Lefevre 2014; Szep and Marshall 2013). Thousands of Rohingyas are held in these camps and forced to contact family members to pay a US$2,000 ransom for their release. Those unable to obtain the money are left to eke out a living in the camps—with the constant perils of hunger, beatings, disease, and death. Traffickers often sell Rohingyas who cannot make their ransoms to work on rubber plantations or as bonded laborers on Thai fishing boats. In January 2013, 400 Rohingyas were identified working at a rubber plantation on the Thailand-Malaysia border (Marshall and Lefevre 2014).

Thai government officials, immigration officials, and members of the Thai Royal Police and the Thai Navy have all been implicated in the sale of Rohingyas to human traffickers (Szep and Marshall 2013; Marshall and Lefevre 2014; Associated Press 2014; Human Rights Watch 2014a). The Thai government has responded to these allegations by excluding the Rohingyas entirely from the human trafficking reports it submits to the US State Department (Marshall and Lefevre 2014). Arguing that the Rohingyas are smuggling, not trafficking, victims, in 2014 the Thai Ministry of Foreign Affairs stated that "the plight of Rohingyas who left their homeland is essentially one of people smuggling, not one that is typical of human trafficking" (Thai Foreign Ministry 2014a, 27).

While some Rohingyas are detained by Thai immigration officials and sold to traffickers, even those Rohingyas who avoid the perilous journey through Thailand may nevertheless find themselves enslaved. The majority of the more than 877,000 Rohingyas in Cox's Bazaar Bangladesh live in a refugee camp (UNHCR 2021). Others live on Bhasan Char, a silt island that is under Bangladeshi control. Recent research suggests that child marriage among Rohingya populations has increased (Melnikas et al. 2020). Whereas there were strict prohibitions on child marriage in Burma, socio-religious norms within the group translate into a preference for child marriage among many Rohingyas. In the refugee camps it has become easier for children to be married off when families feel the time is right, notably because there are no longer Burmese authorities who must be bribed as a part of the process (Melnikas et al. 2020).

A considerable cross section of people find themselves enslaved in sex work in Thailand. Across the various identities of victims described here, many female victims share the burden of poor economic prospects and considerable pressure to contribute to the family. Even for Thai women who are able to work in the formal labor market, weak enforcement of progressive constitutional provisions that provide for gender equity may undermine their efforts and drive them to work in the informal labor market. This situation can also serve as a trafficking push factor, encouraging Thai nationals like Katnipa Boontien to seek more lucrative work overseas. A lack of economic protections for women and girls who come from marginalized Hill Tribe communities or are foreigners from surrounding countries similarly entraps them in violent gendered and racialized economic systems (Suchland 2015).

Combating Trafficking in Thailand: Criminal Justice or Victim-Centered?

Consider where Thailand falls on the continuum between the devotion of resources to the prosecution and conviction of human traffickers (the criminal justice approach) and the devotion of their resources to prioritizing the human rights and human dignity of sex-trafficking victims (the victim-centered approach). Using the previously identified factors to determine a country's approach to combating trafficking (see chap. 1), a review of Thailand suggests that the Thai government has prioritized criminal justice at the expense of victim's human rights. This focus may be the result of the pressure exerted by the US State Department's annual Trafficking in Persons Report, which over the years have often criticized the Thai government's approach to fighting trafficking and specifically calling attention to its low rate of trafficking convictions.

Prior to the passage of Thailand's comprehensive 2008 anti-trafficking law, punishments for trafficking-related offenses were contained within the 1997 Prevention and Suppression of Trafficking in Women and Children Act. As the name implies, this law applied exclusively to women and children trafficked for the purpose of sexual exploitation. The 1997 law provided for jail sentences between one and ten years for convictions for trafficking in women and seven years to life for convictions for trafficking in children (US Department of State 2006). While the government initiated 352 arrests in 2005 under this law, with 74 convictions, the average punishment was only three years (US Department of State 2006). The 1997 law failed to provide for any punishment for labor trafficking, which is also a serious problem in Thailand.

The passage of Thailand's 2008 Anti-Trafficking in Persons Act ushered in more aggressive punishments for traffickers and a more thorough legal framework for victims' rights. In addition to covering women and children, the newer law includes protections for male trafficking victims and labor-trafficking victims. The law also provides for the creation of an executive-level anti-trafficking-in-persons committee (Section 15, para. 5 of the law). The committee acts as a means for facilitating cooperation between the various agencies within the government that deal with human trafficking and to ensure implementation of the provisions of the 2008 law. It also addresses public corruption by assigning double punishments for any member of the government or law enforcement who is convicted of a trafficking offense (Section 13, para. 4). The Ministry of Social Development and Human Security is required to provide, as needed by the victim, medical treatment, food, shelter, assistance in obtaining compensation, legal aid, and vocational training (Section 4, para. 33). Further, the government must ensure the safety of the trafficked person during any legal proceedings, particularly if the trafficked person is testifying as a witness (Section 4, para. 36). Though the law permits foreign trafficking victims to secure permission to stay in Thailand to receive medical treatment, participate in legal proceedings, or receive rehabilitation assistance (Section 4, para. 37), over time these provisions have not been enacted in practice.

Criminal Justice?

In assessing whether Thai authorities have emphasized prosecuting and convicting traffickers, we draw on the government's annual reports on arrest, prosecution, and conviction rates as reported in the US Trafficking in Persons Reports (see fig. 4.4). Early efforts by Thai authorities (2002–12) yielded high arrest rates but low prosecution and conviction rates. There are at least two possible explanations for the lack of prosecutions and convictions. Corruption and official complicity in trafficking may help to explain low prosecution and conviction rates. As with the plight of the Rohingyas fleeing genocide in Burma to reach Malaysia, Thai police, immigration officials, and other government officials are often directly involved in and profit from human trafficking. This has the obvious effect of inhibiting the likelihood that any of these corrupt officials will be prosecuted for trafficking-related crimes. In 2010 Thailand was downgraded to the Tier 2 Watch List due to its failure to increase conviction rates from previous years. In 2011 the US State Department noted in the annual TIP Report that the Thai law enforcement personnel were closely connected with traffickers and acted to protect commercial sex venues, labor sweatshops, and the seafood industry from police raids.

However, this trend toward high arrest rates and low but growing prosecution and conviction rates mimics larger global trends (UNODC 2018). As governments began ushering in new and more vigorous anti-trafficking legal regimes in the early 2000s, it took them some time to develop domestic prosecutorial systems that could make effective use of their new laws. Trafficking prosecutions are complex endeavors, frequently involving nationals of many countries, crimes committed across different jurisdictions, and victims who are reluctant to cooperate with law enforcement. Victims may be unwilling to testify or may be deported before they can assist in the prosecution process. Thailand also experienced significant domestic political unrest during the period of analysis. Thaksin Shinawatra's government was ousted in a coup in 2006, followed by protest and political unrest between his supporters and the government in 2009 and 2010. Another coup in 2014 created more upheaval and has left the government in the hands of the military.

Beginning in 2012 the Thai government began vigorously arresting traffickers (see fig. 4.4). This sharp rise in arrests has been followed by growing prosecution and conviction rates beginning in 2013 and continuing consistently through the most recent report in 2019. Growth in these two areas is consistent with our expectations for governments that follow a criminal justice approach to combating trafficking; however, directing resources to expand police presence is another hallmark of a criminal justice approach.

Over time the Thai government has created specialized police units and special task forces to assist with prosecutions. In 2007 the attorney general's

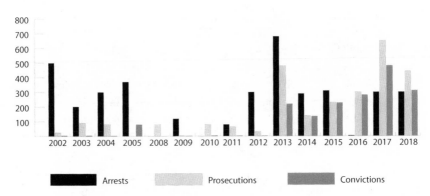

Figure 4.4. Arrests, Prosecutions, and Convictions for Trafficking in Thailand, 2002–18*

*No arrest, prosecution, or conviction data is available for 2006–7.

Source: US State Department Trafficking in Persons Reports 2002–19.

office established the Center Against International Human Trafficking. The eight attorneys who staff the center are responsible for prosecuting trafficking cases in Thailand (US Department of State 2008, 280). In 2009 a new specialized police unit—the Anti–Human Trafficking Division, designed to exclusively address human trafficking—was incorporated into the Royal Thai Police (UNIAP 2010b, 5). The Thailand Internet Crimes Against Children Task Force (TICAC)—a multiagency force that coordinates arrests and prosecutions of those who traffic children—was created in 2015 (US Department of State 2016, 365). In 2016 the government again expanded the attorney general's office, creating a new subunit responsible for guiding and assisting law enforcement and provincial prosecutors in trafficking cases (US Department of State 2017, 388). In 2017 the government also created an expanded task force—the Thailand Anti-Trafficking in Persons Task Force (TATIP), which includes police, NGOs, social workers, and first responders—to assist in screening for potential victims and gathering evidence (US Department of State 2018, 415). Both the TICAC and the TATIP received expanded funding in 2018: 3.6 million baht for TICAC and 9 million baht for TATIP (US Department of State 2019, 454).

Victim-Centered?

Under the terms of the 2008 law, trafficking victims in Thailand are entitled to government financial support and the opportunity to apply for work permits. Yet victims are often detained in shelters against their will as they await long legal processes. In 2016 Tin Nyo Win, a Burmese migrant in Thailand, made headlines when he notified Thai police that his pregnant wife and many other Burmese migrants were enslaved in a shrimp peeling factory in Pathum Thani.

Authorities found approximately 100 Burmese slave laborers, including children, in the factory. Immediately upon being "freed" from slavery Tin Nyo Win and his wife were held in a Thai jail, then eventually detained in a Thai trafficking shelter. In an interview with the *Bangkok Post* (2016b) he explained: "I feel like I have been victimized three times. Once in the shrimp shed, the second time in ... jail and now again in the shelter. Even prisoners know how many years or months they will be in prison, but we don't know anything about how many years or months we'll be stuck here. It's worse than prison."

The Thai system for victim protection is unlike the systems employed by other countries examined in this work. In Thailand, trafficking shelters are run and funded by the central government through the Ministry of Social Development and Human Security (MSDHS) (UNIAP 2014). Over time the number of shelters available for victims has grown from 97 in 2005 to 138 in 2009 (US Department of State 2005, 2009). However, since 2009 the government has not reported the creation of any new shelters.[11] Though it is possible that the government has determined that 138 shelters is sufficient, the pervasive use of immigration detention facilities as a means for holding victims in Thailand suggests that more shelters are needed if victim support is to be a priority in Thailand.

Thailand lacks a central policy or system to provide or to facilitate victim assistance. Even in India, with its federal system and patchwork approach to combating trafficking, the victim-assistance system has been streamlined into one approach that is advanced by the federal government and implemented by state governments. In Thailand we could not find evidence of any similar guiding government policy. Apart from the MSDHS being responsible for assisting victims in shelters and distributing funding, there is no guiding government policy prescribing how victims will be treated or how NGOs will be integrated into that system.[12] This makes the distribution of government funding and provision of victim support challenging.

The implementation of the provisions of the 2008 law has also become a challenge in identifying and supporting foreign trafficking victims in Thailand. Though trafficking victims are supposed to be provided with assistance regardless of their nationality, in practice many foreign nationals are deported to their home countries following long detentions in immigration prisons (US Department of State 2010, 321).[13] By 2011 there were reports that foreign-trafficking victims were being detained against their will in government-run shelters and being denied the ability to work while they assisted the government in prosecuting traffickers (US Department of State 2011). Occasionally the Thai government has reported the number of visas provided to foreign-trafficking victims. In 2011, for example, the Thai government provided thirty visas to foreign labor-trafficking victims and financial support to 103 additional victims

(US Department of State 2012, 339). Sometimes the government only reports the number of work permits provided to foreign victims (128 permits in 2013, 57 in 2014, and 58 in 2015).[14] Compared to the relative size of the foreign-trafficking-victim population in Thailand, the government's provision of these permits and visas only impacts a small portion of trafficking victims who would benefit. More recently, the government has stopped providing concrete numbers of visas or work permits granted—calling into question its commitment to human rights protections for foreign-trafficking victims.

In assessing whether the Thai approach to combating trafficking emphasizes the conviction of traffickers over protecting victims' human rights, it is clear that Thai authorities prioritize the conviction of traffickers. Our analysis reveals that in response to international pressure, the Thai government has dramatically increased support to law enforcement and prosecutors, which over time has contributed to a steep rise in the number of trafficking convictions. Moreover, the progressive 2008 anti-trafficking law, if implemented, would afford expansive protections to both national and foreign sex-trafficking victims. Yet by most accounts, including those contained here, victims in Thai trafficking "shelters" are detained and frequently unable to work, and foreign victims are deported. These shelters better approximate jails or detention centers and they inhibit the human rights of those already victimized by traffickers and slaveholders.

The Role of Women

Two factors are critical for understanding the role of women in the Thai political system. First, while Thai women have historically been represented poorly at all levels of government, since the military took over in a coup and suspended the Constitution in 2014 political representation has suffered, a point elaborated on later. Second, the military takeover has ushered in a period of censorship of anyone the junta deems threatening. In short, while the country has suffered from low rates of female legislative representation for some time, in recent years the political crisis that has enveloped the country has contributed to censorship of political opponents, critics, and advocates who might otherwise be pressuring the government to advance more victim-centered legislation.[15]

Rates of female representation at all levels of Thai politics are low. Between 2008 and 2020 the level of female representation in the Lower House of the National Assembly never surpassed a peak of 16.2 percent, which it achieved in 2020 (see fig. 4.5) (UN Women 2020). For context, 16.2 percent female legislative representation in the Lower House ranks Thailand number 130 of 189 countries ranked by the UN Women and Inter-Parliamentary Union in 2020.

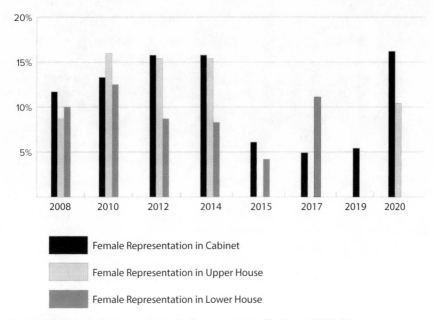

Figure 4.5. Female Representation in Government in Thailand, 2008–20

Source: UN Women and Inter-Parliamentary Union, "Women in Politics," assessed annually between 2008 and 2020. For 2008–16 see Appendix 2B; for 2020 see https://www.unwomen.org/en/digital-library/publications/2020/03/women-in-politics-map-2020.

Iwanaga (2008) argues that low levels of female representation in Thailand are the result of sex-role socialization, which effectively makes the political realm almost exclusively the domain of men (175). The cultural devaluation of women has practical political and policy impacts. Iwanaga's analysis of the complex "structural, institutional and cultural" factors at play in Thailand reveals a diminished level of women's political participation (2008, 176). Low rates of female representation and engagement in formal political roles are consistent with the expectation that a dearth of female representatives will result in a national approach to combating trafficking that emphasizes criminal justice at the expense of victims' human rights.

Since 2014, when the military assumed control of Thailand in a coup, members of the upper house (the Senate) are no longer elected. Of the 250 Senate seats, 194 are appointed by the military, making this body "of, by, and for the military" (Jaipragas and Thongnoi 2019). For this reason, we restrict our assessment of women's political representation to the Lower House.

The low rate of female legislative representation in the Lower House is quite apparent when compared against the rates of female legislative representation in other countries in the Greater Mekong subregion. Figure 4.6 shows

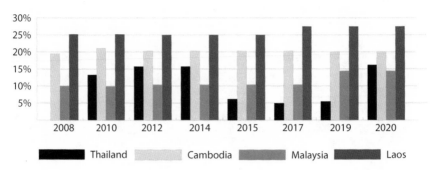

Figure 4.6. Female Representation in the Lower House in Thailand, Cambodia, Malaysia, and Laos, 2008–20

Source: UN Women and Inter-Parliamentary Union, "Women in Politics," assessed annually between 2008 and 2020.

the percentage of female legislative representation in the Lower House of Thailand against representation in Cambodia, Malaysia, and Laos to determine whether there are regional norms at work that discourage female political participation. Laos has the highest rate of female legislative representation in the subregion, averaging 25 percent from 2008 to 2020. In contrast, Thailand is consistently the lowest in the subregion, with just 5 percent female legislative representation in 2017. To put these numbers in a larger global context, in 2020 Laos's rank for female legislative representation is 65 out of the 189 countries (UN Women 2020).

Thailand is a particularly challenging case for assessing the role of women in the legislative process because there are no female cabinet ministers and the rate of female legislative representation in the Lower House is extraordinarily low. While there have been two major legislative reforms in recent years, virtually no evidence can be found that female representatives played any role in their promotion, a fact that is consistent with an approach that is decidedly focused on criminal justice.

Since the passage of the national anti-trafficking legislation in 2008, two major amendments have been added. The first, passed in 2015, increases penalties for traffickers and protects whistleblowers (Chantavanich 2020, 236). The motivation behind this amendment largely came from the official complicity of government officials in trafficking crimes, so it took aim at corruption rather than victim protection. The second amendment was passed in 2017 to revise the definition of exploitation and forced labor to bring it into harmony with the 2000 UN Anti-Trafficking Treaty.

While women have been largely absent from the formal political sphere in Thailand, they have been pioneers in assisting trafficking victims through their work in NGOs. A number of these organizations are working in Thailand and highlighted here are the innovative strategies employed by two Thai-based organizations. The NightLight Foundation started in Bangkok in 1994 with the aim of assisting those adversely affected by the global sex industry. CEO and founder Annie Dieselberg developed a jewelry business, NightLight Design, which provides full-time employment for survivors. Since 2005 the organization has employed 160 women full time, with medical benefits and a savings plan. The foundation also runs a childcare center for the children of women who work for the jewelry design arm of the organization. A NightLight outreach team works in the Nana Sukhumvit district of Bangkok, developing relationships with women and girls in the sex industry. The organization also partners with the International Organization for Migration in rescuing and repatriating foreign women from the bars and brothels in Bangkok. In 2019 NightLight International was recognized by the Royal Thai Police for its work in assisting survivors. In 2019 the organization was also the first to become officially registered as a shelter for trafficking victims in Thailand (Nightlight Bangkok 2019).

A second group, the Foundation of Child Understanding (FOCUS), also known as the Anti-Trafficking Coordination Unit Northern Thailand (TRAF-CORD), started its work in 2002 in an effort to stop the flow of trafficking victims from southern China, Laos, and Burma into northern Thailand.[16] The organization became a certified NGO in Thailand in 2010. TRAFCORD works to protect women and children enslaved in the sex industry in both Thailand and the Greater Mekong subregion. It collects evidence, interviews victims, and coordinates with law enforcement agencies and with other NGOs. Since starting its work in 2002 their staffs have assisted in rescue efforts for Burmese and Thai children forced to work in brothels in the Lampang, Chiang Mai, and Tak provinces. They have also rescued Laotian and Thai women and children from brothels in Chiang Mai, Phayao, Tak, Petchaburi, Choomporn, Nakorn-prathom, Songkla, and Kanjanaburi. More recently FOCUS has assisted boys, who, like those noted earlier, were recruited from the streets and forced into modern slavery in brothels in Chiang Mai and Chiang Rai. The organization also runs a twenty-four-hour crisis hotline to receive calls about child abuse for referral to the police.

Conclusion

This analysis of sex trafficking in Thailand supports the larger argument proposed here, that where the economic rights of women and girls are not protected or enforced in practice, they face a higher probability of being vic-timized by traffickers. In the Thai case, the analysis of the identities of victims shows that the intersection of religion, citizenship status, and gender renders certain groups more likely to be victimized than others. Stateless people who lack citizenship are especially vulnerable to becoming sex-trafficking victims. In Thailand, ethnic Hill Tribe minorities, the Rohingyas, and the children of economic migrants all lack citizenship and tend to be victimized by sex traffickers at high rates.

Political turmoil following the 2014 coup, which left a military junta running the country, has closed off the political space, making it dangerous for civil society organizations, even those advocating for the rights of sex-trafficking victims, to do their work. It is worth noting the extent to which these organizations require anonymity to conduct their work—one of the organizations interviewed requested total anonymity out of fear of government reprisal. What does this say about the political climate in Thailand? At the very least it says that since the most recent coup in 2014, dangers are associated with NGOs being high profile in their work. The military junta seems to be especially effective in closing the gap between arrests, prosecutions, and convictions of traffickers. In each year between 2016 and 2018, Thailand averaged between 200 and 400 trafficking convictions, whereas in the period between 2002 and 2012 there were never more than 5 convictions per year. The difference suggests a strong emphasis on the criminal justice approach to fighting trafficking, which is important in deterring would-be traffickers.

Whereas in India female legislators and cabinet ministers are integral in proposing victim-centered legislation, in Thailand the low rates of female representation have made it difficult to assess the extent to which women are playing these roles. We encountered many female NGO leaders and workers doing the important work of supporting victims but virtually no female legislators working in the Assembly to advance the interests of victims. The patterns uncovered in Thailand—growing authoritarianism and shrinking female legislative participation—foreshadow the findings on Russia.

Notes

1. The most populous country in Southeast Asia in 2010 was Indonesia, followed by the Philippines and Vietnam. For more on historic demographic patterns in the region, see Jones (2013).
2. Cynthia Vejar and Andrew Quach (2013) state that there is quite a bit of controversy surrounding this notion within the Buddhist scriptures and suggest that the inferiority of women may have been a small point buried somewhere in the scriptures that has in practice become broadly accepted.
3. This section of the Thai government progress report on human trafficking lists a series of cases the Thai government was prosecuting against traffickers who were members of the police and military, elected officials, and social workers.

4. The names Burma and Myanmar are used interchangeably.

5. Though the Thai press refers to this case as the "Mae Hong Son prostitution scandal," children are not capable of giving consent to engage in sex work, so here children are considered victims of sex traffickers.

6. Some of the reports also suggest that child victims come from Vietnam and Cambodia (see ECPAT International 2011, 10).

7. Pseudonym used to protect the child's identity. His story comes from Keenapan (2012).

8. For a fascinating account of the history of kathoeys in Thailand, see Totman (2003).

9. An interview with the foundation manager/program coordinator of one Thai anti-trafficking organization, who asked to keep their identity confidential, suggests that the majority of individuals they assist in the north indeed do come from Burma.

10. A pseudonym used by Kimmons to protect the girl's identity.

11. This comes from a review of each US State Department Trafficking in Persons Report published between 2010 and 2019.

12. Interview with NightLight International–Bangkok, August 6, 2014.

13. The interview with NightLight International on August 6, 2014, also confirmed that foreign trafficking victims are often deported following long detentions within Thailand.

14. These numbers can be found in the US Department of State TIP Reports for 2014, 2015, and 2016, respectively.

15. In 2016 the Internal Security Operations Command worked with prosecutors to secure libel charges against three NGO advocates for publishing a book that detailed fifty-four cases of state-sponsored torture against detainees in southern Thailand. Among the three advocates charged with libel was Pornpen Khongkachonkiet, of both the Cross-Cultural Foundation and the chair of Amnesty International Thailand. For more on the charges, which were ultimately dropped, see *Bangkok Post* (2017a).

16. The information contained in this paragraph can be found on the FOCUS/TRAFCORD website: http://www.trafcord.org.

FIVE

Russia

In March 2001, Oxana Rantseva, a twenty-year-old Russian language student, thought she had found a translation job in Limassol, a coastal resort town on the island of Cyprus. According to her father, before she departed she signed a translation contract, but upon arriving in Cyprus she was forced to sign an "artiste" contract that obligated her to dance in a cabaret to maintain her Cypriot visa (Arutunyan 2010). Rantseva's lawyer, Lyudmila Churkina, explained, "Oxana didn't expect that she would have to work as a dancer, and she especially did not expect that she would have to perform [sexual services]" (Arutunyan 2010). Like Oxana, sex-trafficking victims in Europe from post-Soviet countries have reported that once they are employed in the cabarets, they are forced to compel patrons to buy them drinks and that their pay is docked if they do not meet a quota for drink sales. Cabaret owners also force victims to sell sexual services to pay down their growing debt for failing to meet their drink quotas.[1]

Oxana tried to escape. Within three days of arriving in Cyprus she ran from the apartment she shared with other "dancers," leaving a brief note: "I'm tired. I'm leaving for Russia." The owner of the cabaret claims that he found her dancing in another cabaret and took her home in the hopes of eventually deporting and replacing her with another girl from Russia (ECHR 2010, 4). Yet within hours of the cabaret owner taking her to his apartment, Oxana was found dead in front of the apartment building. The balcony door to the owner's fifth-floor apartment was open and a bedspread was tied to the railing of the balcony. Whether foul play was involved or Oxana so desperately wanted to escape the apartment that she was willing to suspend herself from a fifth-floor balcony on a bedspread is unknown, but either scenario is a tragic statement about her circumstances. The exact details of her death were never determined because neither the Russian nor Cypriot governments adequately investigated the mysterious circumstances surrounding her death.[2]

Oxana's case has the unique distinction of being the first human-trafficking case to make it to the European Court of Human Rights (ECHR). Her father petitioned the ECHR, arguing that neither Cyprus nor Russia adequately investigated her death, that the Cypriot government failed to protect her while she was still alive, and that neither government punished those responsible for her death. Her father also argued that Russia did too little to protect his daughter from the threat of trafficking (ECHR 2010, 1). Though her father did not prevail on all counts, the ECHR determined that neither country adequately investigated Oxana's death, that Cyprus was responsible for a violation of Article 4 of the ECHR Convention on Human Rights for failing to protect her from human trafficking, and that both countries were obligated to pay damages (ECHR 2010, 86).

We know about Oxana Rantseva's story because it has gained enormous attention following the ECHR's groundbreaking decision to side with her and against both Cyprus and Russia. The factors contributing to Oxana's path to sex trafficking and ultimately her death are common in Russia: women and girls are promised well-paying service jobs as au pairs, maids, hostesses, or waitresses, both within and outside the county. There are many factors contributing to sex trafficking both within Russia and from Russia to other countries. But among the most powerful are the country's tumultuous transition to a privatized economy, its uniquely weak economic rights for women and girls (especially non-nationals), the widespread official corruption, and a general reluctance within the government and the public at large to confront sex trafficking.

The dearth of economic rights for women and girls disproportionately impacts foreign sex-trafficking victims in Russia. Victim populations in Russia largely come from surrounding post-Soviet countries, including Ukraine and Moldova, and increasingly from Nigeria. Our findings in Russia bear important similarities to those in India and Thailand, where prevailing cultural norms subjugate the lives and power of women and girls relative to their male peers. Yet the Russian case is unique in that both supporters and opponents of Vladimir Putin invoke patriarchal gender stereotypes that reinforce sexism and close off space for feminist activists to prioritize trafficking victims' rights (Sperling 2015). A deep history of sexism in Russia helps to explain its poor legal protections for women's economic rights, which are less necessary in a society in which women are relegated to traditional roles in the home. This absence of women's economic rights creates a higher probability that a country will be a source for sex-trafficking victims. An analysis of the link between the role of women in drafting national legislation and the orientation of anti-trafficking policies runs counter to the expectations of our second hypothesis: while Russian women have been involved in drafting legislation (albeit with very low levels of formal representation in the Duma), the resulting legislation is weakly criminal justice–oriented and virtually silent on victim support. These findings are consistent with the work of comparative political scientists who find that women's representation in Russia overall is largely symbolic, with female politicians often relegated to token roles in the legislature, constrained by informal rules, and unable to advocate for women's interests (Johnson 2016).

Beginning in 2012, Russian authorities initiated an aggressive campaign to severely restrict the activities of foreign-funded civil society groups and to crack down on efforts to promote democracy. The government's campaign to curtail civil society is part of a larger effort to consolidate political power in the hands of the Kremlin and Putin. Caught in the crosshairs of these battles are the hundreds of now-shuttered crisis centers for women. These closing are connected to earlier battles that pitted the Russian state against transnational and local feminists who are often funded by Western governments (Johnson 2009). These groups made critical inroads in bringing the issues of trafficking and violence against women to Russian consciousness in the post–Cold War period, which resulted in the opening of the crisis centers. But as Putin continues to consolidate his power and roll back civil and political rights more broadly, one of many consequences is the deterioration of both women's and trafficking victims' rights in Russia.

Background on Sex Trafficking in Russia

Since the collapse of the Soviet Union in 1991, millions of people in Russia and the former Soviet Republics were left without their social safety net. The transition from a command economy to a privatized economy meant that people could no longer rely on the government to provide for their basic economic security. Living standards deteriorated quickly (Lavigne 2007). Unemployment and wage delays gripped the workforce, and women fared especially poorly in the post-transition environment. Much has been written about the disproportionate impact of the collapse on women (Beneria and Feldman 1992; Human Rights Watch 1995, 1999; Kiblitskaya 2000; Stoecker 2005; Shelley 2010). Among the many policies implemented in the name of privatization in Russia were the elimination of childcare programs, unemployment compensation, and social services. Severe wage delays meant that people frequently worked for months without pay, hoping that they would eventually be compensated. Hyperinflation significantly reduced the value of whatever money people were eventually able to collect. In the face of hyperinflation and without stable incomes, bills added up and were transformed into crushing debt. The desperation for stable work created a sizable pool of potential trafficking victims from within Russia and from many of the former Soviet republics that were also undergoing painful transitions to privatization.

Zoya, a young woman from western Ukraine, accepted what she thought was a job as a maid to pay off her debts. She explains:

Between 1990 and 1998, even until 2000, our government often did not pay any salaries for months. We have accumulated a debt for rent payments.

We could eat somehow, but we could not pay for the apartment. And in 2000 the state obligated us to pay the debt. . . . The condition was that if you don't pay in 2 months, they will evict your family. . . . Traffickers used this situation—they would say, "We will pay your debts; the apartment stays in your possession but you are going with me." . . . Yes, maybe I went to earn money abroad, but I did not know that I will be dressed up and put on some man's lap. I knew that I will clean something and wash; I did not know that I will be servicing men from dawn to sunset and all the money will be taken from me. (Shapkina 2008, 26)

Since 2014 these economic pressures on Russians have only accelerated. The Russian economy collapsed in 2014, and in order to fund the Sochi Olympics the state froze all pension funds for Russian citizens (Churakova and van der Westhuizen 2019).

Factors Contributing to Sex Trafficking in Russia

Sex trafficking in Russia, like in every other place, arises through a variety of avenues of abuse. Here we discuss the most prominent factors that contribute to the problem of sex trafficking in Russia.

The Sexual Revolution and Public Backlash

Just as their social safety net was deteriorating, Mikhail Gorbachev's perestroika ushered in a sexual revolution, which is also important for understanding the response to sex trafficking in Russia (Tverdova 2011; Schuckman 2006). Under the Soviet system sex was understood as a capitalist vice. Women were essential parts of the Soviet labor force, but sex work was not considered legitimate work. As the political strictures of communism fell, so too did the taboo nature of sex. Freedom and sex became inexorably linked for the younger generation (Schuckman 2006; Kon 1995). Tverdova (2011) explains that a consequence of this sexual revolution was a new feeling among some Russian women and girls that they were not ashamed to earn money by selling sex. Prostitution became linked to the new tides of perestroika and liberation (333). The symbol that emerged—of the prostitute as a modern and liberated woman—has come to color Russian public perceptions of sex-trafficking victims. Namely, that these women, like the women from the perestroika era who chose to engage in sex work, are responsible for their fates.

During this time, foreign influence in Russia was also growing—foreign governments and transnational feminist activists colored debates about prostitution and sex work in Russia, which ultimately had implications for trafficking victims. One feminist approach to prostitution based in the United States, the Coalition

Against Trafficking in Women, opposes all forms of prostitution as sex trafficking. Johnson (2009) refers to this as "anti-prostitution" feminism, which seeks to gender the debate by focusing on women and children as victims (112). Another group based in Thailand, the Global Alliance Against Trafficking in Women, adopts a different approach that allows space for adults who engage in sex work. They seek to de-gender the debate and focus on sex workers' labor rights. That both these approaches have become infused in debates about prostitution and sex work in Russia is important, because they represent a divide in approaches to prostitution among the transnational feminists. Ultimately the American-based anti-prostitution group successfully persuaded the George W. Bush administration to link American support for Russian crisis centers with an anti-prostitution pledge (Johnson 2009, 124). The degree of foreign intervention in these debates helps to foreshadow Putin's efforts to curtail foreign-funded civil society organizations beginning in 2012 and presents feminism as foreign and therefore inappropriate for Russia (Orlova 2018).

A subtitle for this chapter could have been "She Should Have Known" to reflect broader sentiments among the Russian public regarding trafficking victims. In a 2014 public opinion poll in Russia commissioned by Russian trafficking expert Mary Buckley, 36.7 percent of respondents suggested that trafficking victims had "themselves to blame" for being trafficked (121). This was an expansive poll, surveying 1,600 respondents, and was part of a larger series of public opinion polls about Russian attitudes on trafficking that Buckley conducted between 2007 and 2014 (Buckley 2018). In the most recent set of responses from 2014, 40.2 percent of those polled suggested that trafficking victims are looking for work abroad due to poor job prospects in Russia (121). Another 27.4 percent of respondents believe that trafficking victims are primarily prostitutes hoping to make more generous wages abroad (121). Buckley's most recent findings are reproduced in table 5.1. Taken together, 64.1 percent of these respondents believed that trafficking victims have either themselves to blame or are prostitutes. These findings help to explain why the national response to combating trafficking in Russia is neither criminal justice–oriented nor victim-centered. The public at large tends to view trafficking victims as responsible for their victimization.

Hypermasculinity and Antifeminist/Anti-LGBTQ+ Resurgence

Buckley's findings—that the Russian public has little sympathy for women who are trafficked for sex—are not surprising in a climate in which Putin and the Kremlin have doubled down on efforts to silence feminists and promote heteronormativity to consolidate power. In 2012, Pussy Riot, a Russian feminist punk art group, released a controversial song, "Punk Prayer," that criticizes Putin and encourages Russians to come out to protest his regime.[3] Pussy Riot

Table 5.1. Perceptions of the Reason for Sex Trafficking in Russia

Answer to the statement "**In your opinion, women and girls who find themselves trafficked into the sex trade abroad . . .**":	Total N=1,600 (%)
have themselves to blame	36.7
have been duped by criminal gangs	40.2
have been sold into slavery by parents and friends	10.3
are looking for work abroad because of a lack of jobs	23.6
are in the main prostitutes, hoping to earn more in other countries	27.4
are victims of the demand in the West for Slavic prostitutes	13.5
are a manifestation of the breakdown in social order and morality	21.5
other	1.4
don't know	4.2
no response	0

Source: Buckley (2018), 121.

played "Punk Prayer" in Moscow's Cathedral of Christ the Savior to simultaneously criticize both Putin's regime and the Russian Orthodox Church for their promotion of traditional conservative family values (Senkova 2018). Members of the group were imprisoned for "hooliganism motivated by religious hatred" (Sperling 2015, 223). The government's harsh crackdown on political speech is consistent with a larger project to adopt hypermasculinity as a foundation for establishing the legitimacy of Putin's authority, Russia's national security, and the country's role in global politics (Orlova 2018, 61). Sperling (2015) recounts the story of Putin's birthday calendar, which features young female students in Moscow State University's journalism department in skimpy clothes offering sexualized quips, implying their attraction to Putin (1). Sperling contends that the Kremlin has ramped up efforts to invoke patriarchal, sexualized gender norms to legitimate Putin's power.

The Kremlin's efforts to deploy hypermasculine rhetoric to legitimate Putin's authority also use homophobic rhetoric against political opponents while passing anti-LGBTQ+ policies into law. Putin's United Russia Party celebrated the annual day of Family, Love, and Fidelity by flying a heterosexual pride flag in 2015 (Suchland 2018, 1074). By 2016 the Kremlin had explicitly outlawed a photoshopped image of Putin's face wearing heavy makeup and superimposed on a gay pride flag because the image had proliferated among LGBTQ+ activists (Baker, Clancy, and Clancy 2019). Beyond invoking homophobic rhetoric against political opponents, in 2013 Putin's government passed the "gay propaganda" law, which criminalizes sharing information with minors about "nontraditional sexual relations" (Human Rights Watch 2018). This war on feminism and the LGBTQ+ community are part of the Kremlin's larger efforts to consolidate authority. The resurgence of hypermasculinity and antifeminist and homophobic policies in Russia have crowded out and vilified proponents of women's rights, including feminists who advocate for the rights of sex workers and trafficking victims.

Deprivation of Women's Economic Rights in Russia

Feminist scholars have highlighted the ways economic and social causes contribute to trafficking. Suchland (2015) shows that a global system of economic violence—namely neoliberalism, the post-Socialist transition, and systems of precarious labor—has the effect of gendering sex-trafficking victimization. One manifestation of this economic violence is the deprivation of women's economic rights. In both law and practice women face extraordinary hurdles in obtaining workplace equality and the cultural status of women in Russia is revealed by this economic inequity. These cultural and economic inequities force them into the informal economy, where they are at greater risk of being targeted and deceived by trafficking recruiters. Much like in India, Russian protections for gender parity in the workplace appear progressive on the surface—the Russian Constitution enshrines the right to equality in the workplace—while a lack of enforcement coupled with newer legislative developments has hollowed out the seemingly progressive approach to gender parity in the workplace. The lack of enforcement of these laws makes women acutely susceptible to sex traffickers. Moreover, the costs of these policies are borne disproportionately by foreign women who come to Russia hoping to find work, making them easy targets for traffickers.

On paper the Russian approach to gender parity in the workplace appears progressive. Article 19 of the Russian Constitution grants equal rights to "all people . . . before the law," and Article 3 of the Russian Labor Code prohibits discrimination in the workplace on the basis of sex.[4] Additionally, Article 37 of the Labor Code provides that individuals should have autonomy in selecting their profession and should be paid free from discrimination: "Everyone shall have the right to freely use his labour capabilities, to choose the type of activity and profession. . . . Everyone shall have the right . . . for labour remuneration without any discrimination whatsoever and not lower than minimum wages and salaries established by the federal law." Yet, despite these policies, many obstacles still exist for women to secure their rights in the workplace. While Article 37 permits individual autonomy in choice of work, Regulation 162, which became a part of the Labor Code in 2000, prohibits women from working in more than 450 different jobs. These positions are in industries that the government considers too physically strenuous or too harmful for women. This list has significant and meaningful effects on job opportunities for Russian women. For instance, in 2012 Svetlana Medvedeva was denied a job as a boat captain because this occupation is on the banned jobs list. After exhausting domestic remedies in Russia to no avail, Medvedeva took her case to the UN Committee on Women, which ruled in her favor (OHCHR 2016). In response to Svetlana's claim at the UN, the UN Committee on the Elimination of Discrimination Against Women called upon Russia to amend and reduce its list because it reinforces stereotypes about the role of women (CEDAW 2016). In April 2019 the Russian Labor Ministry issued an order that would remove 350 of the banned jobs from the list, opening up considerably more opportunities for Russian women in dozens of industries. This order did not take effect until January 2021, so during the period of analysis none of these positions were available to women (*Moscow Times* 2020).

Even in recent instances when the Duma could have prioritized gender equality in the workplace, legislators have chosen not to act. In July 2018 the State Duma speaker, Vyacheslav Volodin, announced that a draft bill focusing on gender equality would no longer be on the State Duma's agenda for legislation (Interfax Russia 2018). The draft bill, which aimed to impose gender quotas on state jobs, was proposed in 2003 and was issued for a second reading in 2018, but it was rejected by the State Duma. Inequities in workplace rights have contributed to persistent wage gaps for women who participate in the formal labor force. In a global analysis of gender pay inequities conducted by the World Economic Forum in 2018, Russia ranked 75th out of 149 countries (World Economic Forum 2018). Deputy Prime Minister Olga Golodets argues that "Russian women's wages are 26 percent lower than those of men" (*Moscow Times* 2017).

Organized Crime

Organized crime plays a role in perpetuating sex trafficking in Russia, though Shelley (2018) contends that traffickers are connected through small networks and are infrequently part of large criminal organizations (156). Shelley suggests "much of human trafficking is not tied to larger criminal networks but is carried out by smaller groups, often family and friends of the victim" (159). Russia is no stranger to illicit trade, though during the Soviet era an illicit trade in goods was largely driven by shortages in consumer goods (Shelley 2018). The collapse of the former Soviet Union created unparalleled opportunities for the once-underground shadow economy to flourish. Putnins and Sauka (2020) use a new methodology for estimating the size of shadow economies in their Shadow Economy Index, finding that between 2017 and 2018 the Russian shadow economy accounted for 44.7 percent of Russia's GDP (2).

Though some victims are recruited by the *mafiya* directly, most often they are recruited by acquaintances, sold to middle-men, and eventually sold to organized crime groups that own a stable of women either in brothels within Russia or outside of the country (Shapkina 2008; Hughes 2002a).[5] In Russia, the word "mafiya" is simply the term for any organized crime group, much like the word "mafia" might be used in the United States. Between 2010 and 2012 approximately 50 percent of traffickers in Eastern Europe and central Asia were female, giving this region the unique distinction of having the single highest rate of female traffickers in the world (UNODC 2014, 67).

Basing her findings on an analysis of 5,200 Russian news articles on trafficking published between 2003 and 2013, McCarthy (2020) shows that Russian female traffickers are involved in all forms of trafficking: for sex, labor, and child trafficking for adoption (83). McCarthy's analysis sheds new light on the ways women take advantage of stereotypical gender roles—as nurturers and thus more trusted and less suspicious than male recruiters—to become highly effective recruiters themselves (85). Public service announcements about the dangers of trafficking tend to feature men as recruiters (Surtees 2008), which gives female recruiters an advantage since women may be perceived as altruistic, nonviolent, and generally unwilling to be involved in crimes that exploit other women (Levenkron 2007, cited in McCarthy 2020). McCarthy's analysis shows that female traffickers in Russia are often "savvy entrepreneurs" who run trafficking operations and even hire male subordinates to work as recruiters (84). The male recruiters use a "lover boy" model of recruitment to romance women before delivering them to traffickers. Recruiters may also be victims themselves, sent back to their town or country of origin by their traffickers to recruit new victims. Hughes (2002a) explains that this may be a rational decision by the victim-turned-recruiter, as an opportunity to briefly return home and gain a respite from the horrors of sex slavery.

Corruption

Bribery and corruption are critical components of most trafficking operations. But in Russia the scale of corruption and bribery—between traffickers on the one hand and the public officials and police on the other—is on an order of magnitude beyond many countries. Transparency International produces annual country rankings based on the perceived degree of corruption within every country around the world. In 2014 Denmark earned the distinction of the number 1 position, meaning that it was perceived to be the least corrupt country in the world. Of the 180 countries in the 2018 rankings, Russia tied with Lebanon, Mexico, Papua New Guinea, and Iran for the 138th position. In 2011 Dmitry Strykanova, a lieutenant colonel in the Russian Foreign Military Intelligence Agency, was convicted, along with ten others, of trafficking 129 women for forced prostitution (Hepburn and Simon 2013, 409). The trafficked victims came from throughout Eastern Europe, including Russia, and were sent to Western Europe and the Middle East between 1999 and 2007 (409). Paradoxically, members of the Russian Ministry of Internal Affairs have also been implicated, but not convicted, in high-profile labor trafficking cases (US Department of State 2010).

Corruption within Russian society is not restricted to high-level officials. Surveys of the Russian public suggest that the police are the least-trusted public institution among the courts, the mass media, the army, the political parties, and the president of Russia, with just 3 percent expressing the highest levels of trust in the police (Gerber and Mendelson 2008, 25). The same study found that on average 9.4 percent of Russian respondents or members of their families had encountered situations wherein they were compelled to offer bribes to the Russian police, illuminating why so many Russians express such little trust in the police overall (18).

This collusion between traffickers and public officials makes a good deal of sense, since many of the traffickers, now involved in organized crime, were once members of the KGB or part of the Russian military. This link gives them critical knowledge of business, weapons, and connections to those still working in official capacities (Caldwell et al. 1999). Traffickers pay bribes at many levels of Russian bureaucracy. Bribes may be paid to border officials to facilitate trafficking or to the police so that they will look the other way. Or the police may simply require victims to provide sex for free in exchange for allowing the trafficking rings to operate. In Moscow a police bus typically is sent to retrieve prostitutes and bring them back to the station once a week so that they can provide *subbortnik*, or free labor, to the police (Hughes 2002a, 21).[6]

Forms of Trafficking and Identities of Victims in Russia

The rocky transition to a capitalist economy coupled with a sexual revolution in the 1990s ushered in many changes that created conditions rife for Russia to become a global hub for commercial sex trafficking—as a source country, a transit path, and a destination country. There are four main types of trafficking in Russia: trafficking for slave labor exploitation, trafficking for sexual exploitation, child trafficking (for sex, labor, and marriage), and trafficking for begging (Tiurukanova and Institute for Urban Economics 2006, 33–50). Though the focus here is on sex trafficking, a major component of the trafficking market in Russia is forced labor from neighboring Common Wealth of Independent State countries. In 2014 there were approximately 5–12 million foreign workers in Russia (US Department of State 2015). The Global Slavery Index estimates that in 2016 approximately 794,000 people were exploited as slaves in Russia (Walk Free Foundation 2018e).

Domestic and International Sex Trafficking of
Russian Women and Girls: The Natasha Trade

In the early to mid-2000s the victimization of Russian women and girls sold into the sex trade abroad attracted such attention in the media and in documentary films that it was given a special name: "the Natasha trade" (Hughes 2015). The stereotypical victim of the Natasha trade is a young Russian woman who is deceived by traffickers and forced into sex work abroad. Though this stereotype permeated popular culture for good reason—Eastern European women and girls were acutely susceptible to sex traffickers in the wild days after the transition—this stereotype did not encompass the full range of threats. Russian women and girls were, and still are, at risk of domestic trafficking.

Russia is divided into eight federal districts. Victims trafficked within Russia are often trafficked from central and eastern regions of the county (the Russian Far East, or RFE; Siberia; and the Urals) into Moscow and St. Petersburg (US Department of State 2015; Khodyreva 2008).[7] The Central Federal District, which includes Moscow, is the center of business and finance and is also a major destination for women trafficked for sex within Russia.[8] Average monthly wages in Moscow in 2013 were approximately 53,953 rubles (or US$1700), which is considerably higher than most other Russian cities. Comparatively, the average monthly income throughout Russia in 2013 was just 25,046 rubles (or US$800) (Rosstat 2020). This income inequality creates a major pull factor, drawing victims to Moscow and St. Petersburg in the hopes of finding well-paying work.

Victims from within Russia tend to be young women and children who are poor and unemployed. Single mothers with children who lack stable incomes are also at risk of becoming sex-trafficking victims within Russia (Tiurukanova and Institute for Urban Economies 2006). Homeless people or those already working in the sex trade are also more likely to be victimized by sex traffickers (32). Victims are often recruited from poor rural areas, such as Siberia and the RFE, and trafficked to the urban centers of Moscow and St. Petersburg.[9] Approximately 70 percent of the victims in the Saratov region, which is in the southwestern part of Russia near the Kazak border, tend to be from rural areas within the region (Hughes 2002a, 26).

Sex-trafficking victims from Russia and other post-Soviet countries share one characteristic that makes them unique among victims in the world: they have comparatively high levels of education (Tverdova 2011; Stoecker 2005; MacWilliams 2003). As Tverdova (2011) explains, a college degree did not insulate women from the wage arrears, unemployment, and hyperinflation that followed the collapse of the Soviet Union. Educated women, like many people in Russia, faced dire economic circumstances following the collapse. Students in college also faced tremendous challenges in trying to pay for their education.

One estimate suggests that as many as 23–35 percent of the young women who find themselves ensnared in sex trafficking abroad were college students on summer break hoping to make money to pay the costs associated with college (MacWilliams 2003).

Russian Orphans Trafficked for Sex Slavery or Forced Begging

Youth is a major contributing factor to victimization in the sex trade in Russia—in Moscow alone there are an estimated 17,000 to 50,000 child-sex-trafficking victims (Tiurukanova and Institute for Urban Economics 2006, 40–41). These are often children who have been abandoned by their parents, raised in orphanages, or homeless. Shelley (2010) explains that many of the estimated 700,000 Russian orphans intentionally avoid orphanages, trying to survive on the street (Fujimura, Stoecker, and Sudakova 2005). They fear orphanages because organized crime often has connections to orphanage administrators and children are forced to beg or work as prostitutes for organized crime groups (Shelley 2010, 180).

Children and orphans in general are both at great risk of falling victim to sex traffickers in Russia. Elena Timofeeva, the CEO of the SafeHouse Foundation, one of the few remaining organizations that assists trafficking victims in Moscow, explains that in 2015 orphans constituted a major focus of her organization's work.[10] Between 2002 and 2005, in Nizhny Tagil in the Ural Federal district, a sex-trafficking syndicate kidnapped at least 30 young women and girls between the ages of thirteen and twenty-five. The girls were raped and beaten. Anyone who refused to cooperate with the traffickers was killed (Latynia 2012). The mass grave uncovered in Nizhny Tagil contained so many of girls and their remains were in such a poor state of decay that police were only able to identify some of the victims (Latynia 2012; *Sydney Morning Herald* 2008).

Women and Girls from CIS Countries, especially Ukraine and Moldova

Russia is also a destination point for intraregional sex-trafficking victims from neighboring post-Soviet countries, including Ukraine and Moldova (US Department of State 2007, 2015). An ILO study on forced labor in Moscow, Omsk, and Stavropol sheds light on the regional variation in victims' nationality within Russia (Tyuryukanova 2006, 35–36).[11] In Moscow, forced labor victims are more likely to come from Ukraine (30 percent) and Moldova (16 percent) than other post-Soviet countries. In Omsk, which is in Siberia and close to Kazakhstan, victims of forced labor come from Uzbekistan (24 percent) and Kazakhstan (13 percent). In Stavropol, in the southwest region of the country in the North Caucasus Federal District, migrants arrived from Uzbekistan (21 percent) and Armenia (18 percent) (35–36). Russia maintains a visa-free zone with nine post-Soviet countries, making the borders porous and relatively easy to cross (Shelley 2010). Average wages in Russia are higher than in these regional peer states, creating a pull factor for people looking for work. Average monthly wages throughout Russia were $856 in 2014, whereas in Moldova average monthly wages were just $291, and in Ukraine were $293 (Interstate Statistical Committee of the Commonwealth of Independent States 2020). Between 2000 and June 2015 the International Organization for Migration assisted 11,237 Ukrainian trafficking victims (IOM Mission in Ukraine 2015a).[12] The largest percentage of these victims, 46 percent, returned home to Ukraine after having been trafficked for sex or labor to Russia (IOM Mission in Ukraine 2015b).[13]

Hostilities between Russia and Ukraine have contributed to increases in trafficking from Ukraine into Russia. The IOM (International Organization for Migration) Mission in Ukraine reports that since the conflict began in 2014, internally displaced persons (IDPs) from the Donbas region in eastern Ukraine and from Crimea are at great risk of falling victim to traffickers (IOM Mission to Ukraine 2015c). Traffickers recruit victims with the promises of refugee status and a brokerage service for emigration. In the first nine months of 2015, the Ukrainian National Migrant Advice and Counter-Trafficking Hotline reported a 68 percent increase in the number of calls received from IDPs as compared to 2014 (IOM Mission to Ukraine 2015c). Trends associated with trafficking in IDPs from Ukraine in 2015 include women and girls abducted and forced into sex slavery or forced labor; men and boys forcibly recruited for exploitation in armed conflict and labor; detainees held by antigovernment forces exploited as forced laborers; and children exploited for begging (IOM Mission to Ukraine 2015c).

Young teenage victims from CIS countries who are exploited as sex slaves in Russia are frequently sold by their parents to acquaintances who promise legitimate work in Russia.[14] An ILO interview in Omsk with a sixteen-year-old girl from Kazakhstan helps to illustrate the dynamics through which regional children come to be victimized by Russian sex traffickers:

There were six children in our family. I am the second. There [in Kazakhstan] people live in poverty, lacking electricity and water. Sometimes we didn't even have bread at home . . . I was thinking about ways to get out of this situation, to help my brothers and sisters and do something for myself. And I met a man by chance. He proposed that I could earn money at market. He came to my parents—I am underage—and he proposed that I work at a market in Samara . . . I can't say exactly the sum [he paid]. Approximately US$300, it was quite a sum, and they let me go. I agreed. (Tyuryukanova 2006, 110–12)

The trafficker created false documents to pass through the Russian border, with the victim posing as his daughter. Upon arriving at an apartment in Russia, the trafficker confiscated the victim's travel documents and forced her to engage in sex work after days of torture, rape, and deprivation of food and water. She earned no money to send home and lived in an apartment with an iron door and bars on the windows, eliminating even the slightest hope of escape. She was interviewed by the ILO after persuading one of the buyers to drive her to Omsk, but she still had no idea how she would return home at the time of the interview (Tyuryukanova 2006, 110–12).

African/Nigerian Women and Girls
In the run up to the 2018 World Cup in Russia, the government dramatically loosened visa restrictions to better facilitate fan travel into Russia. The introduction of a "fan visa" allowed people to enter with only a passport and some evidence that they would be attending a soccer match or World Cup event; they did not need a formal visa to enter the country. The initial fan visas were good for the two weeks before the World Cup plus the ten days after the event, but the Duma extended the fan visa to be valid through the end of 2018. By 2019 it became clear that at least 5,000 of the 650,000 people who had entered Russia by using a fan visa had not left (*Moscow Times* 2019). The Russian police reported that approximately 1,893 Nigerians had entered Russia under a fan visa but had not left as of 2019. That group included many Nigerian women and girls as young as sixteen years old (Vasilyeva 2019). Their stories are familiar. They were promised legitimate work in Russia as shop assistants, hostesses, and waitresses. On arrival, their documents were confiscated and they were told they had incurred as much as US$50,000 in debt that they had to repay before their documents would be returned, and then they were locked in an apartment to work as sex slaves (Vasilyeva 2019).

For instance, Blessing Obuson, a nineteen-year-old single mother from Nigeria, was one of those Nigerian women ensnared by sex traffickers.[15] The trafficker who confiscated her documents and forced her to work as a sex slave was also a Nigerian national. Blessing escaped with the help of an antislavery organization that works specifically to assist Nigerians in Russia. Often families in Nigeria profit from selling their daughters to traffickers in Russia, so their safe return home is not a welcome development. For example, a young Nigerian woman named Ella was rescued from a Russian sex-trafficking ring in

June 2018; when she called her father in Nigeria to tell him what had happened, he threatened to throw her mother out of their home if she did not continue "working" in Russia (Roache 2018).

Forced Marriages and Bride Abductions in the North Caucasus Region

The abduction and forced marriage of teenage brides in Chechnya contributes to sex trafficking and sex slavery in Eastern Europe. Ramzan Kadyrov, the political leader of Chechnya since 2007, has endorsed a series of practices contributing to the decline in women's rights in the region. Kadyrov has vacillated in his support for both polygamy and bride abductions.[16] As a southern Islamic republic within the Russian Federation, there remain cultural gaps between practices in Chechnya and Moscow. During the Soviet era, Russian authorities enforced bans on bride abductions, but following the collapse of the Soviet Union, enforcement against these practices has all but stopped (Buchleitner 2015). As a predominantly Islamic republic, many of the cultural practices within Chechnya are closely similar to those in some central Asian countries, particularly Kyrgyzstan and Kazakhstan. In 2010, Kadyrov supported the practice of shooting "immodestly dressed" women with paintballs to teach them to conform to Koranic scripture (Brooks and Umarova 2010). Kadyrov also attended and posted Instagram photos of himself at the wedding of a forty-seven-year-old Chechen district police chief to his seventeen-year-old bride (Tetrault-Farber 2015). Kadyrov's attendance and promotion of the wedding on social media was particularly significant because the police chief was already married, thus signaling support not only for polygamy but also for the age disparity between the bride and groom.

Bride abductions are a common (though not traditional) practice in central Asia. Young men, often with the help of other young men, snatch teenage girls off the streets and force them into marriage. For the girls, being taken into the home of the boys carries a sort of tainting akin to rape in many cultures. Unwelcome back at home following the abduction, the girls and their families see no other way to preserve the virtue of the girl's family except to marry her off to her abductor. These young brides are often subject to many forms of violence in their new families. The especially weak rule of law in Chechnya, along with Kadyrov's support for practices that contribute to violence against women, have intensified bride abductions in Chechnya. And these practices lead to grim outcomes for women and girls, who are often beaten or killed by their spouses without consequence, emboldening others to engage in these practices (*Caucasian Knot* 2018).

Combating Trafficking in Russia: Criminal Justice or Victim-Centered?

Putin's efforts to consolidate his authority and roll back freedoms for civil society groups has worked to the detriment of women's and trafficking victims' rights in Russia. In recent years the state has equated feminism with foreign intervention and has imprisoned groups such as Pussy Riot in an effort to repress political opposition.[17] Efforts to silence feminists, LGBTQ+ activists, and political opponents more generally has colored the Russian approach to sex trafficking, with virtually no national protections for victims. Using the methodology to assess whether the Russian national approach to supporting victims can be described as victim-centered, namely government support for shelters coupled with progressive foreign visa laws to protect victims' human rights, reveals little evidence of any of these supports.[18]

In the late 1990s, following the demise of the Soviet Union, transnational feminists sought local Russian partners to work with on combating violence against women. In the early days following the transition, Russian feminists collaborated with transnational feminists to develop an extensive women's crisis shelter system in Russia. Money to support democracy and civil society across the post-Soviet world flowed in from the US Agency for International Development (USAID), the Ford Foundation, and other Western sources (Johnson 2009, 57–60; Sundstrom 2006). These efforts contributed to a vibrant women's NGO and crisis center movement throughout Russia (Sundstrom 2002). But following the September 11 terror attacks in the United States, donors shifted their interests, and much of the foreign support to women's crisis centers dried up (Johnson 2009, 61). Later, when the US State Department started offering grants to combat trafficking in persons, a new opportunity for funding emerged, but so too did a new player—the MiraMed Institute and Angel Coalition.

The divide between the conservative American-funded MiraMed Institute and Angel Coalition versus local Russian women's crisis centers emerged, despite some common efforts to combat trafficking in women (Shupiko 2014; Johnson 2009). Johnson (2009) describes the efforts of American professor Donna Hughes, a supporter of the Angel Coalition, publishing an article in the *National Review* that accused the US government of supporting prostitution through USAID funding to the Russian-based crisis shelters (62). The article successfully informed US policy and funding shifted to the MiraMed Institute and away from the women's crisis centers. This is a critically important change because it meant that much foreign funding for Russian centers dried up. As Putin's efforts to push back against foreign influence increased, especially after 2010, little funding was left to support women's shelters of any kind, including ones for trafficking victims.

In terms of the legislative history of combating trafficking in Russia, the issue of trafficking in persons was not addressed by the Russian government until December 2000, when the government signed the UN Protocol to Prevent, Suppress, and Punish Trafficking in Persons. Following the signing of the UN Protocol, various Russian ministries worked on the issue of trafficking, including the Commission on Improvement of the Status of Women under the auspices of the Russian president (Tiuriukanova 2005). In 2001 the commission held a meeting on sex trafficking of women and girls that resulted in a "Program of Action" that gave the ministries a series of tasks for combating trafficking (Tiuriukanova 2005). Placement on the third, or lowest tier of the US Trafficking in Persons Report in 2002, along with pressure from the US government directly, also heightened Russian sensitivity to the issue of trafficking (Buckley 2009).

Responding to pressure from Russian NGOs, the MiraMed Institute, the Angel Coalition, and the US government, the State Duma Committee for Legislation and Judicial Reform between October 2002 and April 2003 created a draft law to combat trafficking (Shupiko 2014; Stoecker and Shelley 2005). The draft law—the development of which appears to have been a model of collaboration between NGOs, IGOs, representatives from government ministries, and members of the state Duma—was led by Elena Mizulina, a state Duma deputy (Stoecker and Shelley 2005, 9). The draft law included victim protection provisions and distributed responsibilities for anti-trafficking efforts to various government entities (Johnson 2009).

Unfortunately, that draft law never saw the light of day. Putin decided in October 2003 to introduce amendments to the criminal code to outlaw trafficking, which resulted in the passage of Putin's amendments to the Russian Criminal Code in December 2003. These amendments introduced Article 127.1 (to combat trafficking) and Article 127.2 (to criminalize the use of slave labor). Noticeably absent from these amendments are any provisions for victim-support services (McCarthy 2009, 7). In 2008 another minor amendment to the 2003 law was passed in response to complaints from the police, who argued that the earlier iteration of the law made it difficult to enforce. McCarthy (2009) explains that the 2008 amendment simply clarified the language of the original law and added one year to the maximum trafficking sentence (6). Following the passage of the 2008 amendment, convicted traffickers in Russia face up to ten years' imprisonment.

Criminal Justice?
Between 2005 and 2009 the Russian police increasingly used Articles 127.1 and 127.2 to prosecute and convict traffickers (see fig. 5.1).[19] Yet even at peak use of these laws in 2009, only ninety-nine traffickers were prosecuted. Beginning in

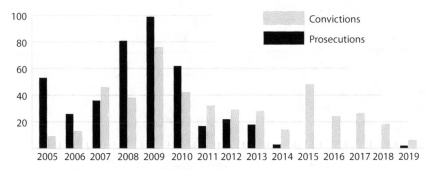

Figure 5.1. Trafficking Prosecutions and Convictions under Articles 127.1 and 127.2 in Russia, 2005–19*

*Between 2015 and 2019 the Russian government did not report official prosecution numbers.

Source: US Trafficking in Persons Reports 2006–20.

2010, both trafficking prosecutions and convictions declined sharply, a trend that continued through 2019. These data suggest that neither prosecution nor conviction rates have steadily increased in Russia during the period of analysis.

Looking exclusively at trafficker prosecutions and convictions under the 2003 law to suggest weaknesses in the Russian anti-trafficking regime misses the other ways that Russian police can prosecute and convict traffickers. Recruitment into prostitution and "organization of prostitution" statutes (Articles 240 and 244 of the Russian Criminal Code, respectively) are often used to convict sex traffickers (UNODC 2009; McCarthy 2015, 2009). For example, in 2007 Russian authorities opened 655 cases charging recruitment into prostitution (violations of Article 240) (UNODC 2009). Police tend to use these other laws, rather than the 2003 anti-trafficking laws, to convict traffickers because the language of the 2003 laws diverges considerably from standard criminal law in Russia (McCarthy 2015). The definitions of trafficking contained in Articles 127.1 and 127.2 follow the recommendation of the UN Protocol to Prevent, Suppress, and Punish Trafficking in Persons, including a requirement for "intent" to exploit the victim (Tiuriukanova 2006, 16–17). Using such a standard makes it difficult to obtain a conviction against a suspected trafficker. For example, an accomplice who transfers a victim from a recruiter to a trafficker may not necessarily have the intent of exploiting the victim, but rather only be motivated to earn the money involved in the transfer (Tiuriukanova 2006, 17). Russian authorities find it difficult to demonstrate the intent of the person involved in the transfer, and therefore tend to use other laws that do not require that they establish intent.

McCarthy (2015, 2009) challenges the received wisdom about why police are disinclined to use anti-trafficking statutes in Russia—namely, that they are corrupt and simply do not care about trafficking victims. Instead, she shows how a single case requires a series of steps through the bureaucratic maze of the Russian legal system. New actors are involved in each step and no single actor is tied to the case or outcome throughout the process, undermining the likelihood that traffickers will ultimately be convicted under the relatively challenging trafficking statutes (McCarthy 2009, 10–13). Compounding these problems are the relics of Soviet-era police practices, which she explains are alive and well today in Russia. Police are motivated to clear/close cases, not open cases they cannot push forward through the process. The complicated nature of trafficking cases, which require establishing intent, victim testimony, and corroborating evidence, simply do not align with the system of promotion within the Russian police (14).

Another way to assess whether the Russian government is prioritizing the prosecution and conviction of traffickers is to analyze Moscow's distribution of funding to specialized anti-trafficking police units. Recall that in India the number of anti-human-trafficking units funded by the government grew consistently from year to year. In the Russian case we find no evidence of the creation of specialized anti-human-trafficking units.[20] Moscow has not ordered that specialized units be created, nor have funds to prioritize combating trafficking been disbursed to law enforcement. Taken together, the declining trafficker conviction rates coupled with the absence of special funding to police suggest that Russian authorities have not adopted a criminal justice approach to fighting trafficking.

Victim-Centered?

Russia's approach to victim support cannot be characterized as victim-centered because anti-trafficking legislation prioritizes conviction of traffickers and does not provide for counseling services, special visas for foreign victims, or funding for shelters. Putin's refusal to fund shelters is likely tied to the wave of largely Western-backed feminist activism that led to the creation of an expansive women's shelter system in Russia in the early 2000s. As Putin and the Kremlin have cracked down on foreign-funded civil society groups since 2012, Western governments have been unable to fund shelters. And because the shelters that have been opened are tied to the work of transnational and domestic feminist activists in Russia, they have been vilified, as Putin and the Kremlin have ramped up efforts to invoke hypermasculine, homophobic rhetoric to consolidate power (Sperling 2015).

The absence of a comprehensive victim-support network at the federal level in Russia means there are no clear regulations to protect sex-trafficking victims. The Federal Migration Service (FMS), which frequently interacts with potential victims, lacks the ability to investigate suspected trafficking cases (US

Department of State 2015). Consequently, foreign trafficking victims are often punished for acts compelled by their traffickers, or deported (US Department of State 2015, 2020). According to FMS official Dmitry Demidenko, in 2013 more than 64,000 foreigners were expelled (Novosti 2014). Though it is likely that many of those deported were trafficking victims, the FMS lacks the ability to investigate their circumstances.

In 2010 the Russian government began encouraging foreign victims to participate in the prosecution of their traffickers, but at the time there was no formal legal option for allowing them to remain in the country (US Department of State 2011). Although during the mid-2000s special trafficking visas were offered to foreign victims in Russia, they were rarely used. Two victims used the visa in 2007, none did in 2008, and at least one did in 2009 (Hepburn and Simon 2013, 407). After 2009 the Russian government stopped reporting the number of victims who used the special visas. Because there are no specialized referral services for foreign-trafficking victims in Russia, the luckiest among this group are deported for residing illegally in Russia (US Department of State 2015). Alternatively, many of the foreign victims were not given the support they needed to be able to stay as witnesses in prosecutions but were also not deported to their home country. Instead, they were simply released from custody to try and make it home on their own or illicitly find work in Russia (US Department of State 2011).

Two major legislative developments in Russia have stifled foreign support for civil society organizations, including women's shelters. These include the passage of Federal Law 121-FZ (known commonly as the Foreign Agents Act) in 2012 and the Yarovaya anti-terror laws in 2018. The Foreign Agents Act provides that any NGO engaging in political activities while receiving funding from a foreign source is considered a foreign agent. Under the law, foreign agents are subject to special reporting requirements and registration with the Ministry of Justice so that they can be placed on the official foreign agents list. Placement on the list carries with it special auditing by the government throughout the year. As Marianna Kosharovsky, the director of the Strategic Resource Alliance at the Human Trafficking Center in Moscow explains, NGOs not considered foreign agents are audited once every three years, making the auditing requirements alone exceptionally burdensome and costly for NGOs labeled as foreign agents (Kosharovsky 2015). The leaders of organizations that fail to register as foreign agents are subject to a two-year prison sentence and heavy fines. Russian authorities have enforced the Foreign Agents Act with zeal. Human Rights Watch (2014) reports that between March and May 2013 alone, hundreds of NGOs in Russia were subjected to inspections and pressured to register as foreign agents.

The two Yarovaya anti-terror laws complicate an already problematic system for identifying and supporting foreign-trafficking victims. These laws are named after their author, Irinia Yarovaya, a conservative female lawmaker. They require Russian telecommunication companies to store all user text chats and phone data for six months in case they are needed by a court order (*Moscow Times* 2018). The laws also make it "a crime for individuals or organizations to provide material assistance to people considered to be in Russia illegally; authorities could prosecute NGOs who assist unlawfully present victims of trafficking" (US Department of State 2019, 10).

The Russian government does not provide funding for shelters or have systems in place to distinguish trafficking victims from other crime victims (US Department of State 2020). Occasionally between 2002 and 2020 reports have indicated that NGOs and intergovernmental organizations opened small shelters in cooperation with local authorities. In 2009 nine shelters were closed, including the IOM shelter in Moscow, which assisted 423 sex- and labor-trafficking victims in the three years of its existence (Hepburn and Simon 2013). In 2013 the Red Cross opened an eight-bed shelter for trafficking victims in St. Petersburg and the IOM partnered with Moscow authorities to make space for trafficking victims in an existing homeless shelter (US Department of State 2014). By 2017 a small shelter run by the Russian Orthodox Church—to assist foreign-trafficking victims between 2012 and 2015—was also shuttered (US Department of State 2017, 337). Both the 2012 Foreign Agents Act and the 2018 Yarovaya anti-terror laws have had a chilling effect on foreign-funded women's shelters in Russia.

As Russia has returned to being an authoritarian-leaning regime, few of the women's crisis shelters that existed in the early 2000s remain today. Yet there are reasons to be somewhat optimistic about both the resurgence of feminism and the creative ways LGBTQ+ activists are opposing Putin in recent years. Some small Russian NGOs also employ cutting-edge trauma-informed therapy to support trafficking victims as they heal from their experiences, which demonstrates resilience despite growing state repression.

The Safe House Foundation is a Russian NGO working to support children, orphans, and both sex- and labor-trafficking victims. It offers a comprehensive approach to victim services, including psychological counseling and trafficking prevention events. The Jewel Girls Program is among the most innovative programs offered by the Safe House Foundation. Jewel Girls brings together both boys and girls who are in difficult situations (orphans, victims of violence, and trafficking victims residing in orphanages or shelters at the time of their participation) for weekly art therapy sessions. Through the program the children are encouraged to discuss the challenges they face and learn to protect themselves from traffickers (Safe House Foundation 2014, 7). Employing art therapy to promote mindfulness has emerged as a best practice for supporting victims of gender-based violence and sex trafficking, showing that the small organizations that have survived in Russia like the Safe House Foundation are ahead of the curve (Sanar Wellness and Polaris Project 2015).

The Role of Women

As Putin and the Kremlin have deployed hypermasculine, heteronormative, and antifeminist policies in recent years, a growing backlash has arisen among feminists, LGBTQ+ activists, and artists. These groups are becoming especially skilled at using art to protest and mobilize against the conservative tide of Putin's United Russia Party. Twenty-seven-year-old Yulia Tsvetkova, an artist from Komsomolsk-on-Amur in the RFE, created a youth center in her small city to introduce young people to feminism and LGBTQ+ issues (Fedorova 2020). When she took on the role of theater director, Tsvetkova produced a performance of the *Vagina Monologues* as well as other productions that challenge traditional gender stereotypes, and conducted some online groups in support of feminism. Her work attracted the attention of the Russian police, who fined her for violating the 2013 "gay propaganda law" and charged her with "production and dissemination of pornographic materials" (Federova 2020). As of summer 2020 Tsvetkova was still awaiting trial, which could result in a six-year prison sentence. Tsvetkova is one of many young feminist/LGBTQ+ activists being targeted for their identities and activism. Local Russian feminists and LGBTQ+ activists, the latter of which Putin refers to using the derogatory term *Gapyropa*, are emerging as critical actors pushing back against Putin's clamp down on civil society and democracy (Buyantueva and Shevtsova 2019).

In the war on progressive civil society actors, especially feminists and LGBTQ+ activists, demonstrates how the United Russia Party, the Kremlin, and Putin make use of the female politicians they actively recruit into office to achieve non-progressive goals. These women's roles can be described as tokenism: female politicians are frequently co-opted by the regime to advance an anti-woman agenda (Johnson 2016). Johnson (2016) shows that female politicians are frequently pigeonholed into roles that help the regime appear as though it is fighting corruption or reducing public anxiety associated with crises. Johnson finds that even the women fast-tracked into prominent roles in the legislature are boxed in "by informal rules and parallel institutions and posts, with virtually no opportunities to advocate for women's interests" (643). Clearly Putin's regime has led to a constriction on civil society and negatively transformed the landscape for women's rights. In addressing the rate of female legislative representation, we are acutely aware that the numbers are less effective in helping explain outcomes than the numbers are in other cases, because female politicians only seek reelection if they have the support of the United Russia Party, and officials in the legislature, whether male or female,

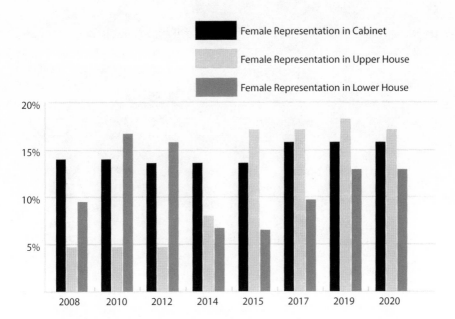

Figure 5.2. Female Legislative Representation in Government in Russia, 2008–20

Source: UN Women and Inter-Parliamentary Union, "Women in Politics," assessed annually for all years in which the UN and the IPU produced a ranking between 2008 and 2020. For data from 2020 see https://www.ipu.org/resources/publications/infographics/2020–03/women-in-politics -2020. For links to all other years see the reference list.

only maintain their positions if they are unyieldingly loyal to Putin (Avdeyeva, Vinokurova, and Kugaevsky 2017).

The Russian legislature, the Federal Assembly, has a bicameral structure— the lower house is the State Duma and the upper house is the Federation Council. Figure 5.2 compares the rate of female representation in the lower house, the upper house, and the cabinet between 2008 and 2020. Over time the rate of female representation in the State Duma has remained relatively stable, averaging and rarely exceeding 14 percent. Female legislative representation in the Federation Council has grown significantly over time, from a low of 4.7 percent in 2008 to a high of 18.2 percent in 2019. Despite the rise in rates of female legislative representation in the upper house over time, Russia's comparative rate of female legislative representation places it 133rd out of 189 countries in 2020 (UN Women and Inter-Parliamentary Union 2020). In 2003 the UN Women and Inter-Parliamentary Union ranked Russia 94th out of 181 countries, illustrating Russia's comparative decline in female legislative representation (UN Women and Inter-Parliamentary Union 2003).

We compare Russia to other states in the region to assess whether regional norms governing female legislative participation exist (see fig. 5.3). It is

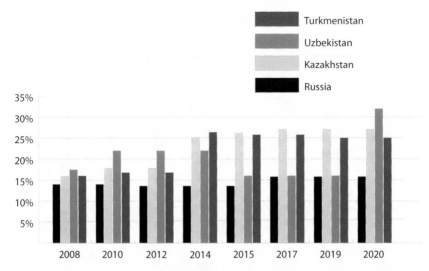

Figure 5.3. Female Legislative Representation in the Lower House in Turkmenistan, Uzbekistan, Kazakhstan, and Russia, 2008–20

Source: UN Women and Inter-Parliamentary Union, "Women in Politics," assessed annually for all years in which the UN and the IPU produced a ranking between 2008 and 2020. For data from 2020 see https://www.ipu.org/resources/publications/infographics/2020–03/women-in-politics-2020.

noteworthy that over time the rates of female legislative representation among regional peer states—including Kazakhstan, Uzbekistan, and Turkmenistan—have grown consistently, while the rate of female legislative representation in Russia has remained flat over the same years. This suggests that even in a primarily autocratic region known for poor protections for women's human rights, Russia trails behind its peers in putting women into token positions in the national legislature. Russia's deviation from the norm that has guided other peer states to incorporate women in the legislature, even if only in superficial ways, speaks to the weak status of women in the country. While female politicians in Russia are not yet advocating for the rights of trafficking victims, recent mobilization by feminists and LGBTQ+ advocates suggests there may soon be more mobilization around women's rights in Russia, including sex-trafficking victims.

Conclusion

Putin's war on feminists and LGBTQ+ activists in Russia colors much of the data related to sex-trafficking patterns, laws, and support for victims. Whereas connections between Western states, transnational feminists, and local feminists imbued late-1990s Russia with a focus on the rights of women and trafficking victims, when Putin returned to the presidency in 2012, women's rights fell off the national agenda. Soon those who sought to protect and promote women found themselves in the crosshairs of Putin's aggressive repression of civil society. In this environment, women's economic rights have suffered and women in the legislature are boxed out of opportunities to promote the interests of women and sex-trafficking victims (Johnson 2016). The large population of sex-trafficking victims from surrounding countries and Nigeria fare especially poorly in this environment. Yet in recent years, as young LGBTQ+ and feminist activists square off against Putin's regime, there is some reason for guarded optimism that their efforts will eventually create space both for advancing women's interests and, ultimately, expanding protections for sex-trafficking victims.

Notes

1. For a specific illustration of the drink quota requirement see Shapkina (2008, 44).
2. The failure of both governments to adequately investigate Oxana's death constitute part of the claims on which her father filed a petition before the European Court of Human Rights.
3. Sperling (2015) challenges the notion that Pussy Riot is a feminist group by showing the many ways the group's lyrics reinforce violence, homophobia, and gendered hierarchies (225–26).
4. For an English version of the Russian Labor Code, see http://www.ilo.org/dyn /natlex/docs/WEBTEXT/60535/65252/E01RUS01.ht. Last accessed January 2021.
5. Author interview of Elena Timofeeva, CEO of SafeHouse Foundation, Moscow, November 10, 2015.
6. Original citation: "Life's Rough on the Streets for Natashas," *Sydney Morning Herald*, June 21, 1997.
7. Khodyreva suggests that between 1999 and 2005 the St. Petersburg Women's Crisis Shelter that she ran assisted Russian sex-trafficking victims from the Russian Far East, the Urals, Siberia, and the southern regions of Russia. The trends associated with trafficking from the east to the west reflect broader migration patterns within Russia (Kleimenov and Shamkov 2005, 34).
8. For example, the Angel Coalition, which was composed of over forty women's organizations, reported that in 2008 its international sex trafficking hotline recorded the highest number of urgent calls for help from Moscow (Angel Coalition 2009, 3).
9. Buckley makes this assertion in a 2012 interview with Voice of Russia Radio. See also Hughes (2002a, 17).
10. Timofeeva interview.
11. It is important to note that these data cover forced labor in seven sectors of the economy, including sex trafficking. We include the data to give the reader a sense of the regional variation in the nationality of victims within Russia.
12. This number includes both sex and labor trafficking.
13. It is important to note that over time the dominant form of trafficking from Ukraine into Russia has flipped: in the early 2000s, Ukrainian victims were more

likely to be trafficked into Russia for sex, but beginning in 2010 Ukrainian victims were more likely to be trafficked for forced labor.

14. On the probability of recruitment through family, acquaintances, and/or social connections, see Tyuryukanova (2006, 41–43).

15. For more on Blessing Obuson and the Nigerian trafficking ring, see *Moscow Times* (2020a).

16. In 2010 Kadyrov expressed his opposition to bride abductions and increased penalties for those convicted of the practice (see Brooks and Umarova 2010).

17. There is heated debate among feminist scholars about whether Pussy Riot could claim legitimate feminist credentials (see Sperling 2015; Mason 2018).

18. In our other cases we examine rates of prostitution arrests as a part of this metric, but Russian authorities do not publish annual citation rates for the administrative offense of prostitution, so this metric was not used. We are grateful to an anonymous reviewer for raising this point.

19. To arrive at these figures we rely on official conviction and prosecution rates as reported to the US State Department by Russian authorities. These numbers can be found in the annual TIP Reports between 2005 and 2020.

20. We used the same methodology in Russia to assess funding for the police as we have in our other cases—TIP Reports and official budgets as reported by the government. Over time, the TIP Reports illustrate that while there are some trainings offered to police, there is no centralized effort to fund and consistently train police to combat trafficking.

SIX

Nigeria

On April 15, 2014, Boko Haram, a terrorist organization operating mainly in northern Nigeria, abducted 276 girls from the Government Girls Secondary School in Chibok, Nigeria. Many in the international community were shocked to learn the girls were taken primarily because they were pursuing an education. For Abubakar Shekau, one of Boko Haram's military leaders, the girls should never have been in school; instead, it was their duty to fulfill their proper roles as wives and mothers. Shekau claimed, "God instructed me to sell them, they are his properties and I will carry out his instructions" (*BBC News* 2014). Boko Haram made good on its threat, perpetrating several additional kidnappings—more than 2,000 women and girls have been taken since 2014— and NGOs have verified that these young women have suffered repeated sexual assaults and have been forced into marriage and service as soldiers (Amnesty International 2015; Human Rights Watch 2019c).

The Chibok abduction generated months of international media coverage and political outrage. However, no real action by the international community materialized to secure the release of the kidnapped girls or to stop further abductions. The kidnappings did bring renewed attention to the problem of human trafficking in sub-Saharan Africa in general and in Nigeria in particular. If Thailand is the eye of the world's human-trafficking storm, Nigeria is the eye of the African storm. Rampant corruption, a growing gap between a wealthy, Western-educated minority and impoverished majority, and the country's heavy reliance on crude oil revenues and remittances from the Nigerian diaspora have created the perfect conditions for human trafficking to thrive.

The Nigerian case clearly illustrates that cultural norms pressure all young Nigerians, especially young Nigerian women, to provide for their families in the absence of strongly protected economic rights. This cultural structure, embodied by the absence of economic and political rights for women, has made young women in the country particularly vulnerable to becoming sex-trafficking victims. Furthermore, despite recent increases in law enforcement efforts to combat trafficking, the relative lack of female representation in government, endemic corruption, and inconsistent funding have made the national response to trafficking incomplete and ineffective.

Background on Trafficking in Nigeria

If nothing else, the Chibok kidnapping in 2014 brought renewed attention to the enormity of human trafficking in Nigeria. The overwhelming majority of academic and policy discourse to that point had examined Nigeria exclusively as a source country for human trafficking, with a focus on the growing impact of Nigerian organized crime and trafficking networks in Europe (e.g., Carling 2006; Siegel and de Blank 2010). There is certainly good reason why this aspect of Nigerian trafficking has gotten so much attention: the numbers are staggering. In recent years this has become especially true for Italy, which appears to have become a key entry point into Europe for Nigerian sex-trafficking networks (see fig. 6.1). Between 2013 and 2016 Italy saw an almost 600 percent increase in potential trafficking victims arriving to the country by sea; of those migrants, the International Organization for Migration (IOM) estimated that in 2017 as much as 80 percent of the Nigerian women and girls coming into Italy each year are vulnerable to becoming sex-trafficking victims throughout Europe (US Department of State 2017; IOM 2017).

However, neither the actions of Boko Haram nor the consistent flow of victims to Europe tell the full story of human trafficking in Africa's most populous

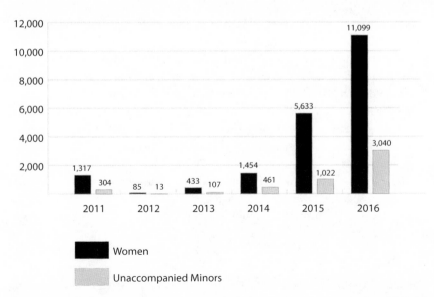

Figure 6.1. Nigerian Women and Unaccompanied Minors Arriving in Italy by Sea, 2011–16
Source: IOM (2017).

nation. As a source, transit, and destination country, Nigeria confronts human trafficking in every one of its states and at all levels of society. Nigerian victims of human trafficking have been identified in at least forty countries, though Europe still serves as the key market for victims (US Department of State 2018; Human Rights Watch 2019d). Domestically, the Walk Free Foundation estimates that over 1.3 million of Nigeria's nearly 200 million citizens are living in modern slavery. A more telling statistic on modern slavery in Nigeria, however, is the sobering fact that more than 74 percent of Nigerians are at risk of becoming enslaved (Walk Free Foundation 2018d).

Nigeria serves as a regional hub for economic activity in West Africa, including human trafficking. Trafficking networks in the region are facilitated by the freedom of movement allowed among the Economic Community of West African States (ECOWAS). Although ECOWAS began the process of increasing integration among and across its member states, particularly the freedom of movement, in the 1980s member states struggled with executing the policy efficiently and consistently. Beginning in 2000, ECOWAS implemented a uniform passport based on the European Union passport that citizens can use to travel between member states (Adepoju, Boulton, and Levin 2010). However, even with the standardized passport, poor and inconsistent training of and corruption among immigration and border officials make it easy for traffickers to bypass the regulations at border crossings and, according to many scholars and NGOs, have led to a growth in both regional and international trafficking centered on Nigeria (Nwogu 2006; Human Rights Watch 2019d).

Sex trafficking, both domestic and international, is the most notorious form of trafficking in Nigeria and possibly the most prevalent. Sex trafficking takes many forms in Nigeria—including commercial sex work, forced marriage, and trafficking in infants and pregnant women—and is the core focus of national awareness campaigns, advocacy, and law enforcement efforts to combat human trafficking (US Department of State 2018). However, economic and political forces at the same time have ensured the survival and growth of other forms of trafficking, both in Nigeria and across the region. Victims are trafficked for domestic servitude in Nigerian, West African, and European cities. Men and boys are often trafficked for forced and bonded labor in Nigeria's mining, agriculture, and textile manufacturing sectors. Children are also commonly trafficked to hawk goods for street vendors, to beg for Koranic schools, and for use as child soldiers (UNODC 2016; US Department of State 2017).

Factors Contributing to Sex Trafficking in Nigeria

The lack of strong protections for women's economic rights and a weak rule of law in general play important parts in making Nigerian women vulnerable to becoming victims of sex trafficking. This is compounded in the Nigerian case by numerous political, economic, and social factors. While some groups of Nigerian women are certainly more vulnerable than others, *all* women in Nigeria are vulnerable on some level to becoming involved in sex trafficking—whether as victims, customers, or as traffickers themselves. Although each of the various factors outlined here plays a critical role in creating situations of vulnerability for Nigerian women, it is the deprivation of strong economic rights and thus of the ability to effectively combat these other pressures that best explain the degree and forms of sex trafficking in the country.

Economic Boom and Bust

Nigeria's economy is impressive in many ways. According to the International Monetary Fund, Nigeria had the highest GDP in Africa in 2017, at nearly $400 billion (Oyekunle 2019). The country also boasts impressive natural resources: Nigeria is Africa's largest producer of crude oil, and revenue from oil accounts for as much as 70 percent of government revenue and 90 percent of export earnings (Giokos 2017; Human Rights Watch 2019d). Nigeria also has a strong agricultural sector and consistently ranks at or near the top of African nations in farm output. Nigerian cities, especially in the south, are home to a dynamic and growing technology sector, as well as the country's thriving film industry, dubbed Nollywood, which is now recognized as the world's second most prolific non-US film industry after India's Bollywood (Bouillon 2019; Human Rights Watch 2019d).

Despite all the apparent advantages and opportunities in the Nigerian economy, the most obvious factors contributing to all forms of human trafficking in the country are economic—including widespread poverty, income inequality, and high rates of unemployment. The cultural devaluation of women means the dire aspects of the economy in Nigeria are exacerbated for them. Despite being an oil-rich country, Nigeria's economy has long struggled to use the revenue from that industry to provide stability and equality. Since 2014, the combination of falling oil prices and attacks on pipelines by militant groups has intensified long-standing economic disparities. In 2016 Nigeria entered its first recession in decades, and the value of the naira dropped by nearly 50 percent (UNDP 2016). In early 2018 Nigeria passed India to become the country with the largest total number of people—about 87 million—living in extreme poverty (Kharas, Hamel, and Hofer 2018).[1] The International Monetary Fund's 2020 economic outlook for Nigeria was also bleak; the organization predicted the country's GDP would shrink by more than 3 percent (International Monetary Fund 2020).

Nigeria's recent economic troubles are part of larger trends of emigration and brain drain that have characterized Nigerian society since at least the 1980s (Carling 2006). Corruption and financial mismanagement, particularly within the petroleum industry, have cost the country billions in revenue and kept the Nigerian economy from experiencing sustained growth or stability (*BBC News* 2012). For decades this instability as well as scarce employment and educational opportunities have pushed Nigerians to seek international opportunities, increasing the vulnerability of millions to human traffickers. Current estimates of Nigerians living abroad vary widely—between 1.2 and 17 million (*The Economist* 2015b). While it might be unclear just how many Nigerians live abroad, what is undeniable is the economic impact this diaspora has on the lives of people back home. According to the World Bank, Nigerians have received between $18 billion and $21 billion in personal remittances every year since 2007 (World Bank 2017a). For some, especially people in southern Nigeria, remittances from family living abroad account for more than 25 percent of a family's household income (Olowa and Shittu 2012).

Violence, Instability, and Governance

Religious and ethnic violence as well as the emergence of Boko Haram have only added to the economic pressures to leave the country that many Nigerians feel. Boko Haram's insurgency has created a self-perpetuating market of potential trafficking victims in Nigeria and across the broader Lake Chad region. In 2016 approximately 1.4 million Nigerians had been displaced by violence linked to Boko Haram, while state-led violence to quell the militant group displaced nearly twice that many—approximately 2.6 million—throughout the region (Kingsley 2016). These displaced millions have congregated in makeshift refugee and internally displaced person (IDP) camps across northern Nigeria. As several scholars have illustrated, life in these camps is rife with danger (e.g., Lischer 2015). In Nigeria the standard dangers of hunger, disease, and overcrowding have been made worse by inconsistent government support and the inability of international aid organizations to reach or work in the camps safely (Kingsley 2016).

Women and girls face particular threats as a result of the government's ongoing war with Boko Haram and are in danger from all parties to the conflict. Boko Haram targets women and girls, especially those pursuing an education; by 2015 the insurgent group had abducted more than 2,000 women and girls, forcing them into marriage, sex slavery, and armed service (Amnesty International 2015; *BBC News* 2014). Unfortunately, even if these individuals are able to escape, they face suspicion and isolation because many in their communities as well as government authorities assume the women and children were indoctrinated while in captivity or have information that can help in fighting the insurgency (US Department of State 2019). Such obstacles to reintegration increase these women and girls' vulnerability to being trafficked again (Adams 2011; Danish Immigration Service 2008; Kingsley 2016).

The conflict between the government and Boko Haram has also further weakened the rule of law and highlighted endemic corruption and inefficient governance in Nigeria (Human Rights Watch 2019d). In an interview with Nosakhare Erhunmwensee, the president of the NAME Foundation, he cited poor governance as a key factor contributing to trafficking: "Looting of the treasury by the political class has led to the decay in infrastructures and the debasement of our patrimony. As a way of making it in life, people move to more conducive environments for a better life."[2] When combined with the displacement and danger faced by IDPs and refugees living in camps in northern Nigeria and beyond, the lack of strong governance makes these individuals particularly vulnerable to victimization. NGOs operating in the Lake Chad region cite countless examples of camp authorities, government officials, and members of the security forces exploiting individuals living in the camps, especially women and children, in multiple ways (US Department of State 2019). Reports from these NGOs and international aid workers have alleged that, using their positions of power, officials have forced camp residents into performing sexual favors or engaging in prostitution in exchange for food or freedom of movement within and outside the camps; other victims are funneled into regional and international sex-trafficking networks (Kingsley 2016; US Department of State 2019). The conflict has further reduced the availability of support from both social services and extended families (Human Rights Watch 2019d). The women living in refugee and IDP camps have exceptionally few options to resist the demands of officials and few from whom they can seek assistance or protection.

Prestige, Duty, and Patronage

The wide range of oppressive social pressures and cultural demands related to duty and patronage are pervasive in Nigerian society and are linked to the vulnerability of millions of Nigerians to all forms of human trafficking. Our focus is on the expectations on young Nigerians to contribute financially to their families, the prestige and social standing that comes with international employment, and the pressure to build a family that includes biological children.

As in the case of Thailand, children in Nigeria are raised with a strong sense of duty to contribute to the family economically from a young age (Abubakar 2018). Children from lower-income families in particular begin work very early in life: 25 percent of children between the ages of 5 and 14 are involved in some form of labor (UNDP 2016). Failing to contribute to the family's finances is considered shameful, and the individual is seen as a failure in their community. This sense of shame is often so strong that even victims of sex trafficking who escape their traffickers struggle with the fact that their freedom comes at the cost of their ability to contribute to the family's economic well-being. Former trafficking victim Kemi spent three years in forced prostitution in Italy before escaping her traffickers and her deportation back to Nigeria. However, after arriving in Nigeria, Kemi did not return to her family; "I was ashamed to go back home . . . I was ashamed to go back with nothing" (*BBC News* 2015).

The pressure to fulfill their duty to financially support family members is compounded by the social stature that having a family member living and working abroad brings to a Nigerian family. This sense of prestige is reflected in a rising consumer culture across Nigeria generally and in Benin City—the central hub of Nigerian sex trafficking—in particular (Carling 2006). There is a growing desire for Nigerian families to not only *be* more financially stable but to *appear* to be so as well. According to Erhunmwensee, this "is most visible in family gatherings like burial[s], wedding[s,] and cultural ceremonies [where] they show off their sibling[s] living abroad [who] have graced their occasion."[3] As this consumer culture expands, there is an impetus to make more money and to make it quickly (Ede, Chiaghanam, and Kalu 2019). The pressure, then, for young Nigerians is immense, especially for young women, who are traditionally more generous in the financial support they give to their families (Carling 2006).

Beyond the responsibility to support their families, most Nigerians face obligations from embedded notions about the patron-client relationship. A patron-client culture is still prevalent in Nigeria and creates hierarchies of personal interactions that Nigerians must navigate in their daily lives. Maintaining these relationships is important both as a patron and as a client. "Every person nurtures the relationship and shows loyalty toward their contacts higher up in the system. In return, they are rewarded with resources to which these contacts have access" (Carling 2006, 17). The expectation of both parties is that this relationship will be reciprocal; a client's work is rewarded by the patron with access to new opportunities or positions of power. Traffickers often capitalize on this relationship in recruiting potential victims.

Young Nigerians face an additional cultural pressure to contribute to their families that adds to the growth of trafficking in the country: procreation. For many Nigerians, childless marriages are unnatural and infertile couples experience tremendous pressure to have children (Fehintola et al. 2017; Makinde 2015; see also Ncube and Ticharwa 2017). However, there are also stigmas against surrogacy and adoption (Makinde 2015; Omeire et al. 2015), making it paramount for many Nigerian families to accept a child as the couple's own. Illegal and secret adoptions are a way to have children without the couple's infertility becoming public knowledge. On the other side of this coin, there are strongly negative attitudes toward unwed mothers and illegitimate children. These two forces combine to create a persistent victim pool of unwed pregnant women and a ready market of childless couples for human traffickers to exploit.

Cultural Expectations Regarding Women's Roles in Society

In many ways it is difficult to generalize about women's roles in Nigerian society. The growth of Nigeria's economy has created a variety of employment opportunities at a range of economic and professional levels in recent decades. Although most of these opportunities continue to be dominated by men, women in Nigeria have begun to make inroads in the public and professional spheres (Nettikkara 2015). Conversely, the ways the Nigerian economy developed has contributed to a tremendous level of income inequality and a sizable difference in the daily realities of the educated, relatively well-off minority and the less educated poor majority. These differences are reflected in the experiences of Nigerian women and girls, particularly in areas such as access to infertility treatment and education (Onuoha 2020). Even the Nigerian pluralistic legal system allows for and supports differences in how women are treated. Under the Nigerian legal system, Islamic and customary laws are considered applicable alongside statutory laws, creating important regional differences in societal expectations of women and the range of rights they enjoy (Human Rights Watch 2019d).

Regardless of the differences among religious, ethnic, and economic groups, Nigerian society is at its core patriarchal, which has important and negative consequences for most Nigerian women, even if the specific manifestations of that patriarchy vary (Mahdi 2020). There are strong cultural beliefs about the value of daughters in Nigeria that have clear implications for human trafficking. In their 2010 study of the perceptions Nigerian women and children have of how and why trafficking occurs, S. Abdulraheem and A. Oladipo found that over 50 percent of interviewees identified "parental discrimination favoring boys over girls" as a key contributing factor to trafficking, second only to poverty (cited in Ukwayi, Angioha, and Aniah 2019).[4]

The lower value that families may place on their daughters has lasting impacts, especially in education and marriage. According to UNICEF, Nigeria has the largest number of children out of school—10 million, or approximately one-fifth of the total worldwide out-of-school population—and most of the children not attending school are girls (Human Rights Watch 2019d; Bro and McCaslin 2019). This has contributed to a sizable gap in literacy rates between men and women. Based on a government survey, the average literacy rate is approximately 80 percent for men and 59 percent for women; literacy rates for women are even lower in northern Nigeria. Education for girls in Nigeria is further hindered by the widespread practice of child marriage. Nigeria has the second-highest number of child brides in the world. Two in ten Nigerian girls are married by the age of fifteen, while more than half are married by age eighteen (Human Rights Watch 2019d).

Deprivation of Women's Economic Rights

Although on paper there are several legal protections for women meant to ensure their safety and equality, substantial failings in these laws contribute directly to weakened economic rights and opportunities for women. The gaps in current laws as well as the absence of their strong enforcement significantly increase the vulnerability of Nigerian women and girls to mistreatment and violence, including human trafficking.

The Nigerian Constitution enshrines the right to nondiscrimination based on sex as well as equality before the law (Human Rights Watch 2019d). However, this formal nondiscrimination is weakened or limited for women and girls in a variety of ways. The right to nondiscrimination based on gender is not specifically applied to employment and there is no legal provision for equal pay for equal work. Further, the constitution includes language that legitimizes child marriage, which is in direct conflict with the Nigerian Child Rights Act (Human Rights Watch 2019d; Bro and McCaslin 2019). In a broader sense, Nigerian law has a consistent gap in defining the age of maturity and thus who is considered and protected as a child. In particular, the constitution sets a subjective standard regarding married women: a woman is considered of mature age upon marriage but husbands are, simultaneously, given considerable power over their wives to the extent of being legally able to treat them as children (Human Rights Watch 2019d).

According to the World Bank, women have made important strides in the Nigerian economy, participating in the labor force at 50 percent, compared to men who participate at 60 percent. However, women still face legal restrictions on their ability to engage in employment as well as widespread harassment in the workplace. Legal restrictions include prohibitions on certain types of work for women, but not for men; it is illegal, for example, for women to work night shifts in manual labor jobs (Bro and McCaslin 2019). Additionally, there are mixed protections for women in terms of sexual harassment. The 2015 Violence Against Persons Prohibition Act (VPPA) does prohibit various acts of gender-related abuse that could fall under the broader umbrella of sexual harassment, including coercion, forced financial dependence or economic abuse, and emotional, verbal, and/or psychological abuse. However, not all states have fully implemented the VPPA, and several northern states also use Sharia law, which has provisions that are contradictory to civil law (Orjinmo 2020). Moreover, under current Nigerian law there are no civil remedies available for women who experience sexual harassment at work (Bro and McCaslin 2019).

The disparity between the prohibitions in the VPPA and the lack of civil remedies for harassment is part of a larger problem of violence against women in Nigeria. A survey published in 2019 indicated that one in three Nigerian girls may have "experienced at least one form of sexual assault by the time they reach 25" (Orjinmo 2020). In June 2020 this issue came to a head in a very public way as the country learned of four shocking cases of sexual violence across the country, including the rape and murder of Vera Uwaila Omosuwa, a twenty-two-year-old university student whose body was left inside a church (Dark 2020; Human Rights Watch 2020b; Orjinmo 2020).

Victims of sexual violence in Nigeria regularly face ridicule and victim-shaming from their communities and law enforcement. Victims, their families, and even their legal representation are often encouraged, and at times threatened, by law enforcement to "resolve" the issue privately with the perpetrator, especially if the perpetrator and/or his family are well known or wealthy (Dark 2020; Ewang 2020). Nationwide protests about the sexual assault of women erupted in early June 2020, much like those India experienced in 2012. In response to the public activism, the government made some attempts to begin addressing the problem, but it is yet to be seen how impactful these efforts will be on societal views and cultural acceptance of sexual violence against women.

For many the environment created by Nigeria's problematic system of laws makes working in the formal sector difficult, if not impossible (Bro and McCaslin 2019; Mahdi 2020). Ultimately, leaving home to seek employment in the informal sector in urban centers in Nigeria or going to work or school abroad offers the only opportunity for women to improve their and their family's economic prospects. Indeed, for many families "having a daughter travel to Europe is the only way to escape extreme poverty" (Carling 2006, 30). The desperation to find work in this climate makes many Nigerians, especially women and girls, particularly vulnerable to traffickers.

Forms of Sex Trafficking in Nigeria

Like in every other country, sex trafficking in Nigeria happens in a variety of ways through a variety of channels. Here we discuss the most prominent types of sex trafficking found there.

Commercial Sex Work

Like in Thailand, sex trafficking is a notorious aspect of Nigeria's international reputation. However, unlike in Thailand, sex trafficking in Nigeria is associated with international commercial sex work and in particular the trafficking of Nigerian women into forced prostitution in Europe. Despite the focus on Europe in the literature and in media accounts, Nigerian women and girls are trafficked for commercial sex work both regionally and internationally. The international dimension of trafficking out of Nigeria may get the most attention because of how widespread it is: Nigerian sex-trafficking victims have been identified in at least forty countries, with South America and the Middle East emerging as the newest growth markets for victims (Ede, Chiaghanam, and Kalu 2019; US Department of State 2018).

There is a considerable degree of mixed information regarding just how much the potential victims of this form of sex trafficking know about what awaits them. According to Human Rights Watch, and affirmed during interviews with Nosakhare Erhunmwensee, a lack of understanding about human trafficking is a key factor in leaving Nigerian women and girls vulnerable to the recruiting tactics of traffickers (Human Rights Watch 2019d). On the other hand, some sources indicate at least some women—especially those who live in or near the country's urban centers—are aware of the problem of sex trafficking and of the high probability that an offer of work or education in Europe will involve a certain amount of sex work (Bowers 2012; Mancuso 2014; Okonofua et al. 2004). For instance, Okonofua et al. (2004) find that 44 percent of the interviewed women and girls in Benin City are familiar with someone currently engaged in sex work outside of Nigeria, and 32 percent said they had been approached about sex work opportunities abroad. It seems that for some women the limited amount of sex work they incorrectly anticipate having to engage in is a small price to pay for the earning potential and prestige that comes from working abroad (Mancuso 2014).

Unfortunately, what is clear is that regardless of whether these victims are aware of the realities of sex trafficking or not, they are all unprepared for the level of exploitation they actually encounter. According to Destiny, a young woman trafficked from Nigeria to Spain, "If you live in Benin [City], there are many girls who come back from [Spain] with lots of money. They told us they had to have sex sometimes . . . we are not stupid, but I did not know I would be beaten and raped and have to have sex every night of the week" (*BBC News* 2016, 1). Destiny's experience is typical of women trafficked for commercial sex work abroad. Many Nigerian women and girls trafficked for prostitution begin their journey anticipating educational or employment opportunities in Europe. However, their destination is frequently a different country than they were promised and on arrival they are informed that all the expenses incurred on their behalf by the traffickers—including travel costs, forged documents, food, and lodging—are a debt they must repay before they can go free. Unfortunately for these victims, this form of debt bondage rarely ends, and usually the total debt owed only increases over time. As is seen in so many cases, the debt is simply part of the ruse. Even when victims offer to engage in other types of work to pay off their debts, their traffickers refuse, violently forcing them into prostitution (Human Rights Watch 2019d).

The victims of Nigerian sex trafficking, especially in Europe, are often controlled by other Nigerian women, called madams. The madams handle the day-to-day recruitment and management of sex workers, which includes maintaining control of the sex workers, ensuring they work (whether in a brothel or on the streets), and addressing any health concerns that may impact their ability to work, such as pregnancy. Under the close watch of these madams, victims are forced to work under extreme and dangerous conditions.

> Women and girls said that madams made them engage in forced prostitution for long hours with no time to rest. Many [said] that madams made them have sex with customers even while ill, menstruating, pregnant, or soon after childbirth or having undergone forced abortions. In some cases, madams told them to put unsanitary materials, such as mattress foam or wipes, in their vaginas to block menstrual blood or bleeding from abortions so that they could have sex with customers. (Human Rights Watch 2019d)

For many victims the only path to escape is through deportation. Although being deported returns victims to Nigeria and frees them from the direct control of their traffickers, the victims then face new challenges. Familial expectations that working abroad translates to financial success and social prestige is felt even more acutely after escaping a trafficking situation. As Kemi's story highlights, many women feel ashamed that they were not able to change their family's economic status while working for their traffickers (*BBC News* 2015). This shame is compounded by the fact that most women's situations are even less hopeful than they were before they were trafficked. These women and girls have no increased educational or job experience and now must contend with the psychological and physical trauma of their ordeal (Human Rights Watch 2019d). Further, once back in Nigeria they are often viewed by their families and communities as "spoiled" because of their time as sex workers. This societal victim-blaming, combined with a perceived inability of these women to contribute to a family economically, makes them failures in their expected roles as women. Therefore many victims do not return to their homes or families, even if they are repatriated to Nigeria (*BBC News* 2015; Madueke 2015).

Child and Forced Marriages

Child marriage is a pervasive problem in Nigeria, compounded by legal ambiguities about the rights, protections, and even definition of children. However, unlike in India, we found no evidence of bride trafficking in Nigeria. Simultaneously, Boko Haram and, more recently, the Islamic State–West Africa (ISIS–WA) have become notorious for abducting girls and forcing them into various forms of slavery, including forced marriage. While it is clear that child marriages and forced marriages are important elements in the dynamics of Nigerian sex trafficking, the distinctions between these two types of involuntary marriage are difficult to define and it is not entirely clear when or where trafficking happens.

However, what these two forms of involuntary marriage do share is that they are often only one aspect of exploitation suffered by the victim. For example, girls taken both by insurgents and security forces are forced to act as domestic servants, child soldiers, and sex slaves in addition to the possibility of forced marriage (Global Slavery Index 2017; UNODC 2016; US Department of State 2019). The story of Aisha, a young woman abducted by Boko Haram in 2014, is indicative of this pattern. According to Aisha, some of the young women held in captivity with her were forced to marry fighters within a week of being taken; others, like herself, were held as sex slaves and trained as soldiers. Aisha told Amnesty International that during her three months in captivity she was repeatedly raped, she witnessed more than 50 people—including her own sister—killed by insurgents, and she was forced to participate in an attack on her own village (Amnesty International 2015).

For other victims, forced marriage is simply a continuation of other forms of sex slavery and intersects with commercial sex work. Adaura's story, as told to Human Rights Watch, is indicative of this reality. Adaura accepted a position for domestic service in Libya but was in fact trafficked for prostitution and held through debt bondage and force. After being sold off by her madam as a personal sex slave, Adaura managed to escape and start a relationship with a man who planned to marry her. Unfortunately, both Adaura and her fiancé were taken hostage by Libyan members of ISIS. Adaura's fiancé was killed; she was allowed to live because she was pregnant at the time, but she was forced to marry one of the fighters. Adaura was kept in the forced marriage until she was rescued and repatriated three years later (Human Rights Watch 2019d).

Finally, we cannot ignore child marriage as it exists as a cultural practice. As a 2019 Human Rights Watch report on the state of trafficking in Nigeria notes, most girls wed in child marriages are from poor and rural parts of the country. As in India, these families often have few alternatives for supporting their daughters. The tendency toward child marriage also appears to be higher among polygamous families that have large numbers of family members to care for as well as the cultural support for keeping multiple wives (Human Rights Watch 2019d). It is possible that trafficking occurs in some of these cases along the lines of India's bride trafficking; however, there are also many cases that are a result of cultural practice and do not contain the required elements to be considered human trafficking.

Forced Pregnancy and Infant Trafficking

Children are commonly trafficked around the world for both sex work and forced labor. In Nigeria, however, the market in children has expanded to include infants and pregnant mothers. UNESCO first reported on the problem of "baby harvesting" in Nigeria in 2006. At that time the practice largely involved young pregnant women who were unmarried and could not or did not want to keep their children after birth. Clinics, orphanages, and maternity homes would shelter these young women, caring for them until they gave birth, and then sell the child to wealthy infertile couples. UNESCO reported that the young mothers were paid off in return for signing papers to relinquish all claims to their children (UNESCO 2006).

UNESCO's early assessment of baby harvesting in Nigeria may have painted an accurate picture of the practices as they existed at the time, but it is difficult to know for certain. What is clear is that UNESCO's 2006 description of a somewhat symbiotic relationship between young unwed mothers and childless couples differs considerably from the infant-mother trafficking networks thriving in Nigeria today. Some young women may still find mutually beneficial—albeit illegal—arrangements with couples looking to adopt a child secretly. However, more common are baby factories disguised as orphanages, maternity homes, clinics, and religious centers where women with unwanted pregnancies go for assistance but are, instead, exploited (Makinde 2015; US Department of State 2018). Young pregnant women are targeted and taken to these facilities by traffickers who prey on them in much the same way young women desperate for employment or educational opportunities are recruited—by offering a way out and an opportunity to improve their situation. Other women are abducted and forced into pregnancy (Madueke 2015; Makinde 2015). Since more than 25 percent of women in Nigeria have their first child by age eighteen, many of the young women exploited in these infant-mother trafficking networks are still children themselves (UNICEF 2016).

The infants born in these baby factories face a variety of fates. The best possible outcome is to be sold to couples in illegal secret adoptions. However, because the adoptions are completed on the black market, there is no oversight to regulate to whom these children are given nor how they are treated before or after the adoption (Madueke 2015; Makinde et al. 2016). The other outcomes awaiting these infants involve being funneled into various trafficking networks across Nigeria, being sold to traffickers for use as child soldiers, sex slaves, organ donors, and forced laborers domestically, regionally, and internationally (Makinde 2015).

Recruitment Strategies

Several scholars—as well as former victims—note that in Nigeria the first point of contact for most victims is someone she knows or who has connections to her family. Abdulraheem and Oladipo found that educated people (57.3 percent) and close associates (32.1 percent) were identified as the most common recruiters for human trafficking (cited in Ukwayi, Angioha, and Aniah 2019). As noted earlier, Nigerian human trafficking networks, especially those in Europe, are often singled out in the media for the prominent role women play in the control of trafficking victims (Aghatise 2002; Mancuso 2014; UNODC 2016). Many of these madams are former trafficking victims themselves who were able to repay their debts and buy their way into the trafficking network (Mancuso 2014; UNODC 2016). Using the madams allows the rest of the trafficking network to take full advantage of the social pressures and responsibilities faced by young Nigerian women and girls.

When recruiting victims in Nigeria, human traffickers also take advantage of the pressures of duty, prestige, and patronage as well as the desperation young Nigerians feel to fulfill their families' expectations (Human Rights Watch 2019d). The initial recruitment approach draws on traffickers' knowledge about the families' finances and the victims' need to contribute. The offers of employment or educational opportunities that are used to lure victims become more legitimate when viewed through the lens of the patron-client relationship. In interviews conducted by Human Rights Watch (2019d), victims of sex trafficking identified friends of their parents, neighbors, aunts and uncles, and even childhood friends as the individuals who initiated the recruitment process. As noted earlier, it is unclear how much information average Nigerian women and girls may have about the dangers of trafficking and the ruses used by traffickers. However, when the offers of education, employment, or a path to improving one's life are presented by those you trust most, they are difficult to refuse or question no matter how savvy one might be (Carling 2006; Madueke 2006).

Combating Trafficking in Nigeria: Criminal Justice or Victim-Centered?

In order to address the legal regime pertaining to human trafficking in Nigeria, it is important to understand the structure of that legal system. Nigeria has a tripartite criminal legal system consisting of the Criminal Code, the Penal Code, and customary laws. Although the history of how this structure developed during the colonial era is beyond the focus here, the specifics of how this structure is applied are important for understanding Nigeria's struggle to combat human trafficking (see Ebbe 2003; Morris 1970). Different regions and groups in Nigeria have their own sets of criminal laws. In particular, the Penal Code is the dominant criminal code for northern Nigeria and incorporates elements of Muslim custom and law; the Criminal Code developed out of English common law and applies only in southern Nigeria. Customary law typically refers to unwritten cultural and social laws followed primarily in the south (Ebbe 2003).

While there is certainly some overlap among these three sources of criminal law, there are many areas in which there is no agreement on which set of laws applies, which acts are considered criminal, how perpetrators should be punished, or how to treat victims. National legislations (i.e., the 2003 and 2015 anti-trafficking laws) have attempted to harmonize the country's approach to combating human trafficking through legal forums, but differences in the underlying legal codes stymie these efforts and lead to inconsistent application of anti-trafficking laws.

Nigeria had had laws to address slavery in some form since precolonial times and addressed the issue again when crafting laws upon independence. Before Nigeria ratified the Palermo Protocol in 2001, the primary protections against human trafficking were found in the Nigerian Constitution, which prohibits slavery, and the Criminal Code, which establishes slave-dealing as one of its enumerated offenses against liberty (Human Rights Watch 2019d). However, these protections are inadequate in several ways. The Penal Code used in northern Nigeria did not initially address issues related to trafficking, so prohibitions on slavery were only applicable in the south (Human Rights Watch 2019d; Ebbe 2003). Nigeria's laws also did not account for elements that have proved to be pervasive in Nigerian trafficking, including the role of female traffickers and the unique issues related to domestic human trafficking (Danish Immigration Service 2008).

In 2003 the Nigerian legislature passed the Trafficking in Persons (Prohibition) Law Enforcement and Administration Act, the first legislative effort in Nigeria to create a national framework for combating human trafficking (Bowers 2012; Olateru-Olagbegi and Ikpeme 2006). The law is innovative in many ways, going beyond the requirements of the Palermo Protocol by criminalizing both actual and attempted acts of trafficking as well as creating provisions to prosecute commercial carriers who knowingly transport victims of human trafficking. The 2003 law also formally recognizes domestic as well as international human trafficking (Bowers 2012). However, this initial legislation also has several critical flaws. Some forms of trafficking were left out of the law's definition, including trafficking in organs, and it focuses primarily on sex trafficking while largely ignoring labor trafficking (Olateru-Olagbegi and Ikeme 2006). Provisions covering other forms of trafficking cannot be found elsewhere in Nigerian law, including in the Criminal Code, the Penal Code, the Labour Act, the Immigration Act, the Child Rights Act, and various state laws, but all these provisions have not been enforceable nationwide (Olateru-Olagbegi and Ikeme 2006; Kigbu 2015; Ebbe 2003). Further, the 2003 law does not address trafficking as a whole and instead criminalizes discrete acts within trafficking networks, "like exportation and importation of persons, harbouring, [and] transportation" (Olateru-Olagbegi and Ikpeme 2006, 32).

In 2015 the 2003 anti-trafficking law was repealed and replaced with national legislation intended to address some of these deficiencies. Broadly speaking, the 2015 law aims to achieve three goals: create a comprehensive national legal framework; protect the victims of human trafficking; and facilitate national and international cooperation in anti-trafficking efforts (Human Rights Watch 2019d). The 2015 law prohibits all forms of trafficking and increases the penalties for traffickers (US Department of State 2016). Convicted traffickers are subject to a minimum fine of 1 million naira (approximately US$2,600) and five years in prison for both sex and labor trafficking. For offenses of sex trafficking involving a minor, the minimum penalty is seven years imprisonment. The law also prohibits a practice developed under the 2003 version of the law wherein judges can allow convicted traffickers to pay a fine to avoid prison (US Department of State 2018).

In addition to creating a national framework for combating trafficking, the 2003 law created the National Agency for the Prohibition of Trafficking in Persons (NAPTIP). Indeed, Nigeria was the first African country to enact legislation with an accompanying agency to combat trafficking. The NAPTIP agency began operations in 2004 and is divided into four units: investigation, prosecution, counseling and rehabilitation, and public engagement (Danish Immigration Service 2008). NAPTIP's expressed intentions are to combat human trafficking at all stages and rehabilitate and reintegrate victims; therefore, the agency is involved in both the criminal-justice and victim-centered approaches to combating human trafficking. One aspect parsed out later is how funding and support for the different operational units of NAPTIP indicates a difference in criminal-justice versus victim-centered approaches.

Criminal Justice?

Two of the four operational units of NAPTIP are focused on addressing the criminal-justice side of human trafficking, and it is largely through their work that Nigeria has maintained Tier 2 status in the TIP Reports from the US Department of State. In the 2019 TIP Report for Nigeria, the State Department notes a significant increase in anti-trafficking law enforcement efforts and cites this reason for granting Tier 2 status. Since its launch in 2004, NAPTIP has investigated and initiated prosecutions against suspected traffickers, steadily increasing the number of investigations initiated each year since at least 2014 (fig. 6.2). The agency opened a record number of investigations in the 2018 reporting period, accounting for the increased law enforcement efforts cited by the Department of State (2019). The law enforcement side of NAPTIP's mandate has been made easier since the passage of the 2015 anti-trafficking law, which provides clearer guidelines over and harsher punishments for trafficking offenses.

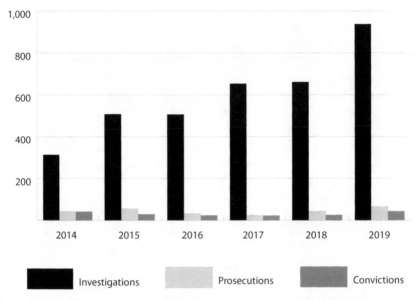

Figure 6.2. Investigations, Prosecutions, and Convictions of Trafficking Cases in Nigeria, 2014–19

Source: US Department of State Trafficking in Persons Reports for Nigeria, 2014–19.

NAPTIP's ability to increasingly pursue law enforcement efforts to combat human trafficking is likely due to steadily growing governmental financial support (fig. 6.3). The agency's budget reached 2.5 billion naira (approximately US$6 million at 2021 exchange rates) before the country experienced a recession in 2016. In that year the money allocated for NAPTIP decreased dramatically, to just over 1.69 billion naira (US$4 million at 2021 exchange rates). In the intervening years the agency has recovered most of these funds, with an allocated budget of 4.3 billion naira (nearly US$11 million at 2021 exchange rates) in 2018 (US Department of State 2019, 2018, 2017, 2016). However, there is broad consensus that despite consistent support from the government, the agency lacks enough resources to fulfill its mandate. To date NAPTIP's funding has been insufficient to allow engagement in proactive anti-trafficking campaigns or to move any of their bases of operation outside major cities (US Department of State 2019). This has encouraged, in large part, NAPTIP's collaborations with NGOs and foreign governments on joint investigations, "training courses, joint intelligence sharing, and mutual legal assistance on trafficking cases" (US Department of State 2018).

In addition to insufficient funding, NAPTIP's most significant challenge in its effort to combat human trafficking through a law enforcement approach

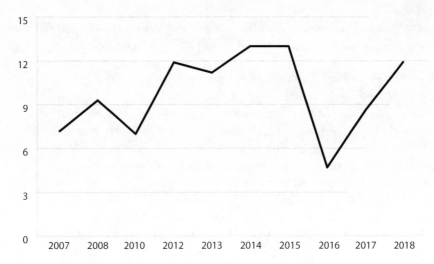

Figure 6.3. NAPTIP Annual Budget, 2007–18

Source: US Department of State Trafficking in Persons Reports for Nigeria, 2008–19.

is Nigeria's relatively weak rule of law. In particular, corruption and a general lack of knowledge about the specific provisions of the 2015 anti-trafficking law among judges have kept conviction rates relatively low. Not until the 2018 TIP reporting period were all convictions of traffickers in Nigeria completed under the provisions of the 2015 law (US Department of State 2019). Between 2015 and 2018 at least some judges found traffickers guilty under the 2003 law. Unfortunately, this also meant that, despite its explicit prohibition in the 2015 law, judges continued to offer convicted traffickers the option of choosing to pay a fine instead of serving the required prison sentence (US Department of State 2018, 2017). While some judges have claimed that the inconsistency in applying the 2015 law is due to lack of knowledge or understanding of the newer law's provisions, NGOs as well as the US State Department also point to pervasive corruption within the judiciary as a source of the problem. Perhaps the most troubling proof of corruption in Nigeria's legal system is that despite persistent allegations of complicity in human trafficking on the part of government officials, Nigeria went four consecutive years without a single prosecution and another five consecutive years with no conviction of any accused government employee.[5] In fact, in the over fifteen years that such allegations have been made, only one Nigerian government official has ever been convicted (US Department of State 2019; US Department of State 2018).

State-level responses to combating human trafficking have been decidedly mixed. The leaders of Edo State—seen as the primary hub for trafficking networks in Nigeria—have recently taken several steps to strengthen their response to trafficking. In early March 2018, "the Oba of Benin—the most powerful religious ruler in Benin City—issued a curse on sex traffickers and revoked all *juju* spells that had been administered by priests to bind victims to their traffickers, which could increase victim identification and victims' willingness to participate in trials against their traffickers" (US Department of State 2018, 12). During that same month the Edo State government drafted and passed its own anti-trafficking legislation, which the governor signed into law on March 23 (Pathfinders Justice Initiative 2018). The goal of these efforts is to address both the spiritual and legal challenges to combating human trafficking and strengthen the application of the 2015 national legislation. Borno State, by contrast, is consistently cited as providing resources and support to the Civilian Joint Task Force (CJTF), a nongovernmental self-defense militia involved in combating Boko Haram. Like Boko Haram, the CJTF has been accused of using child soldiers, abducting girls for use as sex slaves and forced marriage, and assisting the procurement and movement of trafficking victims in the region (US Department of State 2018).

Victim-Centered?
In addition to its law enforcement functions, the NAPTIP also has a unit dedicated to assisting victims with recovery, rehabilitation, and reintegration into society. There are currently ten such command units in cities across the county and ten accompanying shelters for housing victims of trafficking. "Through these shelters, NAPTIP provide[s] access to legal, medical, and psychological services, as well as vocational training, financial empowerment, and business management skills" (US Department of State 2018, 21). According to the NAPTIP, victims are permitted to stay in a shelter for up to six weeks; extended stays are granted under certain circumstances, primarily if the victim is in the process of assisting law enforcement in an investigation or legal action (US Department of State 2019). This unit coordinates with law enforcement to provide protection for trafficking victims from reprisals from their traffickers (Bowers 2012). The NAPTIP further acts as an umbrella organization for addressing victim assistance once victims leave their care and is tasked with coordinating its activities with state-level ministries, NGOs, and other agencies providing support to victims (Danish Immigration Service 2008). The NAPTIP also hosts a hotline for victims of trafficking and provides mentors and training for law enforcement on proactively identifying potential victims of trafficking.

Unfortunately, reports from various NGOs as well as from the TIP Reports make clear that Nigeria's approach to victim assistance is troubling at best. While the 2019 TIP Report highlights the significant increase in the NAPTIP's law enforcement efforts, it also notes the government's markedly decreased efforts in identifying or protecting victims of human trafficking. There are numerous structural problems in the NAPTIP's approach to victim assistance. Although the 2015 anti-trafficking law states that the NAPTIP will only be responsible for assisting victims of human trafficking, the government regularly refers other types of victims to NAPTIP command centers and shelters for assistance (US Department of State 2019), which strains its already modest resources. The 2014 TIP Report for Nigeria noted that only one-fifth of NAPTIP's total budget went to the counseling and rehabilitation unit; all remaining funds were disbursed to the other three divisions.

In addition to these structural barriers to the NAPTIP's victim assistance efforts, victims and human rights advocates have expressed serious concerns regarding which victims are sent to shelters, how the shelters are run, and how victims are treated while staying in shelters. There are no official guidelines for determining which victims should be sent to NAPTIP-run shelters. The agency provides only the most comprehensive version of victim assistance through its own shelters. Accordingly, any victims deemed ineligible to go to NAPTIP shelters are completely cut off from critical services. Those who seek clarity on this process often receive contradictory and confusing information. The head of the NAPTIP command center in Benin told Human Rights Watch, "All victims should be put in a shelter. . . . It depends on individual circumstances" (Human Rights Watch 2019d, 9).

Even for victims who are considered eligible for placement in a NAPTIP shelter, the treatment they receive is less than ideal. As noted earlier, NAPTIP's official policy is that victims are allowed to stay in its shelters for no more than six weeks; however, some victims have been allowed to remain for up to three months. NAPTIP only runs "closed shelters," which has significant consequences for victims. Victims staying in NAPTIP shelters are not permitted to leave without a chaperone, even when they wish to leave the shelter entirely. School-age children are not permitted to stay in the shelters because they are expected to attend school, which would not be possible while staying in a closed shelter. These children, therefore, are referred to the foster care system rather than to trafficking-victim-specific services (US Department of State 2018). Many victims reported that they were not permitted to have visitors or allowed to contact their families directly. Further, trafficking victims are provided with little to no information about any criminal or civil legal proceedings that are taking place ostensibly on their behalf (Human Rights Watch 2019d).

The coordination between the victim assistance side and law enforcement efforts is equally troubling. Although the NAPTIP states that victims are only encouraged to assist law enforcement in prosecuting cases against traffickers, the US State Department (2019) identifies this involvement as a requirement for staying in a NAPTIP shelter. Further, while the 2015 anti-trafficking law expressly prohibits the prosecution of trafficking victims for any illegal actions they were forced to do by their traffickers, NGOs have identified a consistent pattern of arrest and detention for certain types of trafficking victims. In particular, the Nigerian military regularly detains, screens for intelligence value, and pursues criminal prosecutions against trafficking victims having an alleged connection to either Boko Haram or ISIS–WA (US Department of State 2018). Although the Nigerian government denies it, since 2013 thousands of children formerly forced into serving as soldiers have been held in Nigerian military prisons (Becker and Ewang 2020).

At the state level, Edo State is leading the way in subnational anti-trafficking efforts, and the national government has encouraged other states to follow Edo's lead. Although advocates had hoped that Edo State's approach would be more victim-centered than the national government's approach, the Edo State task force has been limited to public awareness campaigns and coordination with the NAPTIP to resolve any conflicts between the national and state anti-trafficking laws (Pathfinders Justice Initiative 2018; US Department of State 2019).

As this evidence makes clear, Nigeria's anti-trafficking regime faces significant challenges and is woefully insufficient to meet either the criminal-justice or victim-assistance needs of the country's serious problem of trafficking. Despite the challenges Nigeria faces moving forward, it is still possible to assess where the country's anti-trafficking response to date falls on the criminal-justice and victim-centered spectrum. It is evident that the Nigerian government, especially at the national level, has invested significant time and resources in pursuing a criminal justice approach to combating trafficking. Unfortunately, this has come at the expense of providing support to trafficking victims, which has continued to decline over time.

The Role of Women

The decline in Nigeria's focus on victim-centered approaches to combating trafficking tracks closely with an overall decline in the representation of women in Nigeria's national government (see fig. 6.4). In 2014, the year leading up to the revision and replacement of the 2003 anti-trafficking legislation, women were relatively well represented in both the Nigerian cabinet (24 percent of ministers) and Parliament (between 6 and 7 percent of each house). Since that time, the percentage of female ministers in the cabinet and members of both Houses of Parliament have steadily declined. By 2020, women's representation was half what it had been just six years prior (UN Women and Inter-Parliamentary Union 2020). Despite, or perhaps because of the Nigerian laws that support a quota system—an approach that results in lower female representation than is found in other African states—women's participation remains abysmally low.

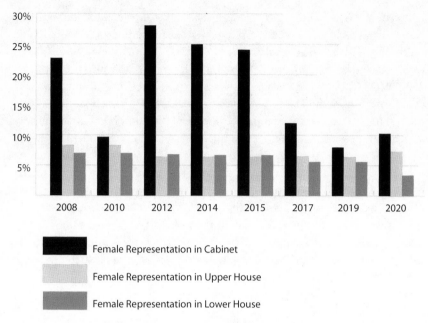

Figure 6.4. Female Representation in Government in Nigeria, 2008–20

Source: UN Women and Inter-Parliamentary Union, "Women in Politics," assessed annually for all years in which the UN and the IPU produced a ranking between 2008 and 2020.

Many of the same factors that contribute to women's vulnerability to human trafficking—patriarchy, violence, and poor economic conditions—are also keeping women from being actively involved in Nigerian politics. Although the United Nations is actively working to help train candidates and provide support to women interested in engaging in politics at all levels, Nigeria is far from reaching the goal set in the 2006 National Gender Policy of 35 percent female representation in both elected and appointed positions. In fact, since the goal was set in 2006, female representation has steadily declined (UN Women and Inter-Parliamentary Union 2019).

Although their representation in the national government has declined and is quite low, Nigerian women have found other ways to be involved in anti-trafficking efforts. State governments seem to offer a few more opportunities to women interested in politics, though they are still limited. The role of women in state governments, most notably the attorney general, may explain Edo State's leadership in combating human trafficking at the state level (Anyabuike 2020). In the world of advocacy and nongovernmental victim support, Amina Titi Atiku-Abubaker, the wife of a former vice president of Nigeria, is a notable figure. She founded the Women Trafficking and Child Labour Eradication

Foundation (WOTCLEF) to help raise awareness of trafficking among young Nigerians as well as support them in ways that make them less vulnerable to traffickers. Titi Atiku-Abubaker and WOTCLEF were driving forces behind the 2003 anti-trafficking legislation and helped draft the original version in 2001. WOTCLEF has also been at the forefront of victim assistance. Over the course of its more than twenty years in existence, the organization has assisted more than 10,000 victims, helping with repatriation and rehabilitation as well as providing vocational training and micro-credit (Vanguard 2018).

In addition to WOTCLEF, several women's religious organizations are active in the fight against human trafficking and regularly provide victim support and campaign for stronger legislation and enforcement (see Anyabuike 2020). Further, as noted earlier, the June 2020 protests to address violence against women in Nigeria are generating important dialogues among women from all walks of life (Orjinmo 2020). Unfortunately, our findings indicate that the lack of women in positions of power in Nigeria place all such efforts at a distinct disadvantage in the fight against human trafficking.

Conclusion

We have shown that trafficking in Nigeria supports both core arguments of this work. Nigeria's relatively weak rule of law, patriarchal culture, and growing economic inequality have systematically reduced the economic opportunities and protections available to women and girls. Additionally, violence and corruption have weakened the few cultural and familial structures in place across Nigeria, driving young Nigerians out of their homes—and, often, out of their country—in search of a better, safer, and more successful life. Nigeria's steady decrease in female representation in parliamentary and ministerial positions reduces the choices women face in developing strategies and initiatives for combating trafficking and, perhaps more importantly, assisting and reintegrating victims of sex trafficking. In Nigeria, as in all the other countries described throughout this work, the common thread is the diminution of the value of women. Intractable patrimony is the consistent and persistent barrier to progress in combating human trafficking. There are certainly recent reasons for hope, but whether real change is on the horizon for Nigeria's women remains to be seen.

Notes

1. This article uses data drawn from the World Poverty Clock run by the World Data Lab. In the methodology section for the World Poverty Clock it is recognized that determining overall poverty rates in Nigeria is particularly challenging given

the diversity of economic growth and stability in the country, especially between northern and southern parts of the country. However, these authors are confident that not only is the number of those living in extreme poverty increasing, it is doing so rapidly and will continue to do so for the foreseeable future (World Data Lab 2020).

2. Author interview of Nosakhare Erhunmwensee, October 27, 2019. NAME organization has an active Facebook page explaining the work it does to assist trafficking victims in Nigeria: https://www.facebook.com/namefoundation/.

3. Erhunmwensee interview.

4. Nearly 17 percent of the women and children interviewed had experienced trafficking prior to participating in this survey.

5. The 2019 TIP Report did acknowledge that NAPTIP initiated seven and completed four prosecutions for trafficking-related offenses against government officials during the reporting period. However, none of these actions resulted in a conviction.

SEVEN

Brazil

In 2014 and 2016 Brazil played host to two major international sporting events: the 2014 FIFA Men's World Cup and the 2016 Summer Olympic Games. Prior to the 2014 event, Brazil's sex workers, like many of their compatriots, expected a huge economic windfall from the influx of tourists the events would bring (Brasileiro 2013; Silverman 2017). However, the anticipation of an increased demand for sex workers also brought an expectation that not all of the demand for sex workers could be filled by Brazil's legally recognized and autonomous prostitutes.

News stories circulated in the months leading up to both the World Cup and the Summer Olympics with horror stories of sex trafficking in Brazil. Many of these stories focused on the exploitation of children in clubs across major urban centers such as São Paulo and Rio de Janeiro. The stories of Jessica and Ana Gabriela are two common examples of this coverage. Jessica, a sixteen-year-old prostitute, was arrested in a club raid in September 2013. In an interview she admitted she only narrowly escaped being lured into what most likely was an attempt at sex trafficking: "One of her regular clients, a Spaniard . . . promised to take her to Europe. 'I told him I was 18 and I was getting my passport . . . I paid 500 reals for a fake ID and was saving money to buy a fake passport. But in the end, I was afraid to go'" (Brasileiro 2013, 2). By contrast, fifteen-year-old Ana Gabriela was not already working as a prostitute when she was recruited to work in Rio de Janeiro. She was offered a job at a bar on the beach near the World Cup venues, but when she arrived in Rio she was taken to a favela, a Brazilian slum, and forced into prostitution, working near the sporting venues along Copacabana Beach (Ridley 2016).

These personal accounts and other widely circulated reports detailing the anticipated increase in sexual exploitation brought on by mega sporting events describe a sexual and moral panic in Brazil over the country's problems with sex tourism and human trafficking. While some scholars dispute the connection between mega sporting events and increases in human trafficking, the panic Brazilian activists and officials felt in the lead-up to the World Cup and Summer Olympics brought renewed attention to the issue of human trafficking in Brazil (see Blanchette and de Silva 2016; Mitchell 2016). Additionally, the responses to trafficking from key actors—including the Brazilian government, religious organizations, and anti-trafficking activists and NGOs—prior to these two events make clear that Brazil is a cautionary tale and dialogues about human trafficking in Brazil highlight the need for academics, activists, and policymakers to more critically examine their own assumptions in their efforts to combat and prevent sex trafficking.

As demonstrated so far, the combination of discrimination and limited opportunities available to women in education, employment, and political leadership have a serious and negative impact on state responsiveness to human trafficking. The cultural and economic devaluation of Brazilian women and girls, especially those from Indigenous and Afro-Brazilian backgrounds or who are transsexual or transgender, make this population extremely vulnerable to sex trafficking. However, Brazil's case also involves issues of consent as it relates to autonomous sex work. The same cultural and social barriers that make cisgender and transgender women vulnerable to sex trafficking also devalue their independent choices to purposely engage in sex work. Existing moral hierarchies relating to gender identity and the role of consent complicate the national response to all forms of human trafficking and create more opportunities and vulnerabilities for traffickers to exploit.

Trafficking in Brazil

Brazil has a long history of slavery stretching back at least to the colonial era and quite possibly even earlier. After becoming a Portuguese colony in the sixteenth century, Brazil quickly became one of the world's largest slave economies. By the mid-nineteenth century, approximately 5 million slaves were brought to Brazil from Africa to work on sugar and rubber plantations and in gold and diamond mines—more than eleven times the number of enslaved people brought to North America (Dolby 2018; Bourcier 2012; Goldstein 2003; Okediji 2004). In 1888 Brazil became the last country in the Americas to abolish slavery; however, by that time Brazil's economy was highly labor-dependent. The country's booming industries, particularly coffee, gold, and diamonds, soon made Brazil an attractive destination for immigrants. Drawn by the promises of employment and success, more than 4 million European and Japanese migrants immigrated to Brazil before the Great Depression (Bourcier 2012; Nakamura 2008; Sowell 1996).

Brazil's historical relationship with slavery has strongly influenced its modern experience with and approach to human trafficking. As the largest economy in Latin America, Brazil has become a central hub for migration in the region and is now recognized as a source, transit, and destination country for legal migration, human smuggling, and human trafficking. Much of the human trafficking that happens in South America is domestic or regional. The size of South American states, their diversity, and their distance from the rest of the world provide strong markets for most human traffickers, without the need to take on the added risks and costs of moving victims abroad. For example, in 2014 nearly 80 percent of all identified victims of trafficking in South American countries were trafficked within their country of origin (UNODC 2016). This trend was reinforced in 2002 when Argentina, Bolivia, Brazil, Chile, Paraguay, and Uruguay signed an agreement as part of their association with the Southern Common Market (MERCOSUR) to allow the free movement of labor among their countries (Andrees, Nasrik, and Swiniarski 2015).

In many ways human trafficking in Brazil reflects regional trends. An urban area known as the Northern Triangle—made up of parts of the cities of Foz do Iguazú in Brazil, Cuidad del Este in Paraguay, and Puerto Iguazú in Argentina—is known for having especially porous borders, making it a popular passage not only for legal migration but also for the smuggling and trafficking of humans and illegal goods, including drugs (Walk Free Foundation 2018). Brazil also has a long-standing open-door policy for Venezuelan migrants fleeing instability, economic insecurity, and violence in their home country (Human Rights Watch 2019b). It is no surprise, then, that alongside the more than 350,000 Brazilians living in conditions of modern slavery, Paraguayans and Venezuelans are commonly identified among those trafficked to Brazil (Walk Free Foundation 2018). By contrast, although it has gained a great deal of media and policy attention, international trafficking into and out of Brazil is much more limited and accounts for a relatively small percentage of the country's trafficking victims (UNODC 2016).

Brazil differs from its South American neighbors in at least one important respect: forced labor, not sex trafficking, may be its most dominant form of human trafficking. And, while it may be more difficult to ascertain in Brazil than in other countries, the enormity of Brazil's problem with forced labor is well known and regularly recognized as being more pervasive than in other parts of Latin America (UNODC 2016). Forced labor, or *trabalho escravo*, is driven largely by many of the same labor-intensive industries that emerged during the colonial era: ranching, coffee, logging, and mining. Traditionally, victims of forced labor in Brazil have been men and boys; however, women and girls are often trafficked into forced labor as domestic workers or into the country's growing textile industry (Walk Free Foundation 2018). In addition to forced labor, there is evidence of certain types of sex trafficking in Brazil, including forced prostitution of women and the sexual exploitation of children. Brazilians, especially transsexual and transgender women, are also often exploited through debt bondage: after migrating voluntarily for sex work they find they cannot repay the costs charged by those facilitating their migration.

Factors Contributing to Sex Trafficking

Several interrelated and mutually reinforcing factors increase the vulnerability of Brazilians to sex trafficking, including long-standing economic and cultural inequality, endemic corruption in government generally and law enforcement specifically, and discrimination against and sexualization of women and girls. Additionally, Brazil is unique in that it is undeniable that the moral entrepreneurs most active in combating sex trafficking in the country are also responsible for perpetuating false narratives about the nature of that trafficking, thus increasing the vulnerability of women and girls. Further, although all Brazilian women face some of these factors, they are most acutely experienced by the Indigenous and Afro-Brazilian communities because these groups are culturally disadvantaged. Strong cultural ideas about gender roles and sexuality also make transsexual and transgender Brazilians, especially those with a feminine identity, particularly vulnerable to economic insecurity, violence, and human trafficking.

Diversity and Inequality

Although Brazil's history has led to an impressively diverse population, it has also created lasting inequality along racial, economic, and geographic lines. The key sources of inequality in Brazil overlap with and reinforce one another, making specific segments of the population particularly vulnerable to exploitation. Above all, race continues to be a consistent predictor of poverty and victimization. For most of Brazil's history as an independent country, white Brazilians made up the majority of the country's population. However, according to the 2010 census, for the first time a majority of Brazilians—50.7 percent— identify as having African ancestry, or being Afro-Brazilian, than any other racial category (Phillips 2011). Several reasons have been offered for the shift in Brazil's demographics, but the most common may be broader acceptance of Black identity. According to the former minister for racial equality, "people are no longer scared of identifying themselves or insecure about saying: I'm black and black is beautiful" (Bailey and Telles 2014, 243). Brazil's demographic shift, at least in part, can be traced to the way Brazilians understand race as being based on appearance rather than ancestry only. Additionally, some scholars have shown that the race with which Brazilians identify can be influenced by social factors and perceptions of others (Bailey and Telles 2014).

Race, then, is a more fluid concept in Brazil, and the racial identity a person chooses can change. Historically this fluidity has reinforced racial inequality and the social perception of darker skin as being "less than" (Lovell 2006). Indeed, some studies have shown that changes in one's social and economic standing influence racial identity; for example, as Brazilians achieve higher levels of education and income, they begin to identify with lighter-skinned racial categories than one previously chosen (Bailey and Telles 2014; Lovell 2006). Despite the growing acceptability of Black identity in Brazil, darker skin tones continue to have a more negative cultural connotation than lighter skin tones; this bias can also lead to economic and political consequences.

Over time, as inequalities developed along racial lines, similar differences emerged among Brazil's five geographic regions: the north, northeast, center-west, southeast, and south. The north and northeast regions are the poorest, least developed, and among the least populated. The northeast, in particular, is home to approximately half of the nation's poor and is considered to have the largest concentration of rural poverty in Latin America (Gacitúa Marió and Woolcock 2008; van Klaveren et al. 2009, 28). The opportunities that do exist in the northeast are concentrated in the region's few coastal urban areas. By contrast, most of Brazil's wealth, income, development, and populations are concentrated in the southern regions. The southeast is home to the country's two largest metropolitan and economic centers, São Paulo and Rio de Janeiro. Although this region is made up of only 11 percent of Brazil's landmass, it is home to more than 40 percent of the population and accounts for more than half of the country's GDP (Azzoni 2014). Since the nineteenth century, large inequalities between and within regions have facilitated and incentivized the migration of people from the poor rural areas to the large urban centers and from the less-developed north to the wealthier south (Castilho, Evrard, and Charrier 2017). This push to migrate in search of better economic opportunities creates an ideal environment for human trafficking.

The intersection of racial and geographic inequality has created extensive economic inequality in Brazil. In 2018 the Walk Free Foundation estimated that the richest 5 percent of Brazilians earn as much as the other 95 percent of the population and that a majority of those in the richest group are white (Walk Free Foundation 2018; Phillips 2011). Poverty and race are strongly correlated, as Afro-Brazilian and Indigenous individuals are between two and three times more likely to be living in poverty than white Brazilians. Although Brazil has made notable efforts to address poverty and reduce economic inequality through taxes and cash transfer programs such as Bolsa Familia, high levels of both poverty and inequality persist. Indigenous and Afro-Brazilians are often unable to close such economic gaps themselves because they also have lower levels of education, which often leads to lower-wage employment in the informal sector and provides less economic security and limits access to social services (Lustig 2015).

The realities of economic inequality and persistent poverty have direct impacts on individuals' vulnerability to human traffickers. The majority of identified victims of both forced labor and sex trafficking come from the north and the northeast. Because of the lack of economic opportunities, residents in these regions are primed to take any offers made by traffickers for work in regional coastal cities or in urban areas in the more prosperous south and southeast (Castilho, Evrard, and Charrier 2017). The victims most commonly trafficked for sexual exploitation—Afro-Brazilian women and girls—face added pressure. Men often work in labor-intensive industries in isolated areas, leaving women behind as the heads of households. This family dynamic further weakens their economic security because the women are often illiterate or have limited education and lack the technical skills to make them competitive in the labor market—if employment opportunities are even available in their area. Many of these women and children also have histories of physical and/or sexual abuse and drug addiction, which further increase their vulnerability to traffickers (Langberg 2005).

Corruption and Violence
Corruption among public officials is perhaps the single most important factor in facilitating human trafficking in Brazil. According to Elba Tavares, a transsexual sex worker in Rio de Janeiro, Brazil "is a half-developed country. What is most developed here is crime and corruption, that's well developed. . . . And when the government is not worth anything, nothing else is" (Phillips and Cheibub 2020, 126). Corruption has proven to be particularly widespread among both law enforcement and politicians in Brazil, and several studies have shown that the public sees both of these groups as being highly involved in trafficking and other criminal activities (Bales 2005; Studnicka 2010).

Brazil's police forces, in particular, are a source of fear rather than protection for the country's most vulnerable communities. According to its own statistics, the police force in Rio de Janeiro was responsible for the deaths of more than 600 people in the first four months of 2020. While instances of most other crimes decreased significantly as lockdown policies went into place in Brazil in response to the global COVID-19 pandemic, instances of police killings increased 43 percent (Muñoz 2020b). Most of the victims of these police killings are Black men, and the police are well known for indiscriminate gunfire—ostensibly in self-defense—while conducting operations in the favelas. Human Rights Watch has spent more than a decade monitoring police behavior in Brazil and have found that "in poor neighborhoods, police open fire recklessly, without regard for the lives of bystanders. Sometimes they wantonly execute people. That they only behave so abusively in poor neighborhoods may explain the lack of uproar over the killings in a society as deeply unequal as Brazil's"

(Muñoz 2020b, 28). The impunity with which these police killings take place in Brazil is reinforced by the words and actions of the country's top politicians. Both Brazilian president Jair Bolsonaro and the Governor of Rio de Janeiro State Wilson Witzel have publicly supported the police killings, even calling for the police to kill more (Canineu 2020; Muñoz 2020b).

Law enforcement routinely engages in numerous other illegal and exploitative enterprises. Militias operating in Brazil that are linked to members of law enforcement and firefighters often take advantage of the poor communities in the country's urban areas. In particular they are known to extort protection money under the guise of security taxes from businesses, control access to and the price of cooking gas, provide stolen or pirated access to cable television and internet services, and of course engage in drug trafficking as well (Wilkinson 2019). These militias have also been tied to some targeted executions of political activists such as Marielle Franco, who was gunned down, along with her driver, Anderson Gomes, in Rio de Janeiro in 2018. Although few homicide cases in Brazil are solved, an arrest was initially made in this case; two suspects—believed to be the shooter and his getaway driver—were arrested nearly a year after the murder (Wilkinson 2019). However, attempts to determine who ordered Franco's execution ended in 2020 when the suspected leader of the militia believed to be responsible for ordering her death was killed in a confrontation with police forces (*BBC News* 2020b).

Corruption among the police and politicians has a direct impact on how trafficking operates in Brazil and how potential victims respond to instances of trafficking in their own lives and families. Federal, state, and municipal officials have been investigated, and sometimes prosecuted, for their involvement in prostitution, child sex trafficking, and forced labor. In 2004 officers from the Brazilian Federal Police and the United Nations identified forty-five state agents who were part of a sex-trafficking ring (Amar 2009). The US Department of State noted that "police officers [have been alleged to] ignore the exploitation of children, patronize brothels, and rob and assault women in prostitution, impeding identification of sex-trafficking victims" (US Department of State 2017, 16). The Brazilian public is aware of the role corruption plays in facilitating various forms of trafficking, including sex trafficking (Huguet and Szabó de Carvalho 2008; Studnicka 2010; Zaluar 2000). In the border areas many families of sex-trafficking victims negotiate directly with brothel owners for the return of victims rather than contacting law enforcement because they have no expectation that the authorities will assist the victims or investigate the traffickers (Ministério da Justiça 2013). These experiences convince potential victims that they are powerless to combat trafficking and prevents them from seeking help in avoiding or escaping trafficking situations.

Discrimination, Sexualization, and Violence

Three primary groups are particularly vulnerable to sex trafficking in Brazil: women, transsexuals and transgender women, and children. As is true in many other countries in Latin America, Brazilians must contend with the cultural devaluation of females and femininity because of the influences of machismo and the political and cultural role of religious conservatism. Brazilian society often emphasizes patriarchy and men's dominance, especially in public spaces. This perspective is paired with the belief that Brazilian women should be submissive "sainted mothers" and primarily focused on the family and the home (Ewing 2014; Lovell 2006). Machismo culture perpetuates the sexual objectification of women and girls and the acceptance of violence against cisgender and transgender women as well as children, especially in private (Barker and Loewenstein 1997; Konstantopoulos et al. 2013; Simões and Matos 2008). These influences are prevalent and appear overtly within poor, nonwhite communities, in both rural areas and urban favelas (Barker and Loewenstein 1997; Ewing 2014). As a result of these cultural influences, all three groups are made more vulnerable by racialization, heteronormative patriarchy, and sexualization, as well as general acceptance of violence against them coupled with an abject failure by the state to provide consistent and efficient protection.

The sexual objectification of women and girls is pervasive in Brazilian media, including in the themes of telenovelas, popular music, and advertising for the country's tourism industry (United Nations n.d.; Dolby 2018). For example, the popular cooking show *MasterChef Junior* instigated several national conversations about Brazil's rape culture and the sexualization of women and girls after sexual comments were directed at a twelve-year-old contestant named Valentina. After Valentina won the competition, "rather than receiving recognition [of] her attributes in the kitchen, she was sexually harassed by Brazilian men who tweeted things such as: "@AnderSoberano: About this Valentina: is it pedophilia if it is consensual?"; "Let me keep quiet so I won't go to jail." All of which was normalized and taken as a joke by those who defended the comments (Marisapr 2016).

The images promoted by the media reveal how men, and the culture in general, view women as sexual objects. In 2010, Instituto ProMundo found that 77 percent of Brazilian men thought it was common to have sex with underage prostitutes. Brazil also ranks fourth globally in adolescent marriage by age fifteen. Several sources note that a common reason adult men seek underage brides is that they are perceived as more obedient, while the girls' families support these marriages as a way to curb the girls' perceived hypersexuality (Dolby 2018). By contrast, transgender women and transsexuals with feminine identities are considered an exotic, taboo, and dangerous middle-ground that many men desire but are afraid to admit (Ferreira 2017). According to Elba Tavares, the clients of trans-women sex workers are frequently married men who are looking for an exotic thrill (Phillips and Cheibub 2020).

Women, children, and transsexual and transgender Brazilians also face considerable and horrific instances of violence throughout Brazil. In 2014 a rape was reported every eleven minutes—more than 47,500 total incidents of rape were reported that year—and in more than 60 percent of those cases the victim was an Afro-Brazilian woman (Dolby 2018). Brazil has one of the highest rates of homicide for women in the world; the national average is 4.4 per 100,000 women, but the rate in some Brazilian states is considerably higher. Roraima State is considered the deadliest in Brazil for women, with a homicide rate of 11.4 per 100,000 women (Human Rights Watch 2017). According to the Brazilian Center for Latin American Studies, more than 92,000 women were killed in gender-related crimes, including rape and domestic abuse, between 1980 and 2020 (Dolby 2018).

The same holds true for the LGBTQ+ community in Brazil, where a death due to homophobia takes place every sixteen hours (Subrinho 2019). Brazil has the highest global murder rate for transgender people, according to Transgender Europe (Phillips and Cheibub 2020). The responses of some individuals to these types of gender-based violence is also telling. In 2015 a sixteen-year-old girl in Rio de Janeiro was gang raped, with video and pictures of the victim later posted to social media. Men across Brazil made jokes about the attack and the victim (Dolby 2018). Although these responses did allegedly shock Brazilian society, there has not been the same kind of organized response and demand for change as seen in response to similar horrific crimes in India and Nigeria.

The violence against cisgender and transgender women and children is not only supported by gender norms and machismo culture, but also allowed to continue by the failure of law enforcement and the judiciary to protect victims and punish perpetrators. Although there are certainly actors within the legal community who genuinely wish to help victims of gender-based violence, Human Rights Watch has found "failures at all points in the trajectory of how domestic violence cases are handled from the moment of abuse forward" (Human Rights Watch 2017, 36). Due to these failures, most cases are closed without convictions or even arrests because the statutes of limitations are routinely allowed to expire. Victims of gender-based violence in Brazil also face the force of gendered norms and discrimination in seeking treatment for physical injuries. Individuals interviewed by Konstantopoulos et al. claim that health care providers in Brazil "either avoid or ignore the overarching problem of violence against women and girls . . . and some healthcare [workers have] negative attitudes toward certain patients (e.g., poor, Black women)" (2013, 1,200). So, even if these women do seek help, there appear to be few safe places they can be guaranteed to find it.

In the case of child and adolescent marriage, Brazilian law itself makes children vulnerable to exploitation. Although the legal age for marriage for both boys and girls is eighteen years, there are important exceptions. Children can marry at sixteen if they have both parents' permission or even younger "in the case of pregnancy or in order to avoid a criminal sentence, namely in the case of statutory rape" (Taylor et al. 2015, 12). These child marriages then become another part of the cycle of violence against women, limiting the ability of girls to pursue education or economic mobility and restricting their social networks and support structures; it also heightens the risk for intimate partner violence (Taylor et al. 2015). For transsexual and transgender women, all of these limitations to protection are further exacerbated by pervasive discrimination against and dismissal of their identities by their families, communities, and law enforcement. When transsexual and transgender victims do seek assistance and protection from the police, they are routinely subjected to further violence and victimization (Ferreira 2017).

Deprivation of Women's Economic Rights
When it comes to gender equality and women's economic rights, Brazil is a country of contrasts. The Brazilian Constitution provides for equal rights and duties for men and women. Dilma Rousseff was elected as the country's first female president in 2015; young women now have literacy rates on par with their male contemporaries, and a consistent majority of university graduates, two-thirds in recent years, are women (Prusa and Picanco 2019; Ceratti 2017). However, in the lived realities of most Brazilian women, equality is only at the surface level. For most women in Brazilian society, equality—especially economic equality—remains far out of reach. No laws exist prohibiting sexual harassment in public places, including in schools, or requiring equal pay for equal work (Tavares 2017). Additionally, the federal antidiscrimination law only prohibits racial discrimination and does not include discrimination based on gender identity or sexual orientation. Although in January 2020 an antidiscrimination law in São Paulo was enacted that did address discrimination based on sexual orientation and gender identity, there is no countrywide law (Soares 2020). In 2019 the Supreme Court declared that these exclusions from the antidiscrimination law are unconstitutional. While this is encouraging, the Supreme Court addressed the issue primarily as a response to an inquiry about a law under consideration by Brazil's Senate at the time that would have mandated prison sentences of up to five years for hate crimes based on sexual orientation or gender identity but would also have introduced religious exceptions to these punishments (Lopes 2019). The Supreme Court's opinion does not serve as a vehicle for policy change nationally; rather, its role is in an advisory capacity to the Senate only.

Women also see practical and individual consequences to the lack of protection for their economic rights. Women earn on average about 25 percent less than men, therefore earning in a year what men earn in just nine months (Muñoz 2018). As seen in many other countries, much of the earnings gap is due to the fact that women are still confined to jobs with lower rates of growth and lower earnings, including jobs in the informal sector (Ceratti 2017). However, unlike many other countries, higher education does not diminish this gap—men with university degrees earn 36 percent more than university-educated women (Muñoz 2018). The gap is even larger for women of color: on average, Afro-Brazilian women earn 7.70 reals (US$2.50) per hour while white women with the same level of education earn 12.50 reals (US$4.02) and white men earn 15.60 reals (US$5.00) (Ceratti 2017).

Conditions are equally problematic for transsexual and transgender Brazilians, who engage in the formal labor force at much lower rates (16.7 percent) than the general population (more than 50 percent). Due largely to the discrimination these individuals face throughout their lives from their families, schools, and society at large, the transsexual and transgender population has much lower rates of education and thus work in much lower-paid and, usually, informal jobs, especially sex work. Numerous studies have found that between 40 and 90 percent of this population is engaged in sex work, with many stating they have never had another job or do not believe they could find one if they looked for it (Lopez and Teixeira 2020; Phillips and Cheibub 2020; da Silva, Luppi, and Veros 2020). On average less than 20 percent of transsexual and transgender Brazilians hold a university degree; indeed, in some parts of Brazil more than 40 percent of this group does not even complete elementary school and another 30 percent drop out between the ages of sixteen and nineteen (da Silva, Luppi, and Veros 2020). Low educational attainment along with low-earning and informal employment lead to high rates of social isolation and suicide among this population. Even for transsexual and transgender Brazilians who do attain high levels of education and participate in the formal labor force, the gender-based bias that exists among cisgender Brazilians reappears, giving those with a masculine identity clear advantages over those with a feminine one (da Silva, Luppi, and Veros 2020).

Moral Panics and Self-Fulfilling Prophecies

Understanding human trafficking in Brazil is a more complex task than for some other countries. In most cases problems in data collection are due primarily to the nature of trafficking as a criminal enterprise. In Brazil, however, the problem is much more complicated; the most common descriptions of human trafficking in Brazil are plagued by poor data collection, confusing and inconsistent definitions in Brazilian law, and moral hierarchies related to women's sexuality and prostitution.

Much of the misinformation about human trafficking in Brazil can be traced to the 2002 Pesquisa Nacional sobre o Trafico de Mulheres, Criancas, e Adolescentes (PESTRAF) study. The study itself has serious methodological problems and, according to Blanchette and da Silva (2012), the authors have resisted discussing publicly how they conducted the study. However, a single report is not solely responsible for making the image of trafficking in Brazil so unclear; rather, it is how this study has been used and recycled by stakeholders over the past twenty years. The results of the PESTRAF study were written with a sense of powerful clarity and confidence; the authors found evidence of extensive and pervasive sex trafficking in Brazil, especially of women and girls. Hundreds of trafficking routes were identified, allegedly run by large international mafias responsible for trafficking thousands of women and girls from Brazil to locations around the world (Blanchette and da Silva 2012). These conclusions have since been used as definitive proof—often the only proof—of sex trafficking in Brazil by many academics, activists, foreign governments (including the US State Department's Trafficking in Persons Reports), and international organizations in their assessments of the state of human trafficking in the country (Blanchette and da Silva 2012; Mitchell 2016).

A close inspection of the study reveals serious defects that call into question the utility of the report's conclusions. From the very beginning of Brazil's efforts to incorporate the Palermo Protocol and to initiate a coordinated effort to combat trafficking, the government's definition of human trafficking has been confusing, inconsistent, and problematic, particularly for its focus on sex work to the near exclusion of all other forms of trafficking. According to the Palermo Protocol there should be a clear distinction between migration for sex work and trafficking for sexual exploitation. The former involves consent of the individual to engage in economic migration, while the latter involves exploitation and the violation of the individual's basic human rights. Brazil's initial definitions of trafficking conflated these two groups of people, essentially making *all* migration for sex work accepted as instances of trafficking and identifying any who assisted in that migration as human traffickers (Blanchette and da Silva 2012; Ministério da Justiça 2013). Although Brazil has since updated its legal definitions to follow the Palermo Protocol more closely, confusion and inconsistency about the differences between human migration, smuggling, and trafficking still remain, even among those tasked with preventing human trafficking and assisting victims (Ministério da Justiça 2013).

Questionable methodology and definitions aside, what made the results of the PESTRAF study so powerful was that they echoed a sex-trafficking narrative already supported by conservative Brazilian politicians, evangelical religious groups, and some sectors of feminist activists. Although prostitution is recognized as a legal profession in Brazil, there is still a great deal of moral opposition to sex work—moral opposition that found its champion in the openly homophobic, misogynistic, and religiously conservative Jair Bolsonaro (Phillips and Phillips 2019; Canineu 2020). Since winning his presidential campaign in 2018 Bolsonaro has made clear, on both domestic and international stages, that he intends to reverse many of the advances made in protecting and promoting the rights of women and the LGBTQ+ community (Muñoz 2020a; Picanço and Prusa 2019). Such actors morally opposed to prostitution have been able to use the problematic legal definitions, events like the World Cup and Summer Olympics, and support from politicians such as Bolsonaro to feed a moral panic in Brazil over human trafficking, focusing that panic specifically on women's sexuality and prostitution (Mitchell 2016).

The consequence of this moral panic is that the real story of human trafficking in Brazil is distorted and many narratives are hidden. Thaddeus Blanchette—a professor of anthropology at Universidad Federal do Rio de Janeiro-Macaé and activist for the rights of Brazil's sex workers, through his work with the Davida Collective and Prostitution Policy Watch—highlighted the extensive media coverage that the "rescue" of the teenage prostitutes was given in 2013, just before the 2014 World Cup.[1] Conversely, in the lead-up to the 2016 Paralympic Games, a reserve colonel in the military police, Pedro Chavarry Duarte, was arrested by police for the alleged sexual assault of a two-year-old girl as well as the attempted bribery of the arresting officers (Becker 2016), but this story received almost no attention outside the Brazilian Portuguese-language press. Further, although Chavarry Duarte was previously arrested for suspected baby trafficking, his 2016 case was delayed by the appeals process and remained unresolved, yet he was still considered a member of the State Police and was receiving a salary in late 2019 (Cardin 2019). It appears, then, that there is a method to the control of the trafficking narrative in Brazil: it strategically hides the roles of certain actors—especially those in authority in public service—and effectively silences the voices of cisgender and transgender women, especially those who choose to engage in sex work.

It may seem that this purposeful muddying of the trafficking narrative would make Brazil a problematic case for our hypotheses. Quite the contrary. In using sex-trafficking narratives to target legal, voluntary sex work, some actors are silencing the voices of women of color and transsexual and transgender Brazilians. Indeed, a consistent statement made by many activists and policymakers in Brazil is that individuals "rescued" from sex work are in fact victims of trafficking, they just do not know enough to realize it (Alessandra 2017; Ministério da Justiça 2013). Rather than supporting the rights of voluntary sex workers, these moral entrepreneurs act as one more constraint on the ability of women to fully realize their economic potential by eliminating what may be their best, if not only, legal path to economic security, which only increases their vulnerability to human traffickers.

Forms of Sex Trafficking in Brazil

Several factors increase vulnerability to human trafficking for cisgender and transgender women and children in Brazil. Moreover, it is very difficult to identify the types of sex trafficking that are actually occurring in the country. Based on our research, there are two types that are certainly occurring on a significant scale: nonconsensual domestic and international sex work and the sexual exploitation of children through forced prostitution.

Nonconsensual Commercial Sex Work

Many of the sensationalized stories of sex trafficking in Brazil are in fact instances of women engaging in voluntary sex work. However, that does not mean there is no trafficking for sex work taking place. Two primary groups of victims are trafficked for commercial sex work in Brazil: cisgender women and girls and transsexual and transgender women. There is some overlap in how this type of trafficking operates for victims, but also distinct differences.

Cisgender women and girls who are trafficked for commercial sex work are most often trafficked domestically or regionally. Unlike in Brazil, prostitution is not a legal or regulated profession in the countries surrounding it, which increases the likelihood of the exploitation of women in sex trafficking. The Ministry of Justice highlighted in particular the trafficking of women from the border areas of Brazil into sex work at brothels in Peru and Bolivia. In both countries the lack of regulations, along with the "demand for cheap sex and for exotic biological types[,] stimulates the search for men and women from different locations," including in Brazil (Ministério da Justiça 2013, 29). Some women willingly migrate to neighboring countries or to other locations within Brazil, looking for autonomous sex work, only to be trafficked to remote locations and forced into sex slavery near mining operations across South America. In Brazil these mining areas are incredibly isolated, often in the poorer north and northeast regions of the country, where there are essentially no public services to support victims or assist them in escaping from their involuntary situations (Walk Free Foundation 2018; Ministério da Justiça 2013).

In addition to domestic and regional trafficking of women and girls, there is some limited evidence of international sex trafficking of Brazilian women. According to the European Union, Brazil is second only to Nigeria in the absolute number of identified victims from non-EU member countries and in the top five for the number of suspected traffickers from non-EU countries (Walk

Free Foundation 2018; Eurostat 2015). In 2016 the report on trafficking by the UNODC did note, contrary to previous reports based on data from the PESTRAF study, that while some Brazilian victims are recruited for international sex trafficking in Europe by foreigners while still in Brazil, it is a rare occurrence (UNODC 2010, 2016). When trafficking does happen, most evidence points to the trafficker and victim sharing a common language as a critical dimension of the traffickers' ruse (UNODC 2016). However, two recent examples in the United Kingdom involved small groups arrested by authorities for exploiting Brazilian women working in English brothels. It is unclear from the accounts whether the women had migrated voluntarily for sex work and were exploited later or if they had been trafficked from Brazil. What is clear from the reports is that debt bondage and violence, including rape, were used once the women were working in the United Kingdom to keep them from leaving the brothels (*BBC News* 2020a; Raffray 2020).

As is the case in the broader human-trafficking literature, there is relatively little information on transsexual and transgender victims of sex trafficking in Brazil (Martinez and Kelle 2013). In some cases transsexual and transgender women who initially enter into sex work voluntarily are later exploited through debt bondage. Often a promise is made that the costs of medical procedures and surgeries will be covered in exchange for the sex work (Teixeira 2019a; Ministério da Justiça 2013). However, it is important to note that this quid pro quo of sex work for medical costs is not in itself considered trafficking by most transsexual and transgender sex workers in Brazil. In fact, Blanchette notes that groups of transsexual and transgender sex workers often form communities where older sex workers help support newer, younger members as they get established in new cities and begin undergoing medical procedures, even if they choose to migrate abroad for sex work.[2] According to these sex workers, the offer to cover medical costs in exchange for sex work only transitions into exploitation when the individuals who have offered to cover medical costs "abuse the situation of vulnerability" through violence, illegal imprisonment, withholding of documents, or forcing the involuntary movement of the person to another location (Ministério da Justiça 2013, 156). Unfortunately, instances of this type of abuse can end tragically for victims. In 2019, police in São Paulo State had open investigations into the deaths of two transgender women. One was apparently murdered by a creditor and the other victim died after an illegal cosmetic surgery procedure where industrial grade silicone was used for body sculpting instead of medical grade silicone (Teixeira 2019a).

Exploitation of Children

While not as prominent as in the Thai case, child sex tourism and trafficking in children for forced prostitution are two large elements of the trafficking landscape in Brazil. According to data from Brazil's federal police, approximately 350,000 children are annually forced into sex slavery, many of them victims of trafficking (Castilho, Evrard, and Charrier 2017; US Department of State 2017, 2014). Because prostitution is legal in Brazil, the country is a popular destination for sex tourism. While much of the sex tourism industry takes place between consensual adults, media portrayals focus on the exploitation of children (see Associated Press 2016, "Brazilian Cops"). While there are likely instances of the use of children as part of the sex-tourism industry, we were unable to identify any clear examples of such exploitation (Walk Free Foundation 2018). In its 2013 report on trafficking in Brazil's border states, the Ministry of Justice did note that activist and service organizations in the region had identified sexual exploitation in some areas and situations connected to sex tourism, including festivals and "fishing tourism in the wetlands" (Ministério da Justiça 2013, 135). Nevertheless, the use of children in sex tourism in Brazil is much rarer than the media portrays it and is certainly less prevalent than in Thailand (Dolby 2018).

What seems to be more common is the exploitation of children in sex slavery, especially in the poorer north and northeast regions (Bureau of International Labor Affairs 2018). The coastal cities in these regions are also associated with sex tourism, which might explain the connection that is often made with the exploitation of children. The reality seems to be that children are trafficked to these locations not because they are sites of sex tourism but because they are locations of considerable development and construction. The children are trafficked to fulfill the sexual demands of the construction crews and migrant workers involved in large mining and construction projects rather than of the tourists (Ministério da Justiça 2013). In a 2013 survey conducted by Childhood Brazil, 57 percent of construction workers said children were being sexually exploited near their construction sites and 25 percent admitted to having used one of these victims for sexual services. Disturbingly, the survey's author concludes that "in the eyes of this population . . . there is no sexual exploitation of children and adolescents. They are not seen as victims or even as children" (Jensen 2016, 43).

Children are driven into exploitative situations for many of the same reasons as adult victims in Brazil: engaging in sex work is simply a matter of survival and there are few legal employment opportunities wherein children can earn enough to support themselves or their families (Abdelgalil et al. 2004; Castilho, Evrard, and Charrier 2017). In fact, to some degree jobs in sex tourism and prostitution have become socially accepted options for desperately poor Brazilian families looking to supplement their incomes. According to Katya, a project leader for one program that works to combat child sex tourism in Recife, a city in the northeast, the problem lies not only in the actions of foreign tourists looking for this type of tourism. The problem is much more complex! In fact, most of the affected families are extremely poor and have several children. Often these families are complicit because they also benefit economically. So they cede their children and receive the promised rewards and, afterwards, they remain silent to avoid compromising their profits. (Castilho, Evrard, and Charrier 2017, 11)

Other victims are lured with the promise of independence and a new life: "For many involved, sex tourism is a synonym of financial independence" (Castilho, Evrard, and Charrier 2017, 13).

Recruitment Strategies

According to the PESTRAF study, most trafficking recruiters in Brazil are men. This is certainly supported by the data on incarceration for trafficking offenses, where the vast majority of people serving prison sentences in Brazil are men. However, there is a growing recognition of the role women play in the recruitment process, especially in the initial stages of contact with a victim. Much like the madams in Nigeria, many of the women who act as recruiters in Brazil are themselves former trafficking victims. These cisgender, transsexual, and transgender women use their "success stories" as a ploy to encourage new victims to accept the opportunities offered by traffickers, and the first point of contact is often a close friend or family member. This is particularly the case for child victims, who are often "recruited" by their own parents (Ministério da Justiça 2013).

Recruiters for sex trafficking make extensive use of debt bondage. Through this tactic traffickers offer to pay certain costs, such as those related to migration—travel, lodging, and visas—or needed to start a new life—covering medical costs in the case of transgender and transsexual victims (Ministério da Justiça 2013; Teixeira 2019a). In order to initiate these recruitments and reach potential victims, human traffickers in Brazil make extensive use of social media and technology. The *Wall Street Journal* (2013) once called Brazil "the social media capital of the universe" because of how quickly its online population of young Brazilians was growing. For example, by 2018 WhatsApp already had more than 100 million users in Brazil. Online platforms provide cheap and simple ways for traffickers to reach large numbers of potential victims in Brazil and in neighboring countries (Dolby 2018; US Department of State 2019). Traffickers are also able to quickly adapt and tailor their recruitment strategies to the interests or needs of potential victims. As federal prosecutor Andre Menezes puts it, "We face here a classic case of modern slavery, in which the chains are not physical, but invisible. We are facing here a case of someone exploiting another person's dreams" (Teixeira 2019a, 12).

Combating Trafficking: Criminal Justice or Victim-Centered?

Human trafficking is addressed by several different pieces of legislation in Brazil, with different types of trafficking addressed by separate laws. Although recent legislation has attempted to make Brazil's legal response to human trafficking more comprehensive, numerous obstacles remain. In particular are the several inconsistent laws available to law enforcement and the judiciary for investigating and prosecuting traffickers, which results in varying rates of conviction and a lack of uniformity in sentencing. Further, inconsistent and competing definitions of "victim" and "human trafficking" undermine both the criminal- justice and victim-centered approaches to combating trafficking in Brazil.

Before ratifying the Palermo Protocol in 2004, Brazil's anti-trafficking laws largely focused on female prostitution (Cunha 2015). After ratification, Brazil revised its criminal code. Perhaps the most important post-Palermo changes made were to Articles 231 and 231a. Article 231 expands Brazil's legal definition of human trafficking to include all victims, regardless of gender, and Article 231a criminalizes domestic as well as international trafficking (Anselmo and Fernandes 2015). Still, the laws only explicitly criminalize activities related to forced prostitution (Cunha 2015). The revised criminal code further narrows the reach of the law by emphasizing the importance of the movement stage of the trafficking process, making it a necessary component of the offense (Hepburn and Simon 2013; Jiang 2015; US Department of State 2016). Under the 2005 anti-trafficking laws, punishment for sex-trafficking offenses ranges between three and eight years in prison and a fine (Cunha 2015).

Trafficking for forced labor and trafficking in children are addressed under other parts of Brazilian law. Labor trafficking is criminalized in Article 149 of the criminal code. Forced labor is categorized as *trabalho escravo*, defined as the act of reducing a person to slave-like conditions (Hepburn and Simon 2013; US Department of State 2016). Trafficking in children is criminalized under Articles 238, 239, and 244a of the Child and Adolescent Statute. Article 238 addresses the sale of children into slavery and/or human trafficking (Cuhna 2015). Selling a child under this article carries a modest penalty of between one and four years in prison and a fine. Article 239 criminalizes the trafficking of children outside of Brazil and can be penalized with up to eight years in prison if the perpetrator uses "violence, grave threat, or fraud" (Cunha 2015, 51). Finally, Article 244a, like Article 231, criminalizes forced prostitution of minors. Traffickers convicted under this article are subject to between four and ten years in prison and a fine (Cunha 2015).

In 2016 the Brazilian government passed a new comprehensive anti-trafficking law to update existing statutes and harmonize the definition of trafficking in Brazilian law with the definition found in the Palermo Protocol. Applying to all forms of human trafficking, Article 149a "criminalizes brokering, enticing, recruiting, transporting, transferring, buying, harboring, or receiving a person by grave threat, violence, coercion, fraud, or abuse for the purpose of organ removal, forced labor (any kind of servitude or conditions analogous to slavery), illegal adoption, or sexual exploitation" (US Department of State 2017, 32).

The new anti-trafficking law addresses several of the deficiencies of earlier legislation. This single law now addresses all forms of trafficking, and all aspects of the trafficking process are criminalized, removing the focus on prostitution and placing emphasis on the movement of victims as a required element of the crime. In addition to increasing the minimum penalty for human traffickers to between four and eight years in prison as well as a fine, Article 149a also calls for the creation of a database of convicted human traffickers (Umlaufi 2019). The law gives judges the option to reduce this sentence by one- or two-thirds for first-time offenders who act alone rather than as part of a criminal organization. Conversely, the penalties can also be increased by one-third to one-half under one of several special circumstances: "The crime was committed by a public official; the victim is a minor or disabled person; there is a personal or familial relationship with the victim; or if the victim was removed from the country" (US Department of State 2017, 19). In addition to introducing harsher punishments, the 2016 law expands the benefits for victims of human trafficking to include legal, social, and health resources (Walk Free Foundation 2018).

Unfortunately, some aspects of Brazil's earlier trafficking laws were not maintained in the 2016 legislation. The most obvious element lacking from Article 149a relates to the use of force, fraud, or coercion in the trafficking of children. Under international law these three elements are not required to characterize an instance of trafficking when the victim is a child; inducement of the victim is sufficient to meet the threshold for an offense of trafficking of children. However, Brazil's most recent anti-trafficking legislation does not exempt instances of child trafficking from demonstrating that force, fraud, or coercion were used, though such an exemption does still exist in Article 244a of the Child and Adolescent Statute (US Department of State 2017; Bureau of International Labor Affairs 2018). One consequence of these conflicting laws is that child victims are often referred to as child prostitutes rather than as victims of sex trafficking, which means they are frequently overlooked by both law enforcement and victim services (Dolby 2018). The lack of a comprehensive anti-trafficking law is further complicated by the fact that Article 149a does not supersede the preexisting laws that address trafficking offenses. Instead, the laws operate, at least for now, side by side. This introduces several competing definitions of trafficking as well as wide variation in the potential sentences traffickers face, with no clear indication of which options should be applied and under which circumstances.

Criminal Justice?

It is difficult to fully assess from a criminal justice perspective how well the 2016 comprehensive anti-trafficking law is operating. The law is still relatively new, so only three years of data are available for review (fig. 7.1) and in recent years the Brazilian government has been reporting less information to foreign governments and international actors (US Department of State 2019, 2018, 2017). However, the data does give some limited cause for optimism regarding implementation of Article 149a. In 2016 investigations and prosecutions of human trafficking took place under both the new and old versions of Brazil's anti-trafficking laws, with most of them being completed under the older laws (US Department of State 2017). Articles 231 and 231a of the 2005 anti-trafficking law were used in 103 investigations and 104 prosecutions. By contrast, 40 investigations and 34 prosecutions were conducted under Article 149 for instances of forced labor. Only 22 investigations and 3 prosecutions were conducted using Article 149a, which includes Brazil's new, expanded trafficking definition (US Department of State 2017). Beginning in 2017 investigations and prosecutions have been conducted under Articles 149 and 149a only (US Department of State 2019, 2018). Unfortunately, since Article 149a includes elements of both labor and sex trafficking, we are unable to determine how many of the cases tried under that part of the updated law relate to sex trafficking.

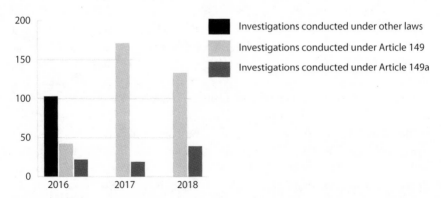

Figure 7.1. Trafficking Investigations Conducted in Brazil, 2016–18
Source: US Department of State Trafficking in Persons Reports 2017–19.

Despite this potential cause for optimism, there are several ongoing challenges to implementing the law efficiently or consistently. While the country has one of the highest rates of human trafficking investigations in South America, it also has far fewer prosecutions and convictions (UNODC 2016). In 2015 the US Department of State reported that in 87 percent of trafficking cases, criminal charges were eventually dropped. Even when traffickers are convicted, they find ways to avoid their sentences. In fact, many individuals convicted of trafficking do not serve out their full prison sentences; instead, most serve their time under house arrest, pay a fine, or do community service (US Department of State 2017, 2019). Others delay their sentences through the appeals process, sometimes indefinitely. These appeals can last years, allowing traffickers to avoid their sentences and continue operating their trafficking networks. In 2015 an estimated 102 million appeals cases were pending review in Brazil. The US Department of State reported that sentences were not enforced in eight of every ten trafficking convictions because the decisions were being appealed (US Department of State 2017).

As we noted earlier, the 2016 anti-trafficking law does not supersede the preexisting laws that addressed elements of human trafficking, which creates serious obstacles to identifying victims and coordinating the efforts of the numerous agencies engaged in Brazil's anti-trafficking efforts. For example, while the Brazilian Federal Police has a unit in every state in the country and participates in most trafficking investigations, the efficacy of these units varies considerably (US Department of State 2018). The confusion over who qualifies as a victim of human trafficking further complicates investigative efforts. For example, cases of missing children, including those who may be victims of human trafficking, are rarely handled with urgency by the police: "The law states authorities are required to search for missing children immediately, but many police officers tell families to come back after a child has been missing for 24 hours" (Teixeira 2019b, 22).

A final concern about Brazil's criminal justice approach to combating trafficking is the lack of accountability for public officials suspected of being involved in human trafficking. The story of former reserve colonel Pedro Chavarry Duarte is a telling example. Despite numerous investigations and arrests, he is still on staff with the State Police and living as a free man. In several consecutive Trafficking in Persons Reports the US Department of State has noted its ongoing concern with the lack of information from Brazil about the resolution of cases involving public officials (see US Department of State 2019, 2018). According to Thaddeus Blanchette, this is because there have been no resolution of cases. In addition to the Chavarry Duarte case, Blanchette also references the conviction of one politician's brother who, along with several others, ran a brothel with underage sex workers in 2014. These individuals were sentenced to more than thirty years in prison. However, since then the convictions have all been slowly and quietly overturned and the individuals involved have returned to political positions of power around Brazil.[3]

Victim-Centered?

The inconsistencies with which trafficking cases are pursued directly affects how victims are identified and treated in Brazil. The most glaring oversight in victim identification under existing anti-trafficking laws relates to child trafficking. Since the laws addressing the trafficking of children are handled under separate pieces of legislation—one of which requires coercion while the other, in line with international law, does not—the identification of children as trafficking victims is erratic at best. There are also remarkably few convictions for trafficking offenses involving minor victims, despite the moral panic–based narrative regarding the prevalence of child sex tourism in Brazil (Castilho, Evrard, and Charrier 2017; US Department of State 2013–19). Although this inconsistency was supposedly remedied in the 2016 anti-trafficking law (Article 149a), the focus on forced prostitution in Article 231 continues to be problematic because it brings anti-trafficking efforts (that is, victim identification) into conflict with legalized prostitution. Between the anti-prostitution moral entrepreneurs and genuine confusion over the differences between consensual sex work, human trafficking, and other forms of sexual exploitation among service providers, many victims go unidentified and unaided.

When victims are identified it appears that technically they are not treated as criminals. However, they are frequently not treated as victims either. For example, in 2016 the National Justice Council created a national forum tasked with increasing judicial efficiency in the handling of trafficking cases and ensuring that victims are not penalized for crimes committed as a result of being a victim of human trafficking for at least five years (US Department of State 2013, 17). There are several reasons to be cautious about this information regarding how victims in Brazil are treated, the most important of which relate to the inconsistency with which Brazilian agencies identify trafficking victims. The wording of the 2014 Trafficking in Persons Report is telling in this regard: "The government did not generally detain, fine, or otherwise penalize *identified* victims . . . for unlawful acts committed as a direct result of being trafficked" (US Department of State 2014, emphasis added, 16). Similarly, the State Department report two years later notes that although there have been no reports of victims being prosecuted, given Brazil's "weak identification system[,] it is likely some victims were detained and jailed" (US Department of State 2016, 21). This suspicion seems well-founded considering how women and girls are treated elsewhere in Brazil's judicial system. According to Human Rights Watch, numerous rulings from Brazil's Supreme Court led to a new law in 2018 that placed limits on pretrial detention for mothers and pregnant women. Unless the woman is accused of a violent crime or crimes against her dependents, all pregnant women and mothers of people with disabilities or children under the age of twelve are to be held under house arrest. However, courts have been very slow to implement this law, with some judges ignoring the new guidelines completely (Human Rights Watch 2019a).

Finally, the 2016 anti-trafficking law mandates that several protections be made available to victims of human trafficking, including temporary shelter; legal, social, and health assistance; and protection against retrafficking and other forms of exploitation (Langberg 2005; US Department of State 2017). At present, victim assistance is sorely lacking in Brazil and the assistance that does exist varies considerably by state, by the form of trafficking used, and by the characteristics of the victim involved. The access to services that victims have—and our ability to assess their access—is further hampered by Brazil's weak victim identification mechanisms (US Department of State 2019).

Although the 2016 anti-trafficking law should lead to greater coordination of victim-assistance efforts at the federal level, state governments currently oversee most of the available government-funded assistance for victims of trafficking. Sixteen of Brazil's twenty-seven states currently operate anti-trafficking offices and one responsibility of these offices is to refer identified victims to social assistance centers . In 2016 there were 2,521 of these social services centers in operation across Brazil, though most of these social assistance centers are underfunded and, as in Nigeria, must use their limited resources to assist several types of victims—including victims of domestic abuse, sexual abuse, and other forms of exploitation—in addition to victims of human trafficking. Less than half of the social service centers operating in 2016 were certified to assist victims of human trafficking. And while it should be noted that the percentage of social service centers certified to work with trafficking victims has nearly doubled from 20 percent in 2013 to almost 40 percent in 2016, the percentage has not increased since then (US Department of State 2019, 2017, 2014).

The specific assistance offered to trafficking victims through these government-run offices and social assistance centers is short term and depends on the type of trafficking the victim suffered. Victims of labor trafficking appear to receive the widest array of services, provided primarily by the Ministry of Labor, which are more likely to prevent retrafficking in the long term. The assistance available to these victims includes job training, counseling services, and three months of unemployment pay (US Department of State 2016). Victims of sex trafficking, by contrast, receive fewer services and the assistance that is available is aimed primarily at dealing with the victims' immediate needs. Two shelters in São Paulo State, for example, provide temporary assistance to women who are victims of sex trafficking. In one of these shelters, "female victims . . . and their children [can] receive health benefits, education, food, and housing for three to six months" (US Department of State 2017, 13). Unfortunately, these services are not available in all states and there are still no specialized or long-term shelters for sex-trafficking victims funded by the federal government (US Department of State 2019).

Specific groups of victims face further obstacles to receiving support. There are few resources dedicated to rescuing, sheltering, or rehabilitating child-trafficking victims, meaning they often go without assistance or are sent to centers unprepared to address their experiences with trafficking (Dolby 2018). For transsexual and transgender victims, law enforcement officers often act as hostile gatekeepers to services, seeing these individuals as "less exploitable" than cisgender women and thus not referring them to assistance services for trafficking victims (Fehrenbacher et al. 2020). Finally, while a foreign victim of sex trafficking identified in Brazil is technically entitled to a permanent visa, there is scant evidence that the Brazilian government actually issues such visas (US Department of State 2016–19).

The Role of Women

As with the other aspects of trafficking in Brazil, the role of women is complex, especially as it relates to combating human trafficking. The relative lack of women's voices in the federal government has clearly influenced the country's response to trafficking (fig. 7.2). The biggest change has been in women's

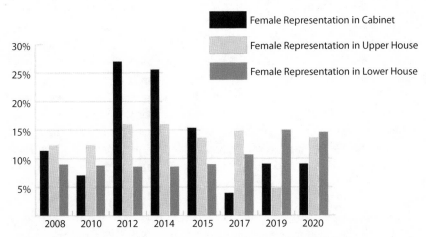

Figure 7.2. Female Representation in Government in Brazil, 2008–20

Source: UN Women and Inter-Parliamentary Union, "Women in Politics," assessed annually for all years in which the UN and the IPU produced a ranking between 2008 and 2020.

representation at the ministerial level, where the percentage of female members of Brazil's cabinet has more than halved since its peak at 27 percent in 2012. This change is clearly tied to the upheaval and corruption scandals of recent presidential administrations, which have consistently moved elected candidates to the right, a trend that culminated in Bolsonaro's presidential election in 2018. Although Bolsonaro's cabinet is certainly more diverse than that of his predecessor, Michel Temer, the presence of female voices is still quite limited and perhaps more symbolic than substantive (Zillman 2016; Fagundes 2020).

The lack of women's representation is even more stark when considering regional trends. According to the World Bank, the average share for female members of Parliament for the Latin American and Caribbean region was 26 percent in 2017 (Ceratti 2017). In 2019 the average share of female representation at the ministerial level among the twelve South American countries was more than 27 percent (UN Women and Inter-Parliamentary Union 2019). Brazil falls short of both (fig. 7.3). While women's representation in the Brazilian Parliament has remained relatively steady since 2014, there is a considerable discrepancy between political quota requirements—which require at least 30 percent of all party-backed candidates to be women—and the number of women who actually hold a seat in the legislature (Tavares 2017). It should be noted that there have been some important successes at the level of state governments, including the historic election of the first two transgender politicians—Erica Malunguinho and Erika Hilton—to São Paulo's state

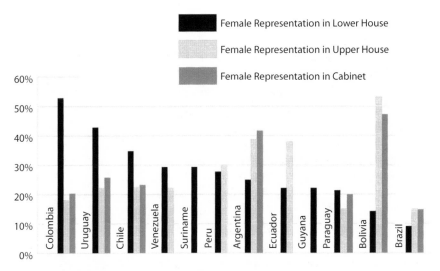

Figure 7.3. Female Representation in Governments of South America, 2019

Source: UN Women and Inter-Parliamentary Union, "Women in Politics," 2019.

legislature (Phillips 2018). Nevertheless, there is still clearly limited representation of women—and no representation of transsexual and transgender Brazilians—at the federal level.

Perhaps a more telling element of women's political representation in Brazil that should be considered is not just whether women's voices are heard, but *which* women's voices are heard. The dialogue about sex trafficking in Brazil is divided between two camps. On one side are conservative politicians, evangelical religious groups, and certain factions of feminists. One of the two women serving in Bolsonaro's cabinet provides an important example. As the minister of women, family, and human rights, Damara Alves has been quick to defend the administration's position on issues related to women's rights despite considerable cuts in the budgets for agencies promoting services for women, including to the Secretariat for Policies by Women (Muñoz 2020a). An evangelical pastor, Alves has also spent much of her career fighting to remove the already restrictive access to abortion that women have in Brazil, going so far as to request a criminal investigation into a magazine that published recommendations from the World Health Organization on safe abortions (Vivanco 2019a). By contrast, Marina Pereira Pires de Oliveira, the Ministry of Justice official who crafted the legislation for Brazil's new anti-trafficking laws in 2005, resigned in 2008. She felt the laws were being "abysmally abused" but was only able to critique the implementation of the anti-trafficking laws after leaving her post; she wrote several "fierce critiques about how these laws were being misused and [were] actually increasing the abuse of women" (Mitchell 2016, 329–30).

On the other side of the anti-sex-trafficking dialogue are traditional feminists, Brazil's sex workers and their advocates, and the LGBTQ+ community. This group holds a more nuanced view of sex trafficking, in line with international law, and advocates for more support and protection for Brazil's sex workers. In effect this side of Brazil's anti-sex-trafficking dialogue works directly with—or are members of—the country's most vulnerable populations, attempting to allow their voices to be heard directly rather than speaking for them. And they do so, frequently, at their own peril. Jean Wyllys, an openly gay politician who worked with the late Gabriela Leite—herself a famous former sex worker and feminist activist—to revise Brazil's 2005 anti-trafficking laws, gave up his seat in Brazil's Parliament in 2019 (Mitchell 2016). Wyllys cited persistent threats to his life and increased violence against the LGBTQ+ community following Bolsonaro's election as the reasons for vacating his seat; he now lives in exile (Vivanco 2019b). Marielle Franco, another politician, feminist, and human rights activist, was killed by former members of law enforcement in what many consider was a targeted execution (Amnesty International 2020). Franco, herself a Black bisexual who formerly resided in one of Brazil's favelas, fought for the rights of Afro-Brazilians, the LGBTQ+ community, and the country's urban poor, and was a strong critic of the corrupt forces within law enforcement agencies (Wilkinson 2019). According to these activists, the federal government, despite its rhetoric, is withdrawing from the fight against exploitation. The journalist and anti-human-trafficking activist Priscila Siqueira noticed this pullback by the government in 2017 under the Temer administration (Alessandra 2017). Siqueira argues that under the Bolsonaro administration things are only getting worse, pointing to the increase in violence against transsexual and transgender Brazilians as well as the broader LGBTQ+ community since Bolsonaro took office (Phillips and Cheibub 2020).

In terms of victim assistance, several NGOs in Brazil are dedicated to advocating for vulnerable Brazilians, including the Davida Collective and Rede Trans, which work to promote the rights and protections of Brazil's sex workers and transsexual and transgender citizens, respectively. However, likely due to the broader nature of discrimination and exploitation of these groups, neither organization is able to focus on assisting victims of human trafficking. There are, instead, several other NGOs focused on assisting victims of sex trafficking and addressing the gaps in governmental assistance. The Brazilian Association for the Defense of Women, Children, and Youth (ASBRAD), founded in 1997 in São Paulo State, works to defend the human rights of vulnerable populations in Brazil. The organization focuses primarily on assisting women and children, though it does also address issues related to transsexual individuals. Like many of the government-funded social assistance centers, ASBRAD assists victims of several types of violence and exploitation. However, one of the organization's four ongoing projects—Projeto Fronteiras—is dedicated to assisting women who are victims of human trafficking. Projeto Fronteiras operates in nine cities near Brazil's borders to help Brazilians returning from international trafficking. Members of ASBRAD meet these women on their reentry, work with the victims to ascertain what happened, and assess their needs. They then provide referrals to institutions for the women to receive health and psychological care (ASBRAD 2020).

ECPAT Brazil, part of ECPAT International, was founded in 1997 and is a coalition of organizations involved with combating four specific areas of exploitation of children: pornography, prostitution, trafficking in children, and child sex tourism. The various member organizations coordinate to address policies and raise awareness across Brazil and at the federal, state, and municipal levels. At the federal level, ECPAT Brazil was one of the organizations directly involved in developing, publicizing, and implementing the 2013 national plan to combat the sexual exploitation of children. It worked in the states of Rio de Janeiro and Pernambuco to provide literature and training for tourism professionals on identifying trafficking victims and preventing child sex tourism. ECPAT Brazil also provided training to educators working in favelas and shelters in the city of Rio de Janeiro to raise awareness of the ways children are sexually exploited and how to identify potential victims (ECPAT Brazil 2020).

Conclusion

The case of Brazil is an important one on which to conclude our analysis. It highlights the vulnerability of cisgender, transgender, and transexual women and girls to gendered economic policies and makes clear the negative impact that violence and discrimination have on the autonomy of women in society, in the workplace, and at home. In Brazil, women's representation in government also is not simply about numbers or about presence; it's about how women choose or are able to make use of their presence in the halls of power, especially in supporting the needs and rights of their fellow countrywomen. Perhaps just as important, an investigation of the popular narratives of human trafficking in this country force a questioning of assumptions of who trafficking victims are and how best to meet their needs. The agenda of the Bolsonaro administration is certainly cause for concern on all human rights fronts, but the continued and tireless work of activists, even at risk to their own lives, shows there may yet be hope.

Notes

1. Author interview of Thaddeus Blanchette, December 19, 2019.
2. Blanchette interview.
3. Blanchette interview.

Conclusion

The driving edge of our inquiry has been the role that the cultural and economic status of women and girls plays in the efficacy and effort of states to ameliorate human trafficking. The objectification, commodification, and structural and cultural oppression of women and girls enables states to ignore or minimally address human trafficking.

Human trafficking and sex slavery disproportionately affect women and girls and deprives them of their most basic human rights, including their dignity and autonomy. This criminal activity, which has such a devasting impact, particularly on women and girls, reaches all corners of the globe. Our case studies have illustrated some cross-national variation in who becomes a victim of trafficking for sex. We show that from Russia to Brazil and from Nigeria to India there are some consistent patterns associated with sex trafficking. While there are geographic variations based on idiosyncratic cultural and structural factors, there are basic patterns that occur around the world. If the international community and state governments are to responsibly and effectively combat human trafficking and protect the victims of sex trafficking, they must develop an understanding of the role that the diminution of women and girls has in exacerbating the problem. Our work takes a step in that direction by addressing two questions. First, who is likely to become a sex-trafficking victim, and what factors help to predict who may be more or less vulnerable to becoming a sex-trafficking victim? In countries that do not protect the basic human rights of women and girls, we find higher rates of sex trafficking. Second, whether national anti-trafficking legislation takes a criminal-justice approach, where prosecuting traffickers is prioritized or privileged over the protection of victims through a human rights–based approach. The more empowered women are in the economy, in the culture, and in the political sphere, both as legislators and NGO advocates, the more likely a commitment to a rights-based approach, rather than a criminal justice approach, is found.

Like much of the mainstream literature on human trafficking, we highlight the role of systemic power differentials and dominance and the degree of legislative empowerment for women when analyzing state approaches to sex trafficking. Our work employs a global quantitative analysis and five in-depth country assessments to explore the foundations of the gendered causes of sex trafficking. We build on Crawford (2017) to argue that understanding the nexus of gender and the systems of social, political, and economic inequity are critical for explaining the dynamics of sex trafficking. For example, where a dominant religious culture creates a rigid gendered hierarchy in which women and girls are inherently second-class citizens, sex trafficking is more prevalent and taken less seriously by the state. Our case studies also focus on the inter-section of gender with other systems of dominance, including politics, culture, and the economy. While we recognize that each of these systems varies from country to country, we find that many of the dynamics are prevalent across the cases. We began with a quantitative analysis, which demonstrated that where women's human rights are protected, a lower probability of sex trafficking occurs. We proceeded to engage in a foundational analysis to understand how the way women are treated in their societies defines how and when women and girls are victimized by sex trafficking. We then tested our approach against established explanations for trafficking.

Over 150 countries have passed national legislation to combat trafficking in response to the most recent global anti-trafficking treaty (UNODC 2016, 48). We considered whether these domestic laws actually ensure that the basic human rights of victims are protected. We show that even in countries that adopt a quasi-rights-centered rather than a criminal justice–centered approach to the protection of trafficking victims, victims' human rights are persistently and widely violated. Even where a trafficking victim's human rights exist on paper (in India, for example), the actual provision of victim services is lacking. We build on this emerging area of research to demonstrate that victims' human rights are more likely to be protected where women have equitable social, eco-nomic, and political rights and are engaged and empowered in the legislative process (Bartilow 2012; Cho, Dreyer, and Neumayer 2014; Schonhofer 2017; Wooditch 2012). We have also shown the role that women have played in the development of national and local anti-trafficking legal regimes, though we found through our analysis that women are frequently stymied in their efforts to introduce victim-centered legislation. We demonstrate across the cases that as levels of female legislative representation have declined, trafficking legis-lation and, more importantly, enforcement of existing legislation has moved away from focusing on victims' human rights. In Russia and Nigeria, which have startlingly low and declining rates of female legislative representation, we find virtually no protections for trafficking victims. And in Russia, foreign vic-tims are not only not supported as victims, they are likely to be deported. The women who run and work for nongovernmental organizations are key actors advocating for or opposing anti-trafficking legislation. The situation in India illustrates the importance of women as agenda-setters. These agenda-setting women operate in both internal and external ways to push the legislatures toward victim-centered and human rights–oriented approaches.

In Russia and Nigeria women also play considerable roles in operating trafficking syndicates, cutting against the stereotypical understandings about gender roles and sex trafficking, which tend to identify men as traffickers and women as helpless victims. Instead, Russian women are running trafficking operations and hiring male subordinates to recruit unwitting victims under the ruse of romantic relationships. In Europe, Nigerian trafficking rings are often run by former female trafficking victims who use their understanding of the victims' circumstances and sense of obligation to contribute to the family to keep them enslaved. Similarly, in Thailand traffickers deploy victims to their villages to share their "success" as a means for recruiting new victims. Clearly women are important actors in the trafficking process, not merely victims duped by men.

Like many others, we have operationalized human trafficking as a process. That process usually involves fraud and deception in contracts for employment. Promises of legitimate work for fair or even enhanced pay are promised to women and girls in desperate economic situations. Only after they arrive at their destination, either within their own country or somewhere abroad, do they learn they have signed on to become slaves. The strategies traffickers use to control their victims and ensure cooperation vary and may include things like locking victims in a hotel or apartment, threatening their families, holding their immigration papers, or threatening to turn them over to the police for charges arising out of immigration violations or prostitution. Even in instances where the victims are not initially forced into sex work, victims find they are stuck with huge debts to the traffickers arising out of their transport and the cost of living. In other cases the victims' families will take out a loan with a very high interest rate that can only realistically be paid back through the forced labor of the woman or girl who is being trafficked. These last two situations entail victims as not only victims of sex trafficking but also debt bondage. These large and growing debts can create an overwhelming economic and psychological burden. The victims feel they must continue to work because of cultural expectations or their fear of reprisals if they do not comply with the demands of the traffickers. In this regard there is very little distinction between sex trafficking and trafficking for labor. The victims in both scenarios are deceived, recruited, transported, relieved of their identity documents, and forced to work while receiving little or no pay and enormous and growing debts that cannot be paid off.

Thematic Findings

Using a comparative case methodology allows us to tease out dominant themes that run through our analysis. Central to our findings is that societies that relegate the status and rights of women and girls create sex-trafficking victims, undoubtably the most important contribution of this volume. But other themes that have emerged from this analysis are worthy of emphasis: the dangers of childhood, the acute vulnerabilities experienced by the Queer and trans community, and the role of public corruption in the maintenance of sex trafficking and sex slavery.

Women's Unequal Status: A Core Factor

We argue that where women are culturally devalued, politically powerless, and economically disadvantaged, human trafficking of women and girls flourishes. This disparate societal treatment creates substantial barriers to improvement for women and girls at the intersection of those disparities. That is, any country that deprives women of basic economic rights reveals itself as a culture that diminishes the value of women. In India, Dalit women and girls find themselves mercilessly trafficked. The overall deprivation of women's economic rights intersects with their lower caste status and abject poverty, making them especially vulnerable to sex traffickers. The Dalits are at a distinct disadvantage because, although laws exist on paper to protect their human rights, there simply is no actual enforcement of these protections.

Like India, weak protections for women and girls in Thailand, driven by their diminished societal value, leads to widespread exploitation. Thailand provides weaker formal protections for the economic and political rights of women than does India and also fails to enforce the few weak protections that do exist. Moreover, laws ostensibly designed to protect religious and personal freedom completely undermine the formal protections that do exist. For the Rohingyas, all of the factors that lessen the rights of women and girls intersect for the worst possible outcome. The Rohingyas are economically and politically powerless and are culturally dismissed as deserving of no rights. It is hardly surprising, then, that virtually no effort is made by national, state, or local governments to assist them.

In Russia the absence of economic rights for women and girls most directly impacts sex-trafficking victims from nearby Ukraine and Moldova and more recently Nigeria. The absence of women's economic rights combined with culturally accepted and politically motivated xenophobia means the groups most likely to be trafficked are left to fend for themselves because of Russia's aversion to supporting sex-trafficking victims.

In Nigeria the absence of protections for women's economic rights and a generally weak and porous rule of law make women more vulnerable to sex trafficking. While some groups of women are certainly more vulnerable than others based on their economic or ethnic status, on some level *all* women in Nigeria are vulnerable to being ensnared in sex trafficking. The absence of substantial economic rights limits the ability of women to overcome other pressures that lead to sex trafficking in Nigeria.

Finally, in Brazil the groups particularly vulnerable to sex trafficking—women, transsexuals and transgender women, and children—all suffer from cultural, economic, and political devaluation. Like in other countries in Latin America, Brazilian culture devalues women and femininity as a result of the history of machismo enforced by the political and cultural position of conservative religiosity. The religion-based emphasis on patriarchy and male dominance intertwines with the cultural dictate that women should be submissive, saintly, and mostly concerned with family and the home. The machismo culture promotes the sexual objectification of women and girls and celebrates violence against both cisgender and transgender women and children. These cultural pathologies are ubiquitous across poor nonwhite communities, both in rural areas and in the urban favelas. These cultural influences lead to these groups being made more vulnerable by racialization, heteronormative patriarchy, and sexualization, as well as general acceptance of violence against them. Combine this economic, social, and political vulnerability with the absence of any effort to protect them by the state, and it is clear the situation is grim with little reason for optimism.

The Dangers of Childhood

One of the more troubling themes emerging from this analysis is the dangers of childhood as a sex-trafficking risk factor. The poor, the orphaned, or children from particular religious communities experience heightened vulnerabilities for becoming sex-trafficking victims. Their pathways to victimization are culturally distinct—in Nigeria, Boko Haram and state security services both abduct girls and use them as domestic servants, child soldiers, and sex slaves. In some tragic instances girls that are used as sex slaves are also trained as soldiers and forced to fight (Amnesty International 2015). Armed conflict between the state and Boko Haram elevates the dangers of childhood, making children more vulnerable to exploitation across a variety of sectors, including sex slavery. In Russia, orphanages can be recruitment sites for traffickers to lure orphaned girls away with the promise of "field trips." Our analysis of bride-trafficking routes between eastern and northern India shows that child sex trafficking occurs regularly under the guise of marriage. For Dalit women and girls the dangers of bride trafficking are especially acute. Dalit women and girls possess such low social status that they are a wife only in name, and better resemble domestic servants and property or sex slaves in practice.

Though prostitution is legal in both Brazil and Thailand, we identify distinct modes of child sex slavery between these two cases that warrant further discussion. Our study of Brazil reveals that, contrary to received wisdom, children are not primarily trafficked for sex in the service of foreign tourists. Rather, they are more likely to be exploited near construction and mining sites by Brazilian workers. In Thailand, Theravada Buddhist philosophy and powerful notions of filial piety combine to teach women and children that they owe a profound debt to their families. In the service of these debts, families may sell daughters or children may feel pressured to engage in sex work to contribute to the family finances. Montgomery's pioneering (2008) study shows that Thai children between the ages of six and fourteen opted into sex work with the full support and knowledge of their parents. Though the paths into sex slavery look distinct across all the cases, they uniformly show that childhood can be a risk factor for sex trafficking.

Queer/Trans Vulnerabilities

In Thailand and Brazil we are especially interested in the challenges facing trans women who are trafficked and intertwined in sex work. Like others who are trafficked, the challenges faced by this cluster of people are enhanced with increased levels of poverty and increased levels of inequality. However, the additional layer of cultural and legal hostility faced by the trans community adds another layer of oppression to manage. These vulnerabilities are particularly acute for the LGBTQ+ communities in Brazil, whose advocates are being targeted for execution by former members of law enforcement (Amnesty International 2020). Even in victim-centered support structures, members of the trans community find themselves unwelcome, ignored, and left to fend for themselves. In prosecutorial support structures they are sent to inappropriate gender-identity incarceration facilities and treated as poorly or worse than any other criminal in the system. Our intersectional analysis of the trans community leads to the inescapable conclusion that they are the least likely to be protected by the state, regardless of which approach to human trafficking the regime chooses.

In Russia we find that both feminists and members of the LGBTQ+ community have been targeted by the Russian state, using hypermasculinity and heteronormativity to consolidate state power. These policies are important for understanding the orientation of national policies to combat sex trafficking because feminists, often with foreign funding, have successfully lobbied and pressured the Russian state to advance progressive victim-centered policies.

Once Putin and the Kremlin initiated the war on feminists and the LGBTQ+ community, those victim-centered policies were replaced by a purely criminal justice–oriented approach. At the time of writing, artists and activists from these communities are pushing back against the conservative authoritarian tide in Russia, but the war appears far from over, leaving trafficking victims to persist without basic support.

Corruption

Corruption plays a persistent and ubiquitous role as a barrier to the amelioration of human trafficking. The Russian mafiyas are both broadly engaged in the business of human trafficking and closely aligned with the autocratic government. It is no stretch to say that the Russian syndicates would be able to exercise a veto over any local or national effort to legally reign in human trafficking. Additionally, the outsized role of the Russian criminal networks in Russian society generally means that there is no social or political cost to be paid by politicians or law enforcement who cozy up to criminal elements. The tolerance of corruption inevitably leads to the tolerance of the corrupting criminal enterprise, which in this case is human trafficking.

In Brazil the police are rightly viewed as being directly and indirectly involved in human trafficking. Not only do the individuals involved in law enforcement tolerate the cluster of crimes endemic to human trafficking; they are often actually traffickers themselves. Law enforcement is primarily seen as an agent of the state and defender of the inequitable and brutal status quo, meaning victims of human trafficking do not consider law enforcement as a source of assistance. When victims perceive that law enforcement moves in concert with the criminal enterprise that victimized them, there is little expectation that laws about human trafficking will be effective. Corruption undermines the ability of either the Russian or the Brazilian system to meaningfully respond to human trafficking.

In Thailand and Nigeria members of the military and police are engaged in human trafficking both locally and nationally. In both places porous borders and economic instability intersect with class and ethnic cleavages, leading to a complete disregard and lack of concern—both politically and legally—for an entire strata of people by both the local and national authorities.

Country-Specific Findings

In chapter 1 we developed an analytical approach to sex trafficking, arguing that in order to account for all of the myriad causes of sex trafficking, we must interrogate the experiences of women and girls. We used women's economic rights as a rough indicator to determine whether women and girls possess equal rights in the workplace and argue that the international community cannot expect a comprehensive and effective human-trafficking amelioration regime so long as women are culturally and politically second-class citizens.

In chapter 2 we presented current data to reveal some global patterns and constants about human trafficking. Our quantitative analysis shows that wherever women's economic rights are not protected, women are at greater risk of becoming victims of sex trafficking. The analysis also shows that any understanding of the drivers of human trafficking is intertwined with understanding the cultural, economic, and political standing of women. Recall that the analysis shows a very strong relationship between GDP per capita and the likelihood a country is a source of human trafficking.

The inverse relationship between economic well-being and security from human trafficking is the foundation of our approach for the remaining balance of the work. We argue that where women have greater cultural, economic, and political status, efforts toward combating human trafficking are more robust and effective. Our use of economic rights as a surrogate for cultural rights is driven by the idea that economic rights are formal and measurable and reflect cultural values. We use political power as a measure to look beyond simple political rights (like voting) to ascertain the actual ability to introduce, obtain, and enforce policy. This large N assessment and overview leads into a nuanced and close evaluation of the specific country cases.

In chapter 3 we demonstrated the ways in which the culture of India, particularly the rigid caste system, intersects with systems of gender dominance to make Dalit women and girls especially vulnerable to sex traffickers. We review the weak enforcement structure in India despite the relatively strong anti-trafficking legislation that is ignored in practice. While the letter of the law ostensibly protects the economic rights of women and vulnerable ethnic minority groups, the lack of enforcement of such laws seriously restricts and limits the economic opportunities available to these groups. Bride traffickers, sex traffickers, and cartels that run brothel-based slavery are more likely to target women and girls in scheduled castes and tribes. Further, female underrepresentation in politics has worsened these vulnerabilities and contributed to a national approach to trafficking in India that has failed at both punishing traffickers and protecting victims. More recently, female-led NGOs and female politicians have pushed for more victim-centered anti-trafficking legislation in India, but there is a very long road ahead before the legal regime can be considered effective.

It is important to note here that in spite of these challenges, India's approach to victim support emerged as the most victim-centered regime among all of our cases. Despite the large size of the victim population and the resources needed to provide for them, the Indian government does better at partnering with NGOs to provide services and support to victims than the others explored in this work. This modest victim-centered orientation at the national level may be due, at least in part, to the role of women, particularly women working at the helm of NGOs that support victims.

In chapter 4 we examined sex-trafficking patterns in Thailand, which is often thought of as the "hub" of sex tourism and trafficking in the region, if not the world. We demonstrate that Buddhist ideology and long-accepted governmental discrimination against the ethnic Hill Tribe people lead them to become especially vulnerable to sex trafficking. Our assessment of Thailand supports the big picture argument of this work: when the economic rights of women and girls are not protected or laws that provide equitable rights are not enforced, vulnerable groups face a higher probability of being ensnared in trafficking. Our assessment of the identities of victims of trafficking in Thailand makes clear that the intersection of religion, citizenship status, and gender leads some groups to be much more likely to be trafficked than others. Those lacking citizenship, the stateless, are particularly vulnerable to sex trafficking. The ethnic Hill Tribe minorities, the Rohingyas, and the children of economic migrants generally lack citizenship and become trafficked at higher rates than others.

The 2014 coup in Thailand that resulted in the military junta taking charge of the country also seriously reduced the political space available for and efficacy of civil society organizations, including those concerned with sex trafficking. Critically, these organizations need a great deal of anonymity to function because they pose an inherent threat to criminal syndicates and a government that tolerates them. Recall that one of the organizations we interviewed about their work were willing to speak to us only on the condition of complete anonymity out of fear of government reprisal. Since the coup, the dangers associated with the work done by NGOs has only increased. The military junta has embraced a criminal-justice approach to trafficking, as well as other problems, and has closed the gap between arrests, prosecutions, and convictions of traffickers. Also recall that from 2016 through 2018, Thailand convicted between 200 and 400 traffickers annually; prior to then, from 2002 through 2012, the number never exceeded five convictions per year. While this suggests an emphasis on and modest success of the criminal-justice approach to fighting trafficking, in policy the victims continue to be left behind. Moreover, no effort has been taken to address the factors that lead to human trafficking, and even this level of increase in prosecutions and convictions equates to only a small impact on the problem, given the ubiquitous nature of trafficking of women and girls in Thailand.

In other cases in our research we showed that women in politically powerful positions, such as legislators and cabinet ministers, are integral in advocating and establishing victim-centered legislation. Thailand has such a low rate of female representation it makes it difficult to find an impact from the women in these roles. Although we encountered mostly female leaders and workers doing the important work of NGOs in supporting victims, there are virtually no female legislators working to advance the interests of victims.

In chapter 5 we turned to sex trafficking in Russia to consider how transitional economies create conditions that enable trafficking. The collapse of the Soviet welfare state and the introduction of a wildly unregulated market system has left women and girls acutely vulnerable to the rapidly expanding sex-trafficking industry. The sex-trafficking patterns, the establishment and enforcement of laws, and the mechanisms for support of victims in Russia serve as a cautionary tale for other economies in transition. Initial enthusiasm over the early efforts of civil society actors and the hope that Russia would follow the pattern often seen in more-democratic societies—in particular, that NGOs actively participate in the construction and passage of comprehensive anti-trafficking legislation—was short-lived. The momentum toward effective and comprehensive legislation ended in 2003 when Putin implemented a weak and ineffective version of anti-trafficking legislation. Since then, a complete lack of government support for trafficking victims has resulted in closed shelters and the elimination of other social-support structures for victims and the almost complete absence of convictions of traffickers. Further, the hostile bureaucratic designation of NGOs as foreign agents and the accompanying governmental interference in their operations and restrictions on funding that went with that designation essentially have led to complete destruction of the presence of an NGO safety net for human-trafficking victims. The tragic result of these policy decisions is that victims of sex trafficking in Russia remain invisible, ignored, and unsupported in a meaningful way. Russia's approach not only will not reduce the problem but will also allow it to flourish and expand.

In chapter 6 we reviewed the situation in Nigeria to show that economically distressed rural women and girls, as well as those living in refugee camps (including camps for the internally displaced) are especially vulnerable to sex traffickers. Trafficking in Nigeria aligns with both of our core arguments: a weak rule of law combined with the patriarchal culture and systematic economic inequality severely restrict the economic opportunities and legal protections available to women and girls. Violence and corruption have taken a toll on the cultural and familial structures in place across Nigeria and have driven young Nigerians out of their homes and even out of the country in search of a better, safer, and more successful life. The steady and persistent decrease in women in political roles in Nigeria has diminished the voice women have in planning and implementing policy to combat human trafficking. Even more important, the reduced political clout of women has also reduced their capacity to assist victims of sex trafficking.

The case of Brazil, reviewed in chapter 7, underscores and introduces an additional vulnerability of gender identity to the familiar themes of cultural and political misogyny, racial disparities, and gendered economic policies that arise from those two aspects of society. Brazil demonstrates the negative impact that violence, a discriminatory culture, and political and economic powerlessness have on the autonomy of women in society, in the workplace, and at home. We also demonstrate that mere female representation in government is an inadequate measure if political elites do not choose to act on behalf of the most vulnerable women in society. The accepted narratives about human trafficking in Brazil call into question some assumptions in the scholarly and international NGO community about the identity and needs of trafficking victims. While the Bolsonaro administration has dismantled many of the rights-protection structures in Brazil, for trafficking and many other dimensions there is certainly some cause for optimism because of the continued and tireless, if risky, work of NGO activists.

We considered cases ranging from democratic India to autocratic Russia, expecting to find a more serious and efficacious effort to combat human trafficking and protect its victims where representative governance is stronger. Instead, we were surprised to find little difference across the cases. Indeed, the consistency of the pathologies of human trafficking is one of the main lessons from our research. Moreover, while the extent to which women and girls are culturally, politically, and economically second-tier members of society may vary across the cases, in no case was it true that women and girls enjoyed equitable rights or standing before the law with males. Accordingly, it is perhaps an expected outcome to see that violent and abusive criminal activity that overwhelmingly targets women and girls is not only tolerated, but in some instances assisted by the governing institutions.

Table 8.1 illustrates our cross-case findings on the first question related to the causes of trafficking. In short, poor countries with high rates of crime and corruption and low respect for the rule of law and protections for the economic rights of women are prime sources for sex-trafficking victims. Our case studies reveal that the forms of trafficking may be distinct—from bride trafficking in India to brothel-based trafficking in Thailand to debt bondage in Nigeria—but the ultimate outcome linking women's economic vulnerabilities to trafficking are startingly consistent. These countries are all major regional source countries for sex-trafficking victims.

When considered in aggregate, our cases present a bleak picture. Generally speaking, NGOs are the primary avenue of amelioration of human trafficking because the governments we examined seldom fully engage in combating human trafficking. The common underlying predicate among all the cases is the absence of economic, social, and political equality for women and girls. Variations in approach make little difference in actual outcomes.

Table 8.1. Causes of Sex Trafficking Compared

	India	Thailand	Russia	Nigeria	Brazil
Poverty	High	High	Moderate	High	High
Crime	Moderate/Low	Moderate	Moderate	Moderate/High	Moderate/High
Corruption	Moderate	High	High	High	High
Respect for the Rule of Law	Moderate	Moderate	Low	Low	Low
Socio-Political Equality for Women	Low	Low	Low	Low	Low
Economic Equality for Women	Low	Low	Low	Low	Low

Assessments of intensity of the causes of human trafficking by country

Addressing the second question on the orientation of national policy, table 8.2 demonstrates that the status of women and girls in any given society determines the level of commitment to combating human trafficking. Again, the variety of approaches taken in the countries does not meaningfully alter the continuum of problems faced by victims of human trafficking. As vulnerabilities intersect by class, race, age, sex, religion, and gender expression—that is, by every aspect of identity that might make a person more vulnerable to being trafficked—the victim of human trafficking faces less support from the state and more barriers to exit from a dire situation.

Critically, while the primary topic of this work is human trafficking, the importance of our analysis goes beyond that particular dimension to the wide deprivation of human rights faced by women and girls around the world. Until gender equity along all three dimensions of culture, politics, and economics becomes a priority for states, NGOs, and the international community, human rights deprivations will continue. However, there may be ways to improve the lot of anyone vulnerable to being trafficked even as we strive to bring equality to the forefront of the debate and make meaningful progress for women and girls.

Table 8.2. Orientation of National Anti-Trafficking Policy/Government Response

	India	Thailand	Russia	Nigeria	Brazil
Human Trafficking Prosecution & Police	High	High	Moderate	Low	High
Human Trafficking Victim Centered	Moderate	Low	Low	Low	Moderate
Human Trafficking Amelioration Successful	Low	Low	Low	Low	Low

Assessments of the range of governmental anti-trafficking responses

Looking Forward

While our work paints a bleak picture of the current status of national anti-trafficking regimes, we offer two policy recommendations drawn from our findings: the need to center equal rights for women at the national level and the noncriminalization of trafficking victims.

There are many camps of activists and scholars committed to a variety of sometimes conflicting policies designed to ameliorate human trafficking. For example, some argue that legalizing sex work is the answer, while others insist that greater levels of policing are required. Some urge a greater allocation of resources from the international community to vulnerable populations and others contend that the adoption of new international protocols must be a first step. We conclude that the various proposals that address only one dimension of the problem are destined to fail. Each, no matter how worthy or compelling, targets a narrow swath of issues that are but symptoms of the underlying pathologies that allow human trafficking to flourish. So long as women are not social, civil, and economic equals, they will continue to be victimized through trafficking. We cannot reasonably expect the countries that consider women to be second-class citizens, or worse, to effectively protect them. Thus, centering the equality of women and girls in national policy will go a long way toward advancing the interests of trafficking victims.

Additionally, at least since the passage of the Palermo Protocol, one of the critical debates has been whether states should emphasize combating human trafficking through a prosecutorial regime or an approach that is centered on victim assistance. The concept of taking victims' rights seriously or establishing a victim-relief structure has not taken hold. Our work here suggests that the underlying diminution of women in society means both approaches result in poor policy outcomes that range from outright failure to little more than small victories at the margin.

An emerging debate may create a pathway for dramatically improving the circumstances of those ensnared in human trafficking apart from improvements in the social, cultural, and political status of women and girls. In short, perhaps the time has come for an international embrace of the principle of noncriminalization, so that any victim of human trafficking is not classified as a criminal nor guilty of any crime or offense committed while ensnared in trafficking or which in some way arose out of their status of being trafficked (see, e.g., Schloenhardt and Markey-Towler 2016). The point is to distinguish between the crimes against victims and the crimes committed by victims unrelated to being trafficked. This approach could remove one of the more significant dimensions of coercion and control currently available to traffickers: the threat that local authorities will arrest and punish the victims of trafficking because of a myriad of offenses, from prostitution to violations of immigration laws to bribery and racketeering.

There is no clear answer in the debate about how a noncriminalization regime could be implemented. Undoubtedly there would be local variations in practice and likely some limits to the immunity from prosecution enjoyed by the victim class. So, while a complete review of how a noncriminalization approach might work is beyond the scope of this project, we embrace this policy concept as an avenue for consideration and implementation. Though possibly contentious, some effort at the implementation of noncriminalization should be embraced because the status quo has failed to make significant improvements for victims of human trafficking around the world.

References

AAWW (Apne Aap World Wide). 2018. Last accessed May 2018. http://apneaap.org/about-us/the-story-of-apne-aap/.

Abbamonte, Jonathan. 2019. "Sex-Selective Abortion in India: Estimates on the Occurrence of Sex-Selective Abortion in India and Some Possible Solutions to Eliminate the Practice." Population Research Institute. https://www.pop.org/sex-selective-abortion-in-india.

Abdelgalil, Sara, R. G. Gurgel, Sally Theobald, and L. E. Cuevas. 2004. "Household and Family Characteristics of Street Children in Aracaju, Brazil." *Archives of Disease in Childhood* 89, no. 9: 817–20.

Abubakar, Ali Abare. 2018. "Child Labor Continues to be a Pressing Problem in Nigeria; Girls Are Especially at Risk." *The World*, July 30, 2018, http://www.pri.org/stories/2018-07-30/child-labor-continues-be-pressing-problem-nigeria-girls-are-especially-risk.

Adams, Cherish. 2011. "Retrafficked Victims: How a Human Rights Approach Can Stop the Cycle of Re-Victimization of Sex Trafficking Victims." *George Washington International Law Review* 43, no. 1: 201–34.

Adepoju, Aderanti. 2005. "Review of Research and Data on Human Trafficking in Sub-Saharan Africa." *International Migration* 43, no. 1–2: 75–98.

Adepoju, Aderanti, Alistair Boulton, and Mariah Levin. 2010. "Promoting Integration through Mobility: Free Movement under ECOWAS." *Refugee Survey Quarterly* 29, no. 3: 120–44. doi: https://doi.org/10.1093/rsq/hdq032.

Aghatise, Esohe. 2002. "Trafficking for Prostitution in Italy: Concept Paper." Expert Group Meeting on Trafficking in Women and Girls, Glen Cove, New York. www.un.org/womenwatch/daw/egm/trafficking2002/reports/EP-Aghatise.PDF.

Akee, Randall, Arnab Basu, Nancy Chau, and Melanie Khamis. 2010. "Ethnic Fragmentation, Conflict, Displaced Persons and Human Trafficking: An Empirical Analysis." *Migration and Culture* 8: 691–716. Bingley: Emerald Group.

Akee, Randall, Arjun Bedi, Arnab Basu, and Nancy Chau. 2014. "Transnational Trafficking, Law Enforcement and Victim Protection: A Middleman's Perspective." *Journal of Law and Economics* 57, no. 2: 349–86.

Aldous, Susan, and Pornchai Sereemongkonpol. 2008. *Ladyboys: The Secret World of Thailand's Third Gender*. Boulder, CO: Maverick.

Alessandra, Karla. 2017. "Vulnerabilidade Social Favorece Aliciamento de Escarvos para trabalho e Sexo, Concordam Debatedores." *Câmara dos Deputados*, August 31, 2017, camara.leg.br/noticias/521855-vulnerabilidade-social-favorece-aliciamento-de-escarvos-para-travalho-e-sexo-concordam-debatedores/.

Alvarez, Maria Beatriz, and Edward J. Alessi. 2012. "Human Trafficking Is More Than Sex Trafficking and Prostitution: Implications for Social Work." *Affilia* 27, no. 2: 142–52.

Amar, Pau. 2009. "Operation Princess in Rio de Janeiro: Policing 'Sex Trafficking,'" Strengthening Worker Citizenship, and the Urban Geopolitics of Security in Brazil." *Security Dialogue* 40, no. 4–5: 513–41.

Amnesty International. 2004. "Myanmar: The Rohingya Minority: Fundamental Rights Denied." May 18, 2004. http://www.amnesty.org/en/library/info/ASA16/005/2004.

———. 2015. "Nigeria: Abducted Women and Girls Forced to Join Boko Haram Attacks." April 14, 2015. https://www.amnesty.org/en/latest/news/2015/04/nigeria-abducted -women-and-girls-forced-to-join-boko-haram-attacks/.

———. 2019. "DRC: ICC Conviction of Ntaganda Provides Long Awaited Justice for Victims of Grotesque Crimes." July 8, 2019. https://www.amnesty.org/en/latest /news/2019/07/drc-icc-conviction-of-ntaganda-provides-long-awaited-justice-for -victims-of-grotesque-crimes/.

———. 2020. "Brazil: Two Years After Killing of Marielle Franco, Rio de Janeiro Authorities Must Solve Unanswered Questions." March 14, 2020. https://www.amnesty.org /en/latest/news/2020/03/brazil-two-years-after-killing-of-marielle-franco/.

Anderson, Bridget. 2016. "Worker, Helper, Auntie, Maid?: Working Conditions and Attitudes Experienced by Migrant Domestic Workers in Thailand and Malaysia." International Labor Organization Regional Office for Asia and the Pacific. https:// www.ilo.org/asia/publications/WCMS_537808/lang-en/index.htm.

Andrees, Beale, Alix Nasrik, and Peter Swiniarski. 2015. "Regulating Labour Recruitment to Prevent Human Trafficking and to Foster Fair Migration: Model, Challenges, and Opportunities." International Labour Organization. https://www.ilo.org /global/publications/working-papers/WCMS_377813/lang—en/index.htm.

Angel Coalition. 2009. "Angel Coalition Report: Moscow." http://www.miramed.org/pdf /AngelCoalition2009.pdf.

Anselmo, Mário, and Guilherme Fernandes. 2015. "An Overview of International Human Trafficking in Brazil." In *The Illegal Business of Human Trafficking*, edited by Maria João Guia, 61–70. New York: Spring International.

Anti-Slavery International. 2009. "Bonded Labour." Accessed May 2016. http://www .antislavery.org/includes/documents/cm_docs/2009/b/1_bonded_labour.pdf.

Anyabuike, Teresa. 2020. "In Edo State, Advocates Aim to Engage the People in Anti-Trafficking Fight." *Global Sisters Report*, April 28, 2020. https://globalsistersreport .org/news/trafficking/column/edo-state-advocates-aim-engage-people-anti -trafficking-fight.

Apodaca, Clair 1998. "Measuring Women's Economic and Social Rights Achievement." *Human Rights Quarterly* 20, no. 1: 139–72.

Appleton, Naomi. 2011. "In the Footsteps of the Buddha?: Women and the Bodhisatta Path in Theravada Buddhism." *Journal of Feminist Studies in Religion* 27, no. 1: 33–51.

Arutunyan, Anna. 2010. "Russian Father Wins Sex Trafficking Case." *Moscow Times*, January 2, 2010.

ASBRAD (Associação Brasileira de Defesa da Mulher da Infância e da Juventude). 2020. "Projeto Fronteiras." http://www.asbrad.org.br/projetos/projeto-fronteiras/.

Associated Press. 2014. "Thailand: 2 Journalists Face Charges." *New York Times*, April 17, 2014. https://nyti.ms/1hRHxkj.

———. 2016. "Brazilian Cops Rescue 8 Kids from Beach Sex-Trafficking Ring." *Daily News*, July 11, 2016. nydailynews.com/news/crime/brazilian-cops-rescue-8-kids -beach-trafficking-ring-article-1.2706992.

Avdeyeva, O. A. 2012. "Does Reputation Matter for States' Compliance with International Treaties?: States' Enforcement of Anti-Trafficking Norms." *International Journal of Human Rights* 16, no. 2: 289–320.

Avdeyeva, Olga A., Dekabrina M. Vinokurova, and Alexandr A. Kugaevsky. 2017. "Gender and Local Executive Office in Regional Russia: The Party of Power as a Vehicle for Women's Empowerment?" *Post-Soviet Affairs* 33, no. 6: 431–51. https://doi.org/10.1080/1060586X.2017.1365806.

Azzoni, Carlos R. 2014. "Regional Disparities in Brazil: Recent Trends and Future Possibilities." Paper presented at the 2014 Regional Studies Association Global Conference. http://www.regionalstudies.org/uploads/Fortaleza_RSA_2014.pdf.

Bailey, Stanley R., and Edward E. Telles. 2014. "From Ambiguity to Affirmation: Challenging Census Race Categories in Brazil." Unpublished manuscript. http://www.sscnet.ucla.edu/soc/faculty/telles/Paper_AffirmationandAmbiguity.pdf.

Baker, Carrie. 2013. "Moving Beyond 'Slaves, Sinners, and Saviors': An Intersectional Feminist Analysis of US Sex-Trafficking Discourses, Law and Policy." *Journal of Feminist Scholarship* 4 (Spring): 1–23.

Baker, James, Kelley Clancy, and Benjamin Clancy. 2019. "Putin as a Gay Icon?: Memes as a Tactic in Russian LGBTQ+ Activism." In *LGBTQ+ Activism in Central and Eastern Europe: Resistance, Representation and Identity*, edited by Radzhana Buyantueva and Maryna Shevtsova, 209–33. Switzerland: Palgrave Macmillan.

Bales, Kevin. 2004. *Disposable People: New Slavery in the Global Economy*. 2nd ed. Berkeley: University of California Press.

———. 2005. *Understanding Global Slavery*. Berkeley: University of California Press.

———. 2007. "What Predicts Human Trafficking?" *International Journal of Applied Criminal Justice* 31, no. 2: 269–79.

Bales, Kevin, and Ron Soodalter. 2009. *The Slave Next Door: Human Trafficking and Slavery in America Today*. Berkeley: University of California Press.

Bangkok Post. 2016a. "Thai Women in Bahrain Sex Racket." May 14, 2016. http://www.bangkokpost.com/news/general/972125/thai-women-in-bahrain-sex-racket.

———. 2016b. "Shrimp Slaves Face Long Wait for Justice." July 2, 2016. https://www.bangkokpost.com/thailand/general/1025733/shrimp-slaves-wait-for-justice.

———. 2017a. "Charges Officially Dropped in 'Torture' Book Case." November 2, 2017. https://www.bangkokpost.com/thailand/general/1352679/charges-officially-dropped-in-torture-book-case.

———. 2017b. "Evil Traffickers Must Face Justice." May 7, 2017. https://www.bangkokpost.com/opinion/opinion/1245130/evil-traffickers-must-face-justice.

———. 2019. "Protecting ASEAN's Most Vulnerable." November 2, 2019. https://www.bangkokpost.com/thailand/general/1785419/protecting-aseans-most-vulnerable.

Barker, Gary, and Irene Loewenstein. 1997. "Where the Boys Are: Attitudes Related to Masculinity, Fatherhood, and Violence Toward Women among Low-Income Adolescent and Young Adult Males in Rio de Janeiro, Brazil." *Youth & Society* 29, no. 2: 166–96.

Bartilow, Horace. 2012. "Gender Representation and International Compliance Against Human Trafficking." Working paper presented at Human Trafficking, International Crime and National Security: A Human Rights Perspective, Goerg-August University of Gottingen, Germany.

BBC. 2014. "The Story of India's Slave Brides." November 25, 2014. http://www.bbc.com/news/world-asia-india-30189014.

BBC News. 2012. "Nigeria: 'Oil-gas Sector Mismanagement Costs Billions.'" October 25, 2012. bbc.com/news/world-africa20081268#:~:text=%20leaked%20report%20into%20Nigeria'sfinancial%20side%20of%20th%20sector.

———. 2013. "Horrors of India's Brothels Documented." Accessed May 2016. http://www.bbc.com/news/world-asia-india-24530198.

———. 2014. "Boko Haram 'to Sell' Nigeria Girls Abducted from Chibok." May 5, 2014. www.bbc.com/news/world-africa-27283383.

———. 2015. "Human Trafficking: The Lives Bought and Sold." July 28, 2015. http://www.bbc.com/news/world-33592634.

———. 2016. "The World of Nigeria's Sex Trafficking 'Air Lords.'" January 27, 2016. bbc.com/news/magazine_35244148.

———. 2020a. "Cheltenham Man Jailed for Trafficking Women from Brazil." June 5, 2020. bbc.com/news/uk-england-gloucestershire-52938942.

———. 2020b. "Marielle Franco Murder: Suspect Shot Dead by Police." February 9, 2020. bbc.com/news/world-latin-america-51439016.

Beck, Nathaniel, Jonathan N. Katz, and Richard Tucker. 1998. "Taking Time Seriously: Time-Series-Cross-Section Analysis with a Binary Dependent Variable." *American Journal of Political Science* 42, no. 4 (October): 1260–88.

Becker, Jo, and Anietie Ewang. 2020. "Nigeria Releases More Children and Youth from Military Prison." Human Rights Watch, March 8, 2020. hrw.org/news/2020/03/08/nigeria-releases-more-children-and-youth-military-prison.

Becker, Sabina. 2016. "Brazil: Pious MP Busted for Pedophilia, Caught Red-Handed." *News of the Restless* (blog). September 20, 2016. https://sabinabecker.com/2016/09/brazil-pious-mp-busted-for-pedophilia-caught-red-handed.html.

Beneria, L., and Feldman S. 1992. *Unequal Burden: Economic Crisis, Persistent Poverty and Women's Work.* Boulder, CO: Westview.

Berger, Herve, and Hans van de Glind. 1999. "Children in Prostitution, Pornography, and Illicit Activities: Thailand." International Labour Organization, January 1, 1999. http://www.ilo.org/asia/whatwedo/publications/WCMS_BK_PB_6_EN/lang—en/index.htm.

Bernat, Francis P., and Tatyana Zhilina. 2011. "Trafficking in Humans: The TIP Report." *Sociology Compass* 5: 452–62. https://doi.org/10.1111/j.1751-9020.2011.00380.x.

Bettio, Francesca, and Tushar Nandi. 2010. "Evidence on Women Trafficked for Sexual Exploitation: A Rights Based Analysis" *European Journal of Law and Economics* 29, no. 1: 15–42.

Biswas, Soutik. 2018. "Why India's Rape Crisis Shows No Signs of Abating." *BBC News*, April 17, 2018. https://www.bbc.com/news/world-asia-india-43782471.

Black, Gordon. 1972. "A Theory of Political Ambition: Career Choices and the Role of Structural Incentives." *American Political Science Review* 66, no. 1: 144–59.

Black, Maggie. 2007. "Ritual Slavery Practices in India: Devadasi, Jogini, Mathamma." International Dalit Solidarity Network. Accessed May 2016. http://idsn.org/wp-content/uploads/user_folder/pdf/New_files/India/WomeninRitualSlavery.pdf.

Blanchette, Thaddeus, and Ana Paula da Silva. 2012. "On Bullshit and the Trafficking of Women: Moral Entrepreneurs and the Invention of Trafficking of Persons in Brazil." *Dialectical Anthropology* 36, no. 1–2: 107–25.

———. 2016. "'Brazil Has Its Eye On You': Sexual Panic and the Threat of Sex Tourism in Rio de Janeiro during the FIFA World Cup, 2014." *Braziliana: Journal for Brazilian Studies* 4, no. 2: 411–54.

Blanton, Robert, Shannon Lindsey Blanton, and Dursun Peksen. 2018. "Confronting Human Trafficking: The Role of State Capacity." *Conflict Management & Peace Science* 37, no. 4 (August): 1–20.

Bollyky, Thomas J., Tara Templin, Matthew Cohen, Diana Schoder, Joseph L. Dieleman, and Simon Wigley. 2019. "The Relationships between Democratic Experience, Adult Health, and Cause-Specific Mortality in 170 Countries between 1980 and 2016: An Observational Analysis." *The Lancet* 393 (April 20): 1628–40.

Bouillon, Sophi. 2019. "Nigeria's Nollywood Film Industry Reels in Foreign Investors." *The Jakarta Post*, July 9, 2019. http://www.thejakartapost.com/life/2019/07/08/nigerias-nollywood-film-industry-reels-in-foreign-investors.html.

Bourcier, Nicolas. 2012. "Brazil Comes to Terms with Its Slave Trading Past." *The Guardian*, October 23, 2012. https://www.theguardian.com/world/2012/oct/23/brazil-struggle-ethnic-racial-identity.

Bowers, Meleena M. 2012. "Room for Improvement: Nigeria's Approach to Trafficking." International Models Project on Women's Rights, September 4, 2012. www.impowr.org/journal/room-improvement-nigerias-approach-trafficking.

Brinham, Natalie. 2012. "The Conveniently Forgotten Human Rights of the Rohingya." *Forced Migration Review* 41: 40–41.

Bro, Alexandra, and Jack McCaslin. 2019. "Nigeria's Laws Hold Women Back, and the Economy Suffers." Council on Foreign Relations, March 8, 2019. cfr.org/blog/nigerias-laws-hold-women-back-and-economy-suffers.

Brooks, C., and A. Umarova. 2010. "Despite Official Measures, Bride Kidnapping Endemic in Chechnya." *Radio Free Europe/Radio Liberty*.

Buchleitner, Jessica. 2015. "The Truth about Bride Kidnapping: An Insider Interview on Chechnya." *Women's News Network*, January 14, 2015. https://womennewsnetwork.net/2015/01/14/truth-about-bride-kidnapping/.

Buckley, Mary. 2009. "Public Opinion in Russia on the Politics of Human Trafficking." *Europe-Asia Studies* 61, no. 2: 213–48.

———. 2018. *The Politics of Unfree Labor in Russia: Human Trafficking and Labour Migration*. Cambridge: Cambridge University Press.

Bureau of International Labor Affairs. 2018. "Child Labor and Forced Labor Reports: Brazil." US Department of Labor. doi.gov/agencies/ilab/resources/reports/child-labor/brazil.

Burke, Jason. 2014. "Few Grieve for the Passing of Mumbai's Red-Light District." *The Guardian*, December 22, 2014. http://www.theguardian.com/world/2014/dec/22/time-running-out-mumbai-red-light-district-kamathipura.

Burke, Mary, Barbara Amaya, and Kelly Dillon. 2019. "Sex Trafficking as Structural Gender-Based Violence: Overview and Trauma Implications." In *The Palgrave International Handbook on Trafficking*, edited by John Winterdyk and Jackie Jones, 452–65. New York: Springer International.

Buyantueva, Radzhana, and Maryna Shevtsova. 2019. *LGBTQ+ Activism in Central and Eastern Europe: Resistance, Representation and Identity*. Switzerland: Palgrave Macmillan.

Caldwell, Gillian, Steve Galster, Jyothi Kanics, and Nadia Steinzor. 1999. "Capitalizing on Transition Economies: The Role of the Russian Mafiya in Trafficking Women for Forced Prostitution." In *Illegal Immigration and Commercial Sex: The New Slave Trade*, edited by Phil Williams, 42–73. Portland, OR: Frank Cass.

Cameron, Sally, and Edward Newman, eds. 2008. *Trafficking in Humans: Social, Cultural and Political Dimensions*. Tokyo: United Nations University Press.

Canineu, Maria Laura. 2020. "One Year of Ruinous Anti-Rights Policies in Brazil." Human Rights Watch, January 15, 2020. hrw.org/news/2020/01/15/one-year-ruinous-anti-rights-policies-brazil.

Cardin, Adele. 2019. "Why Is Convicted Pedophile Still Receiving Salary from Rio State Police?" *Rio Times*, October 4, 2019. https://riotimesonline.com/brazil-news/rio-de-janeiro/why-is-a-convicted-brazilian-pedophile-colonel-not-banished/.

Carling, Jørgen. 2006. "Migration, Human Smuggling, and Trafficking from Nigeria to Europe." International Organization for Migration. http://publications.iom.int/system/files/pdf/mrs23.pdf.

Carver, Terrell. 1996. *Gender Is Not a Synonym for Women*. London: Lynne Rienner.

Castilho, César Teizeira, Barbara Evrard, and Dominique Charrier. 2017. "Child Sex Tourism in the Context of the 2014 FIFA Football World Cup: The Case of the Host City of Recife, Brazil." *Sport in Society* 21, no. 5: 1–19.

Caucasian Knot. 2018. "Women Murdered with Impunity in the Caucasus: Who Is to Blame?" April 18, 2018. https://www.eng.kavkaz-uzel.eu/articles/43113/.

CEDAW (Committee on the Elimination of Discrimination Against Women). 2014. "Concluding Observations on the Combined Fourth and Fifth Periodic Reports of India." July 24, 2014. http://tbinternet.ohchr.org/_layouts/treatybodyexternal/Download.aspx?symbolno=CEDAW%2fC%2fIND%2fCO%2f4–5&Lang=en.

———. 2016. "Views Adopted by the Committee on the Elimination of Discrimination Against Women under Article 7(3) of the Optional Protocol to the Convention on the Elimination of All Forms of Discrimination Against Women (Sixty-Third Session)." February 25, 2016. https://tbinternet.ohchr.org/_layouts/15/treatybodyexternal/Download.aspx?symbolno=CEDAW/C/63/D/60/2013&Lang=en.

Ceratti, Mariana. 2017. "What Does It Mean to Be a Woman in Brazil?: The Answer Will Surprise You." World Bank, March 8, 2017. https://www.worldbank.org/en/news/feature/2017/03/08/ser-mujer-brasil.

CERD (UN Committee on the Elimination of Racial Discrimination). 2007. "Concluding Observations of the Committee: India." May 5, 2007. https://tbinternet.ohchr.org/_layouts/treatybodyexternal/Download.aspx?symbolno=CERD/C/IND/CO/19&Lang=En.

Chandramouli, C. 2013. "Primary Census Abstract: Data Highlights." India Ministry of Home Affairs. http://idsn.org/wpcontent/uploads/user_folder/pdf/New_files/India/2013/INDIA_CENSUS_ABSTRACT-2011-Data_on_SC-STs.pdf.

Chandran, Rina. 2018. "In Thai Tourist Spots, a Hidden World of Male Sex Slavery." *Reuters*, June 13, 2018. https://www.reuters.com/article/us-thailand-trafficking-sexcrimes/in-thai-tourist-spots-a-hidden-world-of-male-sex-slavery-idUSKBN1J91GU.

Chantavanich, Supang. 2020. "Thailand's Challenges in Implementing Anti-Trafficking Legislation: The Case of the Rohingya." *Journal of Human Trafficking* 6, no. 2: 234–43.

Charnysh, Volha, Paulette Lloyd, and Beth Simmons. 2015. "Frames and Consensus Formation in International Relations: The Case of Trafficking in Persons." *European Journal of International Relations* 21, no. 2: 323–51.

Chetry, Pooja, and Rekha Pande. 2019. "Gender Bias and the Sex Trafficking Interventions in the Eastern Border of India-Nepal." *South Asian Survey* 26, no. 2: 117–38.

Cho, Seo-Young. 2015a. 3P Anti-Trafficking Policy Index. http://www.economics -human-trafficking.org/data-and-reports.html.

———. 2015b. "Modelling for Determinants of Human Trafficking: An Empirical Analysis." *Social Inclusion* 3, no. 1: 2–21.

Cho, Seo-Young, Axel Dreher, and Eric Neumayer. 2013. "Does Legalized Prostitution Increase Human Trafficking?" *World Development* 41: 67–82.

———. 2014. "Determinants of Anti-Trafficking Policies: Evidence from a New Index." *Scandinavian Journal of Economics* 116, no. 2: 429–54.

Cho, Seo-Young, and Krishna Chaitanya Vadlamannati. 2012. "Compliance with the Anti-Trafficking Protocol." *European Journal of Political Economy* 28, no. 2: 249–65.

Churakova, Irina, and Amanda van der Westhuizen. 2019. "Human Trafficking in the Russian Federation: Scope of the Problem." In *The Palgrave International Handbook of Human Trafficking*, edited by John Winterdyk and Jackie Jones, 1–22. London: Palgrave.

Cingranelli, David L., David L. Richards, and K. Chad Clay. 2014. "The CIRI Human Rights Dataset." http://www.humanrightsdata.com.

Clinton, Hillary. 1995. "Remarks for the United Nations Fourth World Conference on Women." Beijing, China. Accessed June 2020. https://www.un.org/esa/gopher-data /conf/fwcw/conf/gov/950905175653.txt.

———. 1996. "Women's Rights Are Human Rights." *Women's Studies Quarterly* 24, no. 1–2: 98–101. https://www.jstor.org/stable/40004518.

Crawford, Mary. 2017. "International Sex Trafficking." *Women & Therapy* 40, no. 1–2: 101–22.

Cunha, Danilo Fontenele Sampaio. 2015. "Women Trafficking for Sexual Purposes: The Brazilian Experience after Law N.11.106, of March 28, 2005." In *The Illegal Business of Human Trafficking*, edited by M. J. Guia, 43–59. Switzerland: Springer International.

Dalit Freedom Network. 2016. "Who Are the Dalits?" Accessed May 2016. http:// dalitnetwork.org/who-are-the-dalits/.

Dalla, Rochelle L., and Lee M. Kreimer. 2017. "After Your Honor Is Gone . . .": Exploration of Developmental Trajectories and Life Experiences of Women Working in Mumbai's Red-Light Brothel Districts." *Sexuality & Culture* 21: 163–86.

Dalla, Rochelle L., Trupti Jhaveri Panchal, Sarah Erwin, Jessie Peters, Kaitlin Roselius, Ramani Ranjan, Mrinalini Mischra, and Sagar Sahu. 2020. "Structural Vulnerabilities, Personal Agency, and Caste: An Exploration of Child Sex Trafficking in Rural India." *Violence and Victims* 35, no. 3: 307–30.

Danish Immigration Service. 2008. "Protection of Victims of Trafficking in Nigeria: Report from Danish Immigration Service's Fact-Finding Mission to Lagos, Benin City, and Abuja, Nigeria." https://www.nyidanmark.dk/NR/rdonlyres/BAD16BF3 -A7C8-4D62-8334-DC5717591314/0/Nigeriatrafficking2007FINALpdf.pdf.

Dark, Shayera. 2020. "Nigerians Are Confronting an Underreported Rape Crisis That's Spiked during the Lockdown." Quartz Africa, June 24, 2020. qz.com/Africa/1871793 /Nigerians-confront-rape-culture-crisis-after-dbanj-allegations/.

da Silva, Maria Aparecida, Carla Gianna Luppi, and Marla Amélia de Sousa Mascena Veros. 2020. "Work and Health Issues for the Transgender Population: Factors Associated with Entering the Labor Market in the State of São Paulo, Brazil." *Ciência & Saúde Coletiva* 25 no. 5 (May 1, 2020): 1723–34.

Davis, Jarrett, Elliot Glotfelty, and Glenn Miles. 2017. "No Other Choice: A Baseline Study on the Vulnerabilities of Males in the Sex Trade in Chiang Mai, Thailand."

Dignity: A Journal on Sexual Exploitation and Violence 2, no. 4: 1–36. https://digital commons.uri.edu/cgi/viewcontent.cgi?article=1020&context=dignity.

Davis, Jarrett, and Glenn Miles. 2018. "They Chase Us Like Dogs: Exploring the Vulnerabilities of Ladyboys in the Cambodian Sex Trade." *Dignity: A Journal on Sexual Exploitation and Violence* 3, no. 2: 1–24.

D'Costa, Bina. 2006. "Marginalized Identity: New Frontiers of Research for IR?" In *Feminist Methodologies for International Relations*, edited by Brooke Ackerly, Maria Stern, and Jacqui True, 129–52. Cambridge: Cambridge University Press

Desai, Sonalde, Amaresh Dubey, Brij Joshi, Mitali Sen, Abusaleh Sharif, and Reeve Vanneman. 2010. *Human Development in India: Challenges for a Society in Transition*. Oxford: Oxford University Press.

DiRienzo, Cassandra. 2018. "Compliance with Anti-Human Trafficking Policies: The Mediating Effect of Corruption." *Crime, Law, and Social Change* 70, no. 5: 525–41.

Di Tommaso, M. L., I. Shima, S. Strøm, and F. Bettio. 2009. "As Bad as It Gets: Well Being Deprivation of Sexually Exploited Trafficked Women." *European Journal of Political Economics* 25, no. 2: 143–62.

Dolby, Natasha. 2018. "Domestic Sex Trafficking of Children in Brazil." Center for Human Rights and International Justice at Stanford University. https://humanrights .stanford.edu/publications/domestic-sex-trafficking-children-brazil.

Duggal-Chadha, Aradhna. 2006. "Children and Disasters." *Refugee Survey Quarterly* 25, no. 4: 85–90.

Ebbe, Obi N. I. 2003. "Nigeria." *World Factbook of Criminal Justice Systems*. US Department of Justice Bureau of Justice Statistics.

ECHR (European Court of Human Rights). 2010. "Case of Rantsev v. Cyprus and Russia." Application no. 25965/04. http://hudoc.echr.coe.int/eng?i=001−96549#{%22ite mid%22:[%22001−96549%22]}.

The Economist. 2015a. "The Blights of Boko Haram." January 19, 2015. https://www .economist.com/blogs/graphicdetail/2015/01/daily-chart-10.

———. 2015b. "Secret Weapon: Nigeria's Diaspora Is a Source of Money, Markets, Skills and Ideas." June 18, 2015. https://www.economist.com/news/special-report/2165 4360-nigerias-diaspora-source-money-markets-skills-and-ideas-secret-weapon.

ECPAT Brasil. 2020. "Who We Are." http://ecpatbrasil.org.br/?page_id=119.

ECPAT International. 2006. "Global Monitoring Report: India." Accessed August 2013. http://www.ecpat.net/A4A_2005/PDF/South_Asia/Global_Monitoring_Report -INDIA.pdf.

———. 2011. "Global Monitoring: Status of Action Against Commercial Sexual Exploitation of Children: Thailand." Accessed June 2016. http://www.ecpat.org/wp-content /uploads/legacy/a4a_v2_eap_thailand_1.pdf.

———. 2015. "Situational Analysis of the Commercial Sexual Exploitation of Children: Thailand." Accessed June 2016. http://www.ecpat.org/wp-content/uploads/legacy /SITAN_THAILAND_ENG_FINAL.pdf.

———. 2016. "Regional Report on Sexual Exploitation of Children in Travel and Tourism." Accessed June 2020. https://www.protectingchildrenintourism.org/.

———. 2018. "The Sexual Exploitation of Children in Southeast Asia: Regional Overview." Accessed June 2020. https://www.ecpat.org/wp-content/uploads/2018/02 /Regional-Overview_Southeast-Asia.pdf.

Ede, Victor Ifeanyi, Ozioma Faith Chiaghanam, and Dominic Zuoke Kalu. 2019. "Evaluating the Role of Christian Women Organizations in the Fights against Human

Trafficking in Nigeria." *Journal of Advanced Research in Humanities and Social Science* 6, no. 1: 16–22.

Elias, Juanita, and Shirin Rai. 2015. "The Everyday Gendered Political Economy of Violence." *Politics & Gender* 11, no. 2: 424–29.

Enloe, Cynthia. 2014. *Bananas, Beaches and Bases: Making Feminist Sense of International Politics.* Berkeley: University of California Press.

Eremenko, Alexey. 2014. "Sex Slavery Thrives in Russia Out of Public View." *Moscow Times*, December 1, 2014.

Eurostat. 2015. "Trafficking in Human Beings." Statistical Working Paper. https://ec .europa.eu/anti-trafficking/publications/trafficking-human-beings-eurostat-2015 -edition_en.

Ewang, Anietie. 2020. "Authorities in Nigeria Should Ensure #JusticeForUwa." Human Rights Watch, June 2, 2020. hrw.org/news/2020/06/02authorities-nigeria-should -ensure-justiceforuwa#.

Ewing, Heidi. 2014. "Human Trafficking in Latin America: Culture and Victimization." Master's thesis, Northeastern University. https://repository.library.northeastern .edu/files/neu:3363385/fulltext.pdf.

Fagundes, Murilo. 2020. "Bolsonaro Names First Black Cabinet Member as Education Minister." *Bloomberg*, June 25, 2020. https://www.bloomberg.com/news/articles /2020-06-25/bolsonaro-names-first-black-cabinet-member-as-education-minister.

Fedorova, Anastasiia. 2020. "Activists Speak Out about Russian Artist Yulia Tsvetkova's Prosecution for Feminist Drawings." *Calvert Journal*, June 12, 2020. https:// www.calvertjournal.com/articles/show/11875/russian-queer-artist-yulia-tsvetkova -prosecution-protests.

Fehintola, A. O., F. O. Fehintola, O. A. Ogunlaja, T. O. Awondtunde, I. P. Ogunlaja, U. Onwudiegwu. 2017. "Social Meaning and Consequences of Infertility in Ogbomoso, Nigeria." *Sudan Journal of Medical Sciences* 12, no. 2: 63–77.

Fehrenbacher, Anne E., Jennifer Musto, Heidi Hoefinger, Nicola Mai, P. G. Macioti, Calogero Giametta, and Calum Bennachie. 2020. "Transgender People and Human Trafficking: Intersectional Exclusion of Transgender Migrants and People of Color from Anti-Trafficking Protection in the United States." *Journal of Human Trafficking* 6, no. 2: 182–94.

Feingold, David. 2010. "Trafficking in Numbers: The Social Construction of Human Trafficking Data." In *Sex, Drugs, and Body Counts: The Politics of Numbers in Global Crime and Conflict*, edited by Peter Andreas and Kelly Greenhill, 46–74. Ithaca, NY: Cornell University Press.

Fernquist, Jon. 2012. "Child Labor: The Worst Forms." *Bangkok Post*, February 6, 2012. http://www.bangkokpost.com/learning/learning-from-news/278534/child-labour -the-worst-forms.

Ferreira, Amanda Álvares. 2017. "Travesti Prostitution in Brazil: Reading Agency and Sovereignty through Dissident Sexualities." Master's thesis, Catholic University of Rio de Janeiro.

Fortify Rights. 2016. "EU: Maintain Pressure on Thailand to End Human Trafficking." Accessed June 2016. http://www.fortifyrights.org/publication-20160224.html.

Frank, R. W. 2013. "Human Trafficking Indicators, 2000–2011: A New Dataset." Sydney: University of Sydney.

Fujimura, Clementine K., Sally W. Stoecker, and Tatyana Sudakova. 2005. *Russia's Abandoned Children: An Intimate Understanding.* Westport, CT: Praeger.

Gacitúa Marió, Estanislao, and Michael Woolcock, eds. 2008. *Social Exclusion and Mobility in Brazil*. Washington, DC: World Bank.

Gallagher, Anne. 2010. *The International Law of Human Trafficking*. Cambridge: Cambridge University Press.

Gentry, Caron, and Laura Sjoberg. 2015. "Terrorism and Political Violence." In *Gender Matters in Global Politics*, edited by Laura Shepard, 148–58. London: Routledge.

Gerber, Theodore P., and Sarah E. Mendelson. 2008. "Public Experiences of Police Violence and Corruption in Contemporary Russia: A Case of Predatory Policing?" *Law & Society Review* 42, no. 1: 1–44.

Ghuman, R. S. 2016. "The Sikh Community in Indian Punjab: Some Socio-Economic Challenges." *Journal of Punjab Studies* 19, no. 1: 87–109.

Giokos, Eleni. 2017. "Nigeria's Economy Was a 'Disaster' in 2016. Will This Year Be Different?" *CNN Money*, April 27, 2017. https://www.money.cnn.com/2017/04/27/news/economy/nigeria-oil-growth/index.html.

Gleditsch, Nils Petter, Peter Wallensteen, Mikael Eriksson, Margareta Sollenberg, and Harvard Strand. 2002. "Armed Conflict 1946–2001: A New Dataset." *Journal of Peace Research* 39 no. 5: 615–37.

Glerstorfer, Carl. 2014. "While India's Girls Are Aborted, Brides Are Wanted." *CNN*, September 3, 2014. http://www.cnn.com/2014/09/03/world/asia/india-freedom-project/.

Global Slavery Index. 2017. "Region Analysis: Sub-Saharan Africa." https://www.global slaveryindex.org/region/sub-saharan-africa/.

Goldstein, Donna M. 2003. *Laughter Out of Place: Race, Class, Violence, and Sexuality in a Rio Shantytown*. Berkeley: University of California Press.

Goodey, Jo. 2004. "Sex Trafficking in Women from Central and East European Countries: Promoting a 'Victim-Centered' and 'Woman-Centered' Approach to Criminal Justice Intervention." *Feminist Review* 76: 26–45.

Goscilo, Helena. 1996. *Dehexing Sex: Russian Womanhood Before and After Glastnost*. Ann Arbor: University of Michigan Press.

Government of India Ministry of Home Affairs. 2011. "Census of India 2011: Provisional Population Totals at a Glance." Accessed May 2018. http://www.censusindia .gov.in/2011-prov-results/paper2/prov_results_paper2_ap.html.

Government of India Ministry of Statistics and Programme Implementation. 2021. Accessed July 2021. http://mospi.nic.in.

Government of India National Crime Records Bureau. 2014. "Figures at a Glance: 2014." Accessed May 2018. http://ncrb.nic.in/.

Government of India National Legislature. 1955. Act No. 22, Protection of Civil Rights. Accessed February 2021. https://www.refworld.org/docid/3ae6b57c0.html.

———. 1956. "Immoral Traffic (Prevention) Act." Accessed August 2018. http://wcd.nic .in/act/itpa1956.htm.

———. 1976. "Equal Remuneration Act." Accessed November 2018. http://labour.gov.in /sites/default/files/equal_remuneration_act_1976_1.pdf.

———. 1989. Act No. 33, Scheduled Castes and the Scheduled Tribes Prevention of Atrocities Act. Accessed February 2021. http://www.refworld.org/docid/3ae6b 52a1c.html.

Gowen, Annie. 2013. "Arrest of Indian Diplomat in New York Sparks US-India Tensions." *Washington Post*, December 13, 2013. https://www.washingtonpost.com /world/asia_pacific/arrest-of-indian-diplomat-in-new-york-sparks-us-india

-tensions/2013/12/17/09d1d81e-6714-11e3-997b-9213b17dac97_story.html?utm
_term=.c0ce1f80504a.

Guha, Mirna. 2018. "Disrupting the 'Life-Cycle' of Violence in Social Relations: Recommendations for Anti-Trafficking Interventions from an Analysis of Pathways
Out of Sex Work for Women in Eastern India." *Gender and Development* 26, no. 1:
53–69.

Guinn, D. E. 2008. "Defining the Problem of Trafficking: The Interplay of US Law,
Donor, and NGO Engagement and the Local Context in Latin America." *Human
Rights Quarterly* 30, no. 1: 119–45.

HAQ (Center for Child Rights and Campaign Against Child Trafficking). 2016. "Child
Trafficking in India." Last accessed January 2021. http://haqcrc.org/wp-content
/uploads/2016/06/child-trafficking-in-india-report.pdf.

Harkins, Benjamin. 2019. *Thailand Migration Report.* UN Thailand Working Group on
Migration. https://thailand.iom.int/thailand-migration-report-2019-0.

Heller, Lauren, Robert Lawson, Ryan Murphy, and Claudia Williamson. 2016. "Is
Human Trafficking the Dark Side of Globalization?" *Defense and Peace Economics*
29, no. 4: 355–82.

Hepburn, Stephanie, and Rita Simon. 2013. *Human Trafficking Around the World: Hidden in Plain Sight.* New York: Colombia University Press.

Hernandez, D., and A. Rudolph. 2015. "Modern Day Slavery: What Drives Human Trafficking in Europe?" *European Journal of Political Economy* 38: 118–39.

Hindustan Times. 2018. "Lok Sabha Passes Law to Deal with Human Trafficking, Sex
Workers Not to Be Harassed." July 26, 2018. https://www.hindustantimes.com
/india-news/lok-sabha-passes-law-to-deal-with-human-trafficking-sex-workers
-not-to-be-harassed/story-ZNjxp3q7L9Md971gndf0xM.html.

Hughes, Donna. 2000. "The 'Natasha' Trade: The Transnational Shadow Market of Trafficking in Women." *Journal of International Affairs* 52, no. 2: 625–51.

———. 2002a. "Trafficking for Sexual Exploitation: The Case of the Russian Federation." IOM Migration Research Series. Accessed November 3, 2015. http://www
.iom.int.

———. 2002b. "Prostitution in Russia: Does the US State Department Back the Legalization of Prostitution?" *National Review Online,* November 21, 2002. www.national
review.com.

Huguet, Clarissa, and Ilona Szabó de Carvalho. 2008. "Violence in the Brazilian *Favelas*
and the Role of the Police." *New Directions for Youth Development* 119: 93–109.

Huijsmans, Roy. 2008. "Children Working Beyond Their Localities: Lao Children Working in Thailand." *Childhood* 15, no. 3: 331–53.

Human Rights Watch. 1995. "Russia: Neither Jobs nor Justice, State Discrimination
Against Women in Russia." *Human Rights Watch Report* 7, no. 5. https://www.hrw
.org/legacy/reports/1995/Russia2a.htm#P125_19588.

———. 1999. "Too Little, Too Late: State Response to Violence Against Women." *Human
Rights Watch Report* 13, no. 9. http://www.hrw.org/legacy/reports/1997/russwmn/.

———. 2000. "Owed Justice: Thai Women Trafficked into Debt Bondage in Japan."
September 21, 2000. https://www.hrw.org/report/2000/09/21/owed-justice/thai
-women-trafficked-debt-bondage-japan.

———. 2007. "Hidden Apartheid: Caste Discrimination Against India's 'Untouchables.'"
Accessed May 2018. https://www.hrw.org/report/2007/02/12/hidden-apartheid
/caste-discrimination-against-indias-untouchables.

———. 2013. "Race to the Bottom: Exploitation of Migrant Workers Ahead of Russia's 2014 Winter Olympic Games in Sochi." February 6, 2013. https://www.hrw.org /report/2013/02/06/race-bottom/expl.

———. 2014a. "Cleaning Human Waste: 'Manual Scavenging,' Caste and Discrimination in India." Human Rights Watch, August 25, 2014. https://www.hrw.org/report /2014/08/25/cleaning-human-waste/manual-scavenging-caste-and-discrimination -india#177.

———. 2014b. "Thailand: Protect Rohingya 'Boat Children.'" January 6, 2014. http:// www.hrw.org/news/2014/01/06/thailand-protect-rohingya-boat-children.

———. 2014c. "World Report 2014: Russia, Events of 2013." Accessed December 2, 2015. https://www.hrw.org/world-report/2014/country-chapters/russia.

———. 2017. "'One Day I'll Kill You': Impunity in Domestic Violence Cases in the Brazilian State of Roraima." June 21, 2017. hrw.org/report/2017/06/21/one-day-ill-kill -you/impunity-domestic-violence-cases-brazilian-state-roraima.

———. 2018a. "Hidden Chains: Rights Abuses and Forced Labor in Thailand's Fishing Industry." Accessed June 2020. https://www.hrw.org/report/2018/01/23/hidden -chains/rights-abuses-and-forced-labor-thailands-fishing-industry.

———. 2018b. "No Support: Russia's 'Gay Propaganda Law' Imperils LGBT Youth." December 11, 2018. https://www.hrw.org/report/2018/12/11/no-support/russias -gay-propaganda-law-imperils-lgbt-youth#.

———. 2019a. "Brazil: Mothers at Risk of Illegal Detention." May 20, 2019. hrw.org/news /2019/05/10/brazil-mothers-risk-illegal-detention.

———. 2019b. "Brazil: Venezuelan Children Fleeing Alone." December 5, 2019. hrw.org /news/2019/12/05/brazil-venzeulan-children-fleeing-alone.

———. 2019c. "Nigeria: 5 Years After Chibok, Children Still at Risk." April 15, 2019. hrw .org/news/2019/04/15/nigeria-5-years-after-chibok-children-still-risk.

———. 2019d. "'You Pray for Death': Trafficking of Women and Girls in Nigeria." August 27, 2019. hrw.org/report/2019/08/27/you-pray-death/trafficking-women -and-girls-nigeria#_ftn28.

———. 2020a. "Myanmar: Rohingya Await Justice, Safe Return 3 Years On." August 24, 2020. https://www.hrw.org/news/2020/08/24/myanmar-rohingya-await-justice-safe -return-3-years.

———. 2020b. "Nigeria: Lawyer Says Police Assaulted Her." February 6, 2020. hrw.org /news/2020/02/06/nigeria-lawyer-says-police-assaulted-her.

———. 2021. "Rohingya Arrest in Myanmar Just for Traveling." January 7, 2020: https:// www.hrw.org/news/2021/01/07/rohingya-arrested-myanmar-just-traveling.

Iacono, Eva Lo. 2014. "Victims, Sex Workers and Perpetrators: Gray Areas in the Trafficking of Nigeran Women." *Trends in Organized Crime* 17: 110–28.

ILO (International Labour Organization). 2001. "A Compendium of National Law and Practice." International Labour Conference, 89th Session. Report 3, chap. 3.

———. 2018. "ILOSTAT Database." Accessed September 2018. https://data.worldbank .org/indicator/SL.TLF.CACT.FE.ZS.

The Independent. 1993. "Thais Ban Dictionary Over 'City of Prostitutes' Slur." July 5, 1993. http://www.independent.co.uk/news/world/thais-ban-dictionary-over-city -of-prostitutes-slur-1483226.html.

Interfax Russia. 2008. "The State Duma Did Not Support a Bill on Gender Equality." Last accessed July 2020. https://www.interfax.ru/russia/620559.

International Monetary Fund. 2020. "Real GDP Growth Annual Percent Change." IMF Data Mapper. http://imf.org/external/datamapper/ngdp_rpch@weo/oemdc/advec /weoworld/afq/nga.

Interstate Statistical Committee of the Commonwealth of Independent States. 2020. Last accessed September 2020. http://www.cisstat.com/eng/.

IOM (International Organization of Migration). 2016. "Myanmar." Accessed June 2016. http://www.iom.int/countries/myanmar.

———. 2017. "UN Migration Agency Issues Report on Arrivals of Sexually Exploited Migrants, Chiefly from Nigeria." July 21, 2017. http://www.iom.int/news/un-migration -agency-issues-report-arrivals-sexually-exploited-migrants-chiefly-nigeria.

IOM Mission in Ukraine. 2015a. "Combatting Trafficking in Human Beings in Ukraine." June 30, 2015. http://www.iom.org.ua/en/combating-human-trafficking.

———. 2015b. "Combating Trafficking in Human Beings in Ukraine." September 15, 2015. On file with authors.

———. 2015c. "Human Trafficking in Ukraine: Situation Analysis, September 15, 2015." On file with authors.

IRIN (Integrated Regional Information Networks). 2009. "Burmese Migrant Children Missing Out on Education." June 15, 2009. http://www.irinnews.org/report/84844 /thailand-burmese-migrant-children-missing-out-education.

Iwanaga, Kazuki, ed. 2008. Women's Political Participation and Representation in Asia: Obstacles and Challenges. Copenhagen: NIAS–Nordic Institute of Asian Studies.

Jac-Kucharski, A. 2012. "The Determinants of Human Trafficking: A US Case Study." International Migration 50, no. 6: 150–65.

Jaipragas, Bhavan, and Jitsiree Thongnoi. 2019. "Thailand's Military Appointed Senate Could Steal Election Result, Pheu Thai Party Leader Warns." This Week in Asia, March 21, 2019. https://www.scmp.com/week-asia/politics/article/3002567 /thailands-military-appointed-senate-could-steal-election-result.

Jakobsson, N., and A. Kotsadam. 2011. "The Law and Economics of International Sex Slavery: Prostitution Laws and Trafficking for Sexual Exploitation." European Journal of Law and Economics 35, no. 1: 87–107.

Jensen, Alex. 2016. "Amid Olympic Rush, Brazil's Hotels Join the Fight Against Human Trafficking." Mic. August 4, 2016. https://mic.com/articles/150573/amid-olympic -rush-brazil-s-hotels-join-the-fight-against-human-trafficking#.3RwsFJPFR.

Jiang, Chen. 2015. "Forced Prostitution and Modern Slavery: Brazil's Response." Council on Hemispheric Affairs, April 6, 2015. http://www.coha.org/forced-prostitution -and-modern-slavery-brazils-response/.

Johnson, Janet Elise. 2009. Gender Violence in Russia: The Politics of Feminist Intervention. Bloomington: Indiana University Press.

———. 2016. "Fast-Tracked or Boxed In?: Informal Politics, Gender, and Women's Representation in Putin's Russia." Perspectives on Politics 14, no. 3: 643–59.

Jones, Gavin. 2013. "The Population of Southeast Asia." Asia Research Institute Working Paper Series. Accessed June 2016. http://www.ari.nus.edu.sg/wps/wps13_196.pdf.

Jonsson, Sofia. 2019. "The Complex Relationship between Police Corruption and Sex Trafficking in Origin Countries." Journal of Human Trafficking 5, no. 2: 108–129.

Kaloga, Marissa, Sharvadi Karandikar, Lindsey B. Gezinski, and Rebecca J. McCloskey. 2019. "Health Concerns and Access to Services: Female Sex Workers' Experiences in Mumbai, India." World Medical and Health Policy 11, no. 2: 148–62.

Kara, Siddharth. 2009. *Sex Trafficking: Inside the Business of Modern Slavery.* New York: Columbia University Press.

———. 2010. "Designing More Effective Laws against Human Trafficking." *Northwestern Journal of Human Rights* 9: 123.

Keck, Margaret E., and Kathryn Sikkink. 1998. *Activists Beyond Borders: Advocacy Networks in International Politics.* Ithaca, NY: Cornell University Press.

Keenapan, Nattha. 2012. "Helping Children Living and Working on the Streets in Thailand." UNICEF Publication, March 7, 2012. http://www.unicef.org/education /Thailand_61806.html.

Kempadoo, Kamala. 2012. "Introduction: Abolitionism, Criminal Justice, and Transnational Feminism: Twenty-First Century Perspectives on Human Trafficking." In *Trafficking and Prostitution Reconsidered: New Perspectives on Migration, Sex Work, and Human Rights,* edited by Kamala Kempadoo, Jyoti Sanghera, and Bandana Pattanaik, vii–xlii. Boulder, CO: Paradigm.

Khan, M. Shafiqur Rahman. 2013. "Bride Trafficking within India." In *Human Trafficking: The Stakeholders' Perspective,* edited by Veeredndra Mishra, 45–53. Newbury Park, CA: Sage.

Kharas, Homi, Kristofer Hamel, and Martin Hofer. 2018. "The Start of a New Poverty Narrative." Brookings Institute, June 19, 2018. brookings.edu/blog/future -development/2018/06/19/the-start-of-a-new-poverty-narrative/.

Khodyreva, Natalia. 2008. "Gender Violence and the Cost of Social-Psychological Rehabilitation and Legal Assistance: Russian Federation." Comments given at the First World Conference of Women's Shelters, September 8–11, 2008, Edmonton, AB, Canada.

Kiblitskaya, Marina. 2000. "Russia's Female Breadwinners: The Changing Subjective Experience." In *Gender, State and Society in Soviet and Post-Soviet Russia,* edited by Sarah Ashwin, 55–70. London: Routledge.

Kigbu, S. K. 2015. "Challenges in Investigating and Prosecuting Trafficking in Persons' Cases in Nigeria." *Journal of Law, Policy and Globalization* 38: 146–57.

Kimmons, Sean. 2014. "Sex Trafficking Victims Go Unnoticed in Laos." *The Diplomat,* March 24, 2014. http://thediplomat.com/2014/03/trafficking-victims-go -unnoticed-in-laos/.

Kingdom of Thailand. 1998. Labour Protection Act, B.E. 2541. Accessed April 2020. https://www.ilo.org/dyn/natlex/natlex4.detail?p_lang=en&p_isn=49727.

———. 2010. Home Workers Protection Act, B.E.2553. Accessed April 2020. https:// www.ilo.org/dyn/natlex/docs/ELECTRONIC/93545/109400/F-1826987314/THA 93545%20Eng.pdf.

———. 2015. Gender Equality Act, B.E. 2558. Accessed April 2020. https://www.ilo .org/dyn/natlex/docs/ELECTRONIC/100442/120478/F764760666/THA100442 %20Eng.pdf.

———. 2017. Constitution of the Kingdom of Thailand. Accessed April 2020. https:// www.constituteproject.org/constitution/Thailand_2017.pdf?lang=en.

Kingsley, Patrick. 2016. "The Small African Region with More Refugees than All of Europe." *The Guardian,* November 26, 2016. https://www.theguardian.com/world /2016/nov/26/boko-haram-nigeria-famine-hunger-displacement-refugees-climage -change-lake-chad.

Kleimenov, Mikhail, and Stanislov Shamkov. 2005. "Criminal Transportation of Persons: Trends and Recommendations." In *Human Traffic and Transnational Crime:*

Eurasian and American Perspectives, edited by Sally Stoecker and Louise Shelley, 29–46. Lanham, MD: Roman & Littlefield.

Kon, Igor. 1995. *The Sexual Revolution in Russia*. New York: Free Press.

Konstantopoulos, Wendy Macias, Roy Ahn, Elaine J. Alpert, Elizabeth Cafferty, Anita McGahan, Timothy P. Williams, Judith Palmer Castor, Nadya Wolferstan, Genevieve Purcell, and Thomas F. Burke. 2013. "An International Comparative Public Health Analysis of Sex Trafficking of Women and Girls in Eight Cities: Achieving a More Effective Health Sector Response." *Journal of Urban Health: Bulletin of the New York Academy of Medicine* 90, no. 6: 1194–1204.

Kosharovsky, Marianna. 2015. "Foreign Agents Act Chills Anti-Trafficking Efforts in Russia." *Human Trafficking Center Blog* (blog), November 14, 2015. http://human traffickingcenter.org/human-trafficking/foreign-agents-act-chills-anti-trafficking -efforts-russia/.

Kumar, Raksha. 2013. "Human Trafficking Continues to Ravage Jharkhand." *New York Times*, September 23, 2013. https://nyti.ms/2pdp8bi.

Kumar, Rohan, Niharranjan Mishra, and Pooja Shree Mishra. 2020. "Human trafficking: A Review of the Crime in Odisha, India." *Children and Youth Services Review* 119 (105532).

Laczko, Frank, and Marco A. Gramegna. 2003. "Developing Better Indicators of Human Trafficking." *Brown Journal of World Affairs* 10, no. 1: 179–94.

Landman, Todd. 2018. "Out of the Shadows: Trans-Disciplinary Research on Modern Slavery." *Peace Human Rights Governance* 2, no. 2: 143–62.

———. 2020. "Measuring Modern Slavery: Law, Human Rights and New Forms of Data." *Human Rights Quarterly* 42, no. 2: 303–31.

Landman, Todd, and Bernard Silverman. 2019. "Globalization and Modern Slavery." *Politics and Governance* 7, no. 4: 275–90.

Langberg, Laura. 2005. "A Review of Recent OAS Research on Human Trafficking in the Latin American and Caribbean Region." *International Migration* 43, no. 1–2: 129–39.

Latynia, Yulia. 2012. "Child Abuse in Russia is Routine." *Moscow Times*, December 26, 2012. http://www.themoscowtimes.com/opinion/article/child-abuse-in-russia-is -routine/473633.html.

Lauren, Paul Gordon. 1998. *The Evolution of International Human Rights: Visions Seen*. Philadelphia: University of Pennsylvania Press.

Lavigne, Marie. 2007. *The Economics of Transition: From Socialist Economy to Market Economy*. London: Palgrave Macmillan.

Lehmann, Hartmut, and Maria Giulia Silvagni. 2013. "Is There Convergence of Russia's Regions?: Exploring the Empirical Evidence, 1995–2010." Institute for the Study of Labor, Research Paper Series no. 7603. Accessed October 30, 2015. http://ftp.iza .org/dp7603.pdf.

Lijun, Sheng. 2006. "China-ASEAN Cooperation Against Illicit Drugs from the Golden Triangle." *Asian Perspective* 30, no. 2: 97–126.

Lintner, Bertil. 2003. "Betting on the Border." *Far Eastern Economic Review*, December 4, 2003. http://www.asiapacificms.com/articles/cambodia_casinos/.

Lischer, Sarah Kenyon. 2015. *Dangerous Sanctuaries: Refugee Camps, Civil War, and the Dilemmas of Humanitarian Aid*. Ithaca, NY: Cornell University Press.

Lopes, Marina. 2019. "Brazil's Highest Court Votes to Extend Anti-Discrimination Protections to LGBT People." *Washington Post*, May 23, 2019. https://www

.washingtonpost.com/world/brazils-highest-court-makes-it-a-crime-to-attack
-a-person-based-on-sexual-orientation-gender-identity/2019/05/23/cc28fcce
-7cc8–11e9-b1f3-b233fe5811ef_story.html.

Lopez, Oscar, and Fabio Teixeira. 2020. "As Latin America Locks Down, Trans Sex Workers Struggle to Survive." Reuters, April 24, 2020. https://www.reuters.com /article/us-health-coronavirus-transgender-featur/as-latin-america-locks-down -trans-sex-workers-struggle-to-survive-idUSKCN22613Z.

Lovell, Peggy A. 2006. "Race, Gender, and Work in São Paulo, Brazil, 1960–2000." *Latin American Research Review* 41, no. 3: 63–87.

Lustig, Nora. 2015. "Fiscal Policy and Ethno-Racial Inequality in Bolivia, Brazil, Guatemala, and Uruguay." Commitment to Equity (CEQ) Working Paper Series, no. 22. Tulane University. https://ideas.repec.org/p/tul/ceqwps/22.html.

MacKenzie, Megan H. 2012. *Female Soldiers in Sierra Leone: Sex, Security and Post-Conflict Development*. New York: New York University Press.

MacWilliams, Byron. 2003. "Forced into Prostitution." *Chronicle of Higher Education* 50, no. 6: A34–A36.

Madueke, Eucharia. 2015. "Human Trafficking in Nigeria: Sisters Provide Services, Seek Greater Justice for All." *Global Sisters Report*, April 15, 2015. https://www .globalsistersreport.org/column/justice-matters/trafficking/human-trafficking -nigeria-sisters-provide-services-seek-greater.

Mahdi, Saudatu. 2020. "Coronavirus: 'Status Quo of Women Not Sustainable, Balance Must be Tilted.'" *Africa Report*, June 18, 2020. https://www.theafricareport .com/30333/coronavirus-status-quot-of-women-not-sustainable-balance-must-be -tilted/.

Makinde, Olusesan Ayodeji. 2015. "Infant Trafficking and Baby Factories: A New Tale of Child Abuse in Nigeria." *Child Abuse Review* 26, no. 6: 433–43.

Makinde, Olusesan Ayodeji, Olufunmbi Olukemi Makinde, Olalekan Olaleye, Brandon Brown, and Clifford O. Odimegwu. 2016. "Baby Factories Taint Surrogacy in Nigeria." *Reproductive BioMedicine Online* 32, no. 1: 6–8.

Mancuso, Marina. 2014. "Not All Madams Have a Central Role: Analysis of a Nigerian Sex Trafficking Network." *Trends in Organized Crime* 17, no. 1–2: 66–88.

Marisapr. 2016. "The Hyper-Sexualization of the Brazilian Woman." *Panoramas*, April 26, 2016. panoramas.pitt.edu/art-and-culture/hyper-sexualization-brazilian -woman.

Marshall, Andrew, and Amy Sawitta Lefevre. 2014. "Special Report: Flaws Found in Thailand's Human Trafficking Crackdown." Reuters, April 10, 2014. http://www .reuters.com/article/2014/04/10/us-thailand-rohingya-special-report-idUSBREA 3922P20140410.

Marshall, Monty G., Ted Robert Gurr, and Keith Jaggers. 2019. "Polity IV Project: Regime Characteristics and Transitions, 1800–2018." Dataset Users' Manual. Center for Systemic Peace. http://www.systemicpeace.org/inscr/p4manualv2018.pdf.

Martinez, Omar, and Guadalupe Kelle. 2013. "Sex Trafficking of LGBT Individuals: A Call for Service Provision, Research, and Action." *International Law News* 42, no. 4: 21.

Mason, Jessica. 2018. "Pussy Provocations: Feminist Protest and Anti-Feminist Resurgence in Russia." *Feminist Encounters: A Journal of Critical Studies in Culture and Politics* 2, no. 1: 1–14.

Matthews, Chris. 2014. "Fortune 5: The Biggest Organized Crime Groups in the World." *Fortune*, September 14, 2014.

McCarthy, Lauren A. 2008. "Beyond Corruption: An Assessment of Russian Law Enforcement's Fight Against Human Trafficking." *Demokratizatsiya* (Washington, DC) 18, no. 1: 5–27.

———. 2015. *Trafficking Justice: How Russian Police Enforce New Laws, From Crime to Courtroom*. Ithaca, NY: Cornell University Press.

———. 2020. "A Gendered Perspective on Human Trafficking Perpetrators: Evidence from Russia." *Journal of Human Trafficking* 6, no. 1: 79–104.

McKean, Lise. 2016. "Protecting and Empowering Every Last Girl: An Impact Analysis of Apne Aap Women Worldwide, 2002–2015." Apne Aap Women Worldwide, March 2016. http://apneaap.org/resources/external-reports-and-documents/.

Mearsheimer, John. 2014. *The Tragedy of Great Power Politics*. New York: W. W. Norton.

Melnikas, Andrea, Sigma Ainul, Iqbal Ehsan, Eashita Haque, and Sejeda Amin. 2020. "Child Marriage Practices among the Rohingya in Bangladesh." *Conflict and Health* 14, no. 28.

Mendoza, Dovelyn Rannveig. 2018. *Triple Discrimination: Woman, Pregnant, and Migrant*. Fair Labor Association. Accessed January 4, 2022. https://www.fairlabor.org/report/triple-discrimination-woman-pregnant-and-migrant.

Ministério da Justiça. 2013. "Assessment of Trafficking Persons in the Border Areas." Accessed January 4, 2022. https://issuu.com/justicagovbr/docs/diagnostico_trafico_pessoas_frontei.

Mitchell, Gregory. 2016. "Evangelical Ecstasy Meets Feminist Fury: Sex Trafficking, Moral Panics, and Homoantagonism during Global Sporting Events." *GLQ* 22, no. 3: 325–57.

Montgomery, Heather. 2001. "Child Sex Tourism in Thailand." In *Tourism and the Less Developed World Issues*, edited by D. Harrison, 191–201. Oxfordshire: CAB.

———. 2008. "Buying Innocence: Child Sex Tourism in Thailand." *Third World Quarterly* 29, no. 5: 903–17.

———. 2011. "Prevailing Voices in Debates over Child Prostitution." In *Policing Pleasure: Sex Work, Policy and the State in Global Perspective*, edited by Susan Dewey and Patty Kelly, 146–58. New York: New York University Press.

Morris, H. F. 1970. "How Nigeria Got Its Criminal Code." *Journal of African Law* 14, no. 3: 13754.

Morton, Micah F., and Ian G. Baird. 2019. "From Hill Tribes to Indigenous Peoples: The Localisation of a Global Movement in Thailand." *Journal of Southeast Asian Studies* 50, no. 1: 7–31.

Moscow Times. 2017. "Women in Russia Earn Significantly Less than Their Male Counterparts." September 15, 2017. https://www.themoscowtimes.com/2017/09/15/women-in-russia-earn-much-less-than-men-a58950.

———. 2018. "Russia's 'Big Brother Law' Enters into Force." July 1, 2018. https://www.themoscowtimes.com/2018/07/01/russias-big-brother-law-enters-into-force-a62066.

———. 2019. "5,000 World Cup Fans Never Left." January 25, 2019. https://www.themoscowtimes.com/2019/01/25/5000-world-cup-fans-never-left-russia-police-say-a64290.

———. 2020a. "Russia Investigates Nigerian Prostitution Ring." January 14, 2020. https://www.themoscowtimes.com/2020/01/14/russia-investigates-world-cup-nigerian-prostitution-ring-tass-a68893.

———. 2020b. "Russia Opens 350 Banned Professions to Women, Stripping Soviet-Era Restrictions." May 10, 2020. www.themoscowtimes.com/2019/08/16/russia

-opens-350-banned-professions-to-women-stripping-soviet-era-restrictions
-a66903.

Mukherjee, K. K., and Deepa Das. 1996. "Prostitution in Metropolitan Cities of India." Indian Central Social Welfare Board. Copy of study on file with authors.

Muñoz, César. 2018. "Women's Work for Free in Brazil." Human Rights Watch, October 11, 2018. https://www.hrw.org/news/2018/10/11/womens-work-free-brazil.

———. 2020a. "Brazil's Empty Gestures to Women." Human Rights Watch, January 10, 2020. https://www.hrw.org/news/2020/01/10/brazils-empty-gestures-women.

———. 2020b. "Brazil Suffers Its Own Scourge of Police Brutality." Human Rights Watch, June 3, 2020. https://www.hrw.org/news/2020/06/03/brazil-suffers-its-own -scourge-police-brutality.

Myanmar Government. Department of Population, Ministry of Immigration and Population. 2015. "2014 Myanmar Population and Housing Census." Accessed June 2016. http://www.dop.gov.mm/moip/index.php?route=product/product&path=54_49& product_id=95.

Nakamura, Akemi. 2008. "Japan, Brazil Mark a Century of Settlement, Family Ties." *Japan Times Online*, January 15, 2008. http://www.japantimes.co.jp/news/2008/01 /15/news/japan-brazil-mark-a-century-of-settlement-family-ties/.

Napier-Moore, Rebecca, and Katie Sheill. 2016. *High Rise, Low Pay: Experiences of Migrant Women in the Thai Construction Sector*. International Labour Organization Regional Office for Asia and the Pacific. Accessed January 4, 2022. https://www .ilo.org/asia/publications/WCMS_537743/lang-en/index.htm.

The Nation Thailand. 2013. "13 Girls Rescued after Raid on Karaoke Bar." February 17, 2013. http://www.nationmultimedia.com/2011/02/17/national/13-girls-rescued-after -raid-on-karaoke-bar-30148882.html.

———. 2018. "Eight Get Lengthy Prison Terms over Mae Hong Son Prostitution Racket." April 18, 2018. https://www.nationthailand.com/news/30343420.

Naurla, Smita. 1999. *Broken People: Caste Violence Against India's "Untouchables."* Human Rights Watch, Report/Book Series. https://www.hrw.org/reports/1999/india/.

Ncube, Neddie, and Admit Ticharwa. 2017. "'My Fruits Never Ripen': Risk Factors of Anxiety among Zimbabwean Married Childless Women with Recurrent Miscarriages." *International Journal of Innovative Research & Development* 6, no. 3: 177–83.

Nettikkara, Samiha. 2015. "What It Means to be Female in Nigeria." *BBC Trending*, July 1, 2015. https://www.bbc.com/news/blogs-trending-33239356.

Neumayer, Eric. 2005. "Do International Human Rights Treaties Improve Respect for Human Rights?" *Journal of Conflict Resolution* 49, no. 6: 925–53.

New Straits Times. 2017. "'Girls as Dessert': Thai Sex Scandal Exposes Grim Tradition." June 25, 2017. https://www.nst.com.my/world/2017/06/252011/girls-dessert-thai -sex-scandal-exposes-grim-tradition.

New Times of India. 2018. "Lok Sabha Clears Law to Deal with Human Trafficking." July 27, 2018. https://timesofindia.indiatimes.com/india/lok-sabha-clears-law-to -deal-with-human-trafficking/articleshow/65156682.cms.

Nichols, Andrea, and Erin Heil. 2015. "Challenges to Identifying and Prosecuting Sex Trafficking Cases in the Midwest United States." *Feminist Criminology* 10, no. 1: 7–35.

Nicholson, Andrea, Minh Dang, and Zoe Trodd. 2018. "A Full Freedom: Contemporary Survivors' Definitions of Slavery." *Human Rights Law Review* 18: 689–704.

NightLight Bangkok. 2019. Annual Report. Last accessed June 2020. https://www.night lightinternational.com/wp-content/uploads/2020/06/2019-nightlight-annual -report_compressed.pdf.

Novosti, Ria. 2014. "65,000 Foreigners Deported from Russia in 2013." *Moscow Times*, January 17, 2014. http://www.themoscowtimes.com/news/article/65000-foreigners -deported-from-russia-in-2013/492843.html.

Nwogu, Victoria Ijeoma. 2006. "Nigeria: Human Trafficking and Migration." *Forced Migration Review* 24: 32–33.

OHCHR (United Nations Human Rights Office of the High Commissioner). 2016. "Women's Rights Body Rules on Russian Banned Jobs List Complaint." April 22, 2016. https://www.ohchr.org/EN/NewsEvents/Pages/MedvedevaVRussia.aspx.

———. 2017. "National Human Rights Commission of Thailand (Submission for the Session)." https://www.tbinternet.ohchr.org/_layouts/15/treatybodyexternal/Download .aspx?symbolno=INT/CEDAW/IFN/THA/27198&Lang=en.

Ohlsen, Sarah. 2015. "Commercial Sexual Exploitation of Children: A Status Report for Our Jurisdiction." Multnomah County, January 2, 2015. https://multco.us/file /38173/download.

Okediji, Tade O. 2004. "The Dynamics of Race, Ethnicity, and Economic Development: the Brazilian Experience." *Journal of Socio-Economics* 33, no. 2: 201–15.

Okonfua, F. E., S. M. Ogbomwan, A. N. Alutu, Okop Kifre, and Aghahowa Eghosa. 2004. "Knowledge, Attitudes, and Experiences of Sex Trafficking by Young Women in Benin City, South-South Nigeria." *Social Science & Medicine* 59, no. 6: 1315–27.

Olateru-Olagbegi, Bisi, and Anen Ikpeme. 2006. "Review of Legislation and Policies in Nigeria on Human Trafficking and Forced Labour." International Labour Organization Working Paper. http://www.ilo.org/global/topics/forced-labour/publications /WCMS_083149/lang-en/index.htm.

Olowa, Olatomide W., and Adebayo M. Shittu. 2012. "Remittances and Income Inequality in Rural Nigeria." *International Journal of Finance and Accounting* 1, no. 6: 162–72.

Omeire, Charles Obioma, E. B. J. Iheriohanma, A. Osita-Njoku, and E. Omeire. 2015. "The Challenges of Child Adoption and the Emergence of Baby Factory in South Eastern, Nigeria." *International Journal of Education and Research* 3, no. 8: 63–74.

Onuohu, Chris. 2020. "My Battles Against Childlessness—Ibidun Ituah-Ighodalo." *Vanguard*, June 21, 2020. https://www.vanguardngr.com/2020/06/my-battles-against -childlessness-ibidun-ituah-ighodalo/.

Orjinmo, Nduka. 2020. "#WeAreTired: Nigerian Women Speak Out Over Wave of Violence." *BBC News*, June 5, 2020. bbc.com/news/world-africa-52889965.

Orlova, Alexandra V. 2018. "Russian Politics of Masculinity and the Decay of Feminism: The Role of Dissent in Creating New 'Local Norms.'" *William & Mary Journal of Race, Gender, and Social Justice* 25: 59–86.

Oyekunle, Olumide. 2019. "The Largest Economies in Africa by GDP, 2019." The African Exponent, February 20, 2019. https://www.africanexponent.com/post/9786 -top-six-countries-with-the-biggest-gdp-in-africa.

Pandey, Sonal. 2018. "Review Essay: Trafficking of Children for Sex work in India: Prevalence, History, and Vulnerability Analysis." *Explorations, ISS e-journal* 2, no. 1: 21–43.

Pandit, Ambika. 2018. "Anti-Trafficking Bill Won't Affect Voluntary Sex-Workers: Maneka Ghandi." *Times of India*, July 28, 2018. https://timesofindia.indiatimes.com

/india/anti-trafficking-bill-wont-affect-voluntary-sex-workers-maneka-gandhi
/articleshow/65171249.cms.

———. 2020. "Reporting of a Crime a Must in New Anti-Trafficking Bill." *Times of India*,
March 16, 2020. https://timesofindia.indiatimes.com/india/reporting-of-crime-a
-must-in-new-anti-trafficking-bill/articleshow/74644233.cms.

Parrot, Andrea, and Nina Cummings. 2008. *Sexual Enslavement of Girls and Women
Worldwide.* Westport, CT: Praeger.

Pathfinders Justice Initiative. 2018. "Edo State Human Trafficking Bill Signed Into Law
by Governor Obaseki." May 24, 2018. https://www.pathfindersji.org/edo-state
-passes-new-law-against-humantrafficking/.

Patkar, Priti, and Pravin Patkar. 2000. "Consolidating Protection Against Ever-Escalating
Violation: Case of Prerana's Intervention for Protection of Rights of Victims of
Commercial Sexual Exploitation in India." National Criminal Justice Reference Ser-
vice. Accessed July 2013. https://www.ncjrs.gov/pdffiles1/nij/221040.pdf.

Paul, Stella. 2015. "From Slavery to Self-Reliance: A Story of Dalit Women in Southern
India." Interpress Service, April 21, 2015. http://www.ipsnews.net/2015/04/from
-slavery-to-self-reliance-a-story-of-dalit-women-in-south-india/.

Peksen, Dursun, Shannon Lindsey Blanton, Robert G. Blanton. 2017. "Neoliberal Policies and Human Trafficking for Labor: Free Markets, Unfree Workers?" *Political
Research Quarterly* 73, no. 3: 673–86.

Pettersson, Therese, and Magnus Oberg. 2020. "Organized Violence, 1989–2019." *Journal of Peace Research* 57, no. 4.

Phillips, Dom, and Ian Cheibub. 2020. "'If I Don't Have Sex I'll Die of Hunger': Covid-19
Crisis for Rio's Trans Sex Workers." *The Guardian*, May 21, 2020. https://www
.theguardian.com/global-development/2020/may/21/if-i-don't-have-sex-ill-die-of
-hunger-covid-19-crisis-for-rios-trans-sex-workers.

Phillips, Dom, and Tom Phillips. 2019. "Brazil: Bolsonaro in Homophobi Outburst
as Corruption Scandal Swirls." *The Guardian*, December 20, 2019. https://www
.theguardian.com/world.2019/dec/20/brazil-jair-bolsonaro-homophobic-outburst
-corruption-scandal.

Phillips, Tom. 2011. "Brazil Census Shows African-Brazilians in the Majority for the
First Time." *The Guardian,* November 17, 2011. https://www.theguardian.com
/world/2011/nov/17/brazil-census-african-brazilians-majority.

———. 2018. "Brazil's Fearful LGBT Community Prepares for a 'Proud Homophobe.'"
The Guardian, October 27, 2018. https://www.theguardian.com/world/oct/27
/dispatch-sao-paulo-jair-bolsonaro-victory-lgbt-community-fear.

Picanço, Lara Bartilotti, and Anya Prusa. 2019. "At the United Nations, Brazil Allies
with Ultra-Conservatives on Gender and Sex-Ed." *Think Brazil* (blog), July 22,
2019. https://www.wilsoncenter.org/blog-post/the-united-nations-brazil-allies-ultra
-conservatives-gender-and-sex-ed.

Pimonsaengsuriya, Kritsana. 2008. "Understanding the linkages between child sex tourism and other forms of commercial sexual exploitation of children in East Asia and
the Pacific." *ECPAT International* 328.

Pinzon-Rondon, Angela Maria, Amir Attaran, Juan Carlos Botero, and Angela Maria
Ruiz-Sternberg. 2015. "Association of Rule of Law and Health Outcomes: An Eco-
logical Study." *BMJ* 5, no. 10: e007004.

Prajwala. 2018. "Rescue." Last accessed May 2018. http://www.prajwalaindia.com
/rescue.html.

Prusa, Anya, and L. Picanco. 2019. "A Snapshot of the Status of Women in Brazil: 2019." Wilson Center. https://www.wilsoncenter.org/publication/snapshot-the -status-women-brazil-2019.

Putnins, Talis, and Arnis Sauka. 2020. "The Shadow Economy in Russia: New Estimates and Comparisons and Nearby Countries." Free Network Policy Brief Series. https:// freepolicybriefs.org/wp-content/uploads/2020/03/freepolicybriefs20200316-2.pdf.

Raffray, Nathalie. 2020. "Pair Arrested in Connection with Trafficking Brazilian Women to Work in Wembley Brothels." Kilburn Times. https://www.kilburntimes .co.uk/news/two-arrests-brazilian-women-being-sexually-trafficked-to-wembley -brothes-1-6609454.

Ramzy, Austin. 2015. "Fleeing Thailand, Top Investigator of Human Trafficking Says He Fears for His Safety." New York Times, December 10, 2015. http://www.nytimes.com /2015/12/11/world/asia/thailand-human-trafficking-asylum-australia.html?_r=1.

Rao, Smriti, and Christina Presenti. 2012. "Understanding Human Trafficking Origin: A Cross-Country Empirical Analysis." Feminist Economics 18, no. 2: 231–63.

Raza, Danish. 2014. "When Women Come Cheaper than Cattle." Hindustan Times, March 23, 2014. http://www.hindustantimes.com/india/when-women-come-cheaper -than-cattle/story-EJD38cJ4kaTGVn03LJzUkJ.html.

Rennell, Corey. 2004. "Saving the Youngest Workers." Harvard International Review 26, no. 3: 30–33.

Research Network on the Legal Parameters of Slavery. 2012. "Bellagio-Harvard Guidelines on the Legal Parameters of Slavery." Accessed June 2020. https://glc .yale.edu/sites/default/files/pdf/the_bellagio-_harvard_guidelines_on_the_legal _parameters_of_slavery.pdf.

Ridley, Louise. 2016. "Rio Child Sex Trafficking 'Epidemic' Could Rocket During the 2016 Olympics—Here's Why." Huffington Post UK, August 13, 2016. https://www .huffingtonpost.co.uk/entry/rio-olympics-2016-child-sex-rafficking_uk_57a9a7 efe4b089961b8568b.

Risse, Thomas, Stephen Ropp, and Kathryn Sikkink, eds. 1999. The Power of Human Rights: International Norms and Domestic Change. Cambridge: Cambridge University Press.

Roache, Madeline. 2018. "Putin Doesn't Care About Sex Trafficking." Foreign Policy, July 14, 2018. https://foreignpolicy.com/2018/07/13/putin-doesnt-care-about-sex -trafficking-russia-nigeria-world-cup-soccer/.

Roe-Sepowitz, Dominique, and Khara Jabola-Carolus. 2020. "Research Report: Sex Trafficking in Hawai'i: Part III." https://socialwork.asu.edu/sites/default/files/stir /final_report_sex_trafficking_in_hawaii_part_iii_.pdf.

Rosstat (Russian Federal Statistics Service). 2020. Last accessed July 2020. https://eng .gks.ru/.

Runyan, Anne Sisson, and V. Spike Peterson. 2018. Global Gender Issues in the New Millennium. Abingdon-on-Thames, UK: Routledge.

Rusling, Matt. 2015. "Thailand Is Losing the Fight Against Human Trafficking." Huffington Post, December 12, 2015. http://www.huffingtonpost.com/matt-rusling/thailand -is-losing-the-fi_1_b_8829126.html.

Safe House Foundation. 2014. "Annual Report." Copy on file with authors.

Sahni, Rohini, and V. Kalyan Shankar. 2011. "The First Pan-India Survey of Sex Workers: A Summary of Preliminary Findings." Accessed August 2018. http://www.sangram .org/resources/Pan_India_Survey_of_Sex_workers.pdf.

Sanar Wellness Institute and Polaris Project. 2015. "Promising Practices: An Overview of Trauma-Informed Therapeutic Support for Survivors of Human Trafficking." Accessed January 4, 2022. https://polarisproject.org/wp-content/uploads/2019/09/Sanar-Promising-Practices.pdf.

Sarkar, Kamalesh, Baishali Bal, Rita Mukherjee, Sekhar Chakraborty, Suman Saha, Arundhuti Ghosh, and Scott Parsons. 2008. "Sex Trafficking, Violence, Negotiating Skill and HIV Infection in Brothel-based Sex Workers of Eastern India, Adjoining Nepal, Bhutan, and Bangladesh." *Journal of Health, Population and Nutrition* 26, no. 2: 223–31.

Sarkar, Siddhartha. 2014. "Rethinking Human Trafficking in India: Nature, Extent and Identification of Survivors." *Round Table* 103, no. 5: 483–95.

Sauterey, Anne-Lise. 2008. "Anti-Trafficking Regional Cooperation in Southeast Asia and the Global Linkages from the Geopolitical Perspective: Borders and Anti-trafficking Strategies between Burma, Laos PRD, and Thailand." Paper presented at Seminar on Trafficking and Smuggling organized by the Institute of Asian Studies Chulalongkorn University, Bangkok, May 12, 2008.

Scarpa, Silvia. 2008. *Trafficking in Human Beings: Modern Slavery.* New York: Oxford University Press.

Schloenhardt, Andreas, and Rebekkah Markey-Towler. 2016. "Non-Criminalisation of Victims of Trafficking in Persons—Principles, Promises, and Perspectives." *Gronin-gen Journal of International Law* 4, no. 1: 10–38.

Schonhofer, Johanna. 2017. "Political Determinants of Efforts to Protect Victims of Human Trafficking." *Crime, Law, and Social Change* 67, no. 2: 153–85.

Schuckman, Emily. 2006. "Antitrafficking Policies in Asia and Russia and the Russian Far East: A Comparative Perspective." *Demokratizatsiya* 14, no. 1 (Winter): 85–102.

Sekhar, Datta Sudhangsu, and Mukherjee Kaushik. 2017. "Role Played by Social Workers in Non-governmental Organizations in Preventing Human Trafficking in India." *International Journal of Humanities and Social Science Intervention* 6, no. 12: 34–37.

Selvi, Semmalar. 2020. "The Politics of Sexual and Gender-Based Violence against Dalit Women." Gender Violence in India: A Prajnya Report.

Sen, Sankar. 2005. *Trafficking in Women and Children in India.* New Delhi: Orient Longman.

Sen, Sankar, and P. M. Nair. 2004. "A Report on Trafficking in Women and Children in India: 2002–2003, vol. 1." National Human Rights Commission, UNIFEM, and the ISS Project. Accessed August 2018. https://www.nhrc.nic.in/documents/reportontrafficking.pdf.

Senkova, Olga. 2018. "Grassroots Initiatives, Conflicts and Solidarities of the Feminist Scene in St. Petersburg, Russia." May 2018. http://www.promise.manchester.ac.uk/wp-content/uploads/2019/03/Individual-case-study-Russia-Feminist-scene-in-St-Petersburg.pdf.

Shamin, Ishrat. 2001. *Mapping of Missing, Kidnapped and Trafficked Women and Children: Bangladesh Perspective.* Dhaka, Bangladesh: International Organization for Migration.

Shapkina, Nadezda. 2008. "Operation Help: Counteracting Sex Trafficking of Women from Russia and Ukraine." PhD dissertation, Georgia State University. http://scholarworks.gsu.edu/sociology_diss.

Shared Hope International. 2010. "Anti-Trafficking Report: India." Accessed May 2018. http://sharedhope.org/2010/08/23/408/.

Shelley, Louise. 2010. *Human Trafficking: A Global Perspective*. Cambridge: Cambridge University Press.

——. 2018. *Dark Commerce: How A New Illicit Economy Is Threatening Our Future*. Princeton, NJ: Princeton University Press.

Shepard, Laura, ed. 2015. *Gender Matters in Global Politics*. Abingdon-on-Thames, UK: Routledge.

Shupiko, Denise. 2014. "The Development of the Russian Counter-Trafficking Movement: The Angel Coalition and International Politics on Civil Society, Feminism, and Human Trafficking." PhD Diss., University of Maryland, College Park.

Siegel, Dina, and Sylvia de Blank. 2010. "Women Who Traffic Women: The Role of Women in Human Trafficking Networks—Dutch Cases." *Global Crime* 11, no. 4: 436–47.

Silverman, J. G., M. R. Decker, J. Gupta, A. Maheshwari, V. Patel, B. M. Willis, and A. Raj. 2007. "Experiences of Sex Trafficking Victims in Mumbai, India." *International Journal of Gynecology and Obstetrics* 97: 221–26.

Silverman, Robert. 2017. "How the Olympics Hurt Rio's Sex Workers." Vocativ, May 15, 2017. https://www.vocativ.com/429924/how-olympics-hurt-rio-sex-workers/.

Simmons, Beth, and Paulette Lloyd. 2010. "Subjective Frames and Rational Choice: Transnational Crime and the Case of Human Trafficking." SSRN Network. Accessed November 2018. https://papers.ssrn.com/sol3/papers.cfm?abstract_id=1653473.

Simões, Solange, and Marlise Matos. 2008. "Modern Ideas, Traditional Behaviors, and the Persistence of Gender Inequality in Brazil." *International Journal of Sociology* 38, no. 4: 94–110.

Sjoberg, Laura. 2011. "Conclusion: The Study of Women, Gender, and Terrorism." In *Women, Gender, and Terrorism*, edited by L. Sjoberg and C. E. Gentry, 227–40. Athens: University of Georgia Press.

——. 2009. "Feminist Interrogations of Terrorism/Terrorism Studies." *International Relations* 23, no. 1: 69–74.

Smith, Charles A., and Brandon Miller-de la Cuesta. 2011. "Human Trafficking in Conflict Zones: The Role of Peacekeepers in the Formation of Networks." *Human Rights Review* 12, no. 3: 287–99.

Smith, Charles A., and Heather M. Smith. 2011. "Human Trafficking: The Unintended Effects of United Nations Intervention." *International Political Science Review* 32, no. 2: 125–45.

——. 2012. "Human Trafficking and International Cheap Talk: the Dutch Government and the Island Territories." *Journal of Human Rights* 11, no. 1: 51–65.

Smith-Cannoy, Heather. 2018. "Sex Trafficking and International Law." In *International Human Rights of Women*, edited by N. Reilly, 325–42. Singapore: Springer.

——. 2019. "Deprivation of Citizenship: An Examination of the Rohingya Refugee Crisis." In *Emerging Threats to Human Rights*, edited by Heather Smith-Cannoy, 163–85. Philadelphia: Temple University Press.

Soares, Eduardo. 2020. "Brazil: City of Sao Paulo Enacts Law Punishing Discrimination Based on Sexual Orientation and Gender Identity." Library of Congress Global Legal Monitor, February 26, 2020. https://www.loc.gov/law/foreign-news/article/brazil-city-of-so-paulo-enacts-law-punishing-discrimination-based-on-sexual-orientation-and-gender-identity/.

South Asian Times. 2017. "Two More Arrested in Jalpaiguri Child Trafficking Case." March 4, 2017. http://www.thesouthasiantimes.info/index.php?param=news/164764/India/30.

Sowell, Thomas. 1996. *Migrations and Cultures: A World View*. New York: Basic.

Sperling, Valerie. 2015. *Sex, Politics, and Putin*. Oxford: Oxford University Press.

Stern, Maria. 2017. "Feminist Global Political Economy and Feminist Security Studies?: The Politics of Delineating Subfields." *Politics & Gender* 13, no. 4: 728–33.

Stoecker, Sally. 2005. "Human Trafficking a New Challenge for the United States and Russia." In *Human Traffic and Transnational Crime: Eurasian and American Perspectives*, edited by Sally Stoecker and Louise Shelley, 13–28. Lanham, MD: Roman & Littlefield.

Stoecker, Sally, and Louise Shelley. 2005. "Introduction." In *Human Traffic and Transnational Crime: Eurasian and American Perspectives*, edited by Sally Stoecker and Louise Shelley, 1–12. Lanham, MD: Roman & Littlefield.

Studnicka, Andrea Cirineo Sacco. 2010. "Corruption and Human Trafficking in Brazil: Findings from a Multi-Modal Approach." *European Journal of Criminology* 7, no. 1: 29–43.

Subrinho, Wanderley Preite. 2019. "Brazil Registra Uma Morte por Homofobia a Cada 16 Horas, Aponta Relatório." UOL, February 20, 2019. http://www.noticias.uol.com .br/cotidiano/ultimas-noticias/2019/02/20/brasil-matou-8-mil-lgbt-desde-1963 -governo-dificulta-divulgacao-de-adaos.htm.

Suchland, Jennifer. 2015. *Economies of Violence: Transnational Feminism, Postsocialism, and the Politics of Sex Trafficking*. Durham, NC: Duke University Press.

———. 2018. "The LGBT Specter in Russia: Refusing Queerness, Claiming 'Whiteness.'" *Gender, Place & Culture: A Journal of Feminist Geography* 25, no. 7: 1073–88.

Sundstrom, Lisa. 2002. "Women's NGOs in Russia: Struggling from the Margins." *Demokratizatsyia* 10, no. 2: 207–29.

———. 2006. *Funding Civil Society: Foreign Assistance and NGO Development in Russia*. Palo Alto, CA: Stanford University Press.

Surtees, R. 2008. "Traffickers and Trafficking in Southern and Eastern Europe: Considering the Other Side of Human Trafficking." *European Criminology* 5, no. 1: 39–68.

Sydney Morning Herald. 2008. "Pimp Gets Life for Multiple Murders." April 10, 2008. http://www.smh.com.au/articles/2008/04/11/1207420587423.html.

Szep, Jason, and Andrew R. C. Marshall. 2013. "Thailand's Clandestine Rohingya Policy Uncovered." December 5, 2013. http://www.reuters.com/article/2014/04/10/us -thailand-rohingya-special-report-idUSBREA3922P20140410.

Szep, Jason, and Matt Spetalnick. 2015a. "Special Report: State Department Watered Down Human Trafficking Report." Reuters. Accessed June 8, 2020. https://www .reuters.com/article/us-usa-humantrafficking-disputes-special/special-report -state-department-watered-down-human-trafficking-report-idUSKCN0Q821 Y20150804.

———. 2015b. "India Takes Tough Line on Trafficking Victims Who Get Special US Visas." Reuters World News, November 4, 2015. https://www.reuters.com/article /us-usa-india-visas-insight-idUSKCN0ST1SN20151104.

Tavares, Paula. 2017. "How Does Brazilian Law See Women?" *World Bank Blogs* (blog), March 20, 2017. https://blogs.worldbank.org/latinamerica/how-does-brazilian-law -see-women.

Taylor, Alice, Giovanna Lauro, Marcio Segundo, and Margaret Greene. 2015. "'She Goes with Me in My Boat': Child and Adolescent Marriage in Brazil." Promundo. https://promundoglobal.org/resources/she-goes-with-me-in-my-boat-child-and -adolescent-marriage-in-brazil/.

Teixeira, Fabio. 2019a. "Brazilian Police Takes Down Trafficking Ring Targeting Trans Women." Reuters, March 13, 2019. reuters.com/article/us-brazil-lgbt-trafficking /brazilian-police-takes-down-trafficking-ring-targeting-trans-women-idUSKCN 1QU2V3.

———. 2019b. "Brazilian Police Want to Test New Tactic in War against Child Trafficking." Reuters, February 21, 2019. https://news.trust.org/item/20190221232421 -shgk0/.

Tetrault-Farber G. 2015. "Russia Sees Exodus of Labor Migrants." *Moscow Times* no. 5544 (2015).

Thai Freedom House. 2014. "Hill Tribes/Indigenous Peoples." Accessed June 1, 2014. http://thaifreedomhouse.org/about-us/hill-tribes-indigenous-people/.

Thai Government. 2015. "Thailand's Progress Report on Anti-Human Trafficking Efforts." March 31, 2015. http://www.mfa.go.th/main/contents/files/media-center -20150430-161606-980768.pdf.

Thai Ministry of Foreign Affairs. 2014a. "Thailand's Anti-Trafficking Progress Exceeds US State Department Criteria for Upgrade." Press Release, June 15, 2014. http:// www.mfa.go.th/main/en/media-center/14/46613-Thailand%27s-Anti-Trafficking -Progress-Exceeds.html.

———. 2014b. "Thai Report to US State Department." June 2014. Copy on file with authors.

Thai National Statistical Office. 2016. "The 2010 Housing and Population Census." Accessed June 2016. http://web.nso.go.th/en/census/poph/cen_poph_10.htm.

Tickner, J. Ann. 2011. "Feminist Security Studies: Celebrating an Emerging Field." *Politics and Gender* 7, no. 4: 576–81.

———. 2001. *Gendering World Politics: Issues and Approaches in the Post–Cold War Era*. New York: Columbia University Press.

Times of India. 2016. "11 Major Incidents of Violence Against Dalits Which Show How Badly We Treat Them." July 25, 2016. https://www.indiatimes.com/news/india /11-major-incidents-of-violence-against-dalits-which-show-how-badly-we-treat -them-258944.html.

———. 2018. "World Day Against Trafficking: Activists Remain Divided on Anti-Trafficking Bill." July 30, 2018. https://timesofindia.indiatimes.com/india/world-day -against-trafficking-activists-remain-divided-on-anti-trafficking-bill/articleshow /65195897.cms.

Tiuriukanova, Elena. 2005. "Female Labor Migration Trends and Human Trafficking: Policy Recommendations." In *Human Traffic and Transnational Crime: Eurasian and American Perspectives*, edited by Sally Stoecker and Louise Shelley, 95–113. Lanham, MD: Roman & Littlefield.

Tiuriukanova, E. V., and Institute for Urban Economics for the UN/IOM Working Group on Trafficking in Human Beings. 2006. "Human Trafficking in the Russian Federation: Inventory and Analysis of the Current Situation and Responses." http:// www.unicef.org/ceecis/Unicef_EnglishBook%281%29.pdf.

Toast Advisory. 2019. *Final Report: Scan of Issue Areas, Trends and Organizations Working in the Area of Child Trafficking in India*. Global Fund for Children. https:// globalfundforchildren.org/wp-content/uploads/2019/11/Toast-Advisory-India -Anti-Trafficking-Mapping-Report.pdf.

Tomasiewicz, Meaghan. 2018. "Sex Trafficking of Transgender and Gender Nonconforming Youth in the United States." Report, Loyola University of Law Center for the Human Rights of Children. https://ecommons.luc.edu/cgi/viewcontent.cgi ?article=1017&context=chrc.

Totman, Richard. 2003. *The Third Sex: Kathoey, Thailand's Ladyboys.* London: Souvenir.

Trivedi, Jennifer, and Luke Juran. 2015. "Women, Gender Norms, and Natural Disasters in Bangladesh," *Geographical Review* 105, no. 4: 601–11.

True, Jacqui. 2012. *The Political Economy of Violence Against Women.* Oxford: Oxford University Press.

Tsutsui, Kiyoteru, and Christine Min Wotipka. 2004. "Global Civil Society and the International Human Rights Movement: Citizen Participation in Human Rights International Nongovernmental Organization." *Social Forces* 83, no. 2: 587–620.

Tverdova, Yulia. 2011. "Human Trafficking in Russia and Other Post-Soviet States." *Human Rights Review* 12, no. 3: 329–44.

Tyuryukanova, Elena. 2006. "Forced Labour in the Russian Federation Today: Irregular Migration and Trafficking in Human Beings." International Labour Organization. http://www.ilo.org/global/topics/forced-labour/publications/WCMS_081997 /lang—en/index.htm.

Uddin, M. Bashir. 2017. "Revisiting Gender-Sensitive Human Security Issues and Human Trafficking in South Asia: The Cases of India and Bangladesh." In *Crime, Criminal Justice and the Evolving Science of Criminology of South Asia*, edited by Shahid M. Shahidullah, 219–45. New York: Springer International.

Ukwayi, J. K., P. U. Angioha, and E. A. Aniah. 2019. "Associate Factor of Trafficking in Women and Children in Calabar, Cross River State, Nigeria." *European Journal of Political Science Studies* 3, no. 1: 1–14.

Umlaufi, Nick. 2019. "9 Facts about Human Trafficking in Brazil." The Borgen Project, September 22, 2019. http://www.borgenproject.org/9-facts-about-human -trafficking-in-brazil/.

UN (United Nations). n.d. "Real Life Stories: Creuza Oliveira, a Domestic Worker in Brazil." Accessed January 4, 2022. http://www.un.org/en/letsfightracism/oliveira .shtml.

UN-ACT (United Nations Action for Cooperation Against Trafficking in Persons). 2015. "Migration Experiences of Lao Workers Deported from Thailand in 2013: Wang Tao/Lao PDR." Accessed June 2016. http://un-act.org/publication/view/human -trafficking-trends-asia-migration-experiences-lao-workers-deported-thailand -2013/.

UNDP (United Nations Development Programme). 2016. "Nigeria: Human Development Indicators." Human Development Reports. http://www.hdr.undp.org/en /countries/profiles/NGA.

UNESCO (United Nations Educational, Scientific and Cultural Organization). 2006. "Human Trafficking in Nigeria: Root Causes and Recommendations." Policy Paper Poverty Series, No. 14.2(E). http://www.unesdoc.unesco.org/images/0014/001478 /147844e.pdf.

———. 2016. "Searching for Identity." Accessed June 2016. http://www.unescobkk.org /fileadmin/user_upload/culture/Trafficking/citizenship/YINDEE_Searchingfor Identity_article_1_.pdf.

UN General Assembly. 2000. Protocol to Prevent, Suppress and Punish Trafficking in Persons, Especially Women and Children, Supplementing the United Nations Convention against Transnational Organized Crime. November 15, 2000. https://www .refworld.org/docid/4720706c0.html.

UNHCR (United Nations High Commissioner for Refugees). 2021. "Refugee Response in Bangladesh: Operational Portal." https://data2.unhcr.org/en/situations/myanmar _refugees.

UNIAP (United Nations Inter-Agency Project on Human Trafficking). 2010a. "The Criminal Justice Response to Human Trafficking: Recent Developments in the Greater Mekong Sub-Region." Accessed July 2014. http://www.no-trafficking.org /resources_rep_maps.html.

———. 2010b. "Mekong Region Country Datasheets/ Human Trafficking." Accessed June 2016. http://www.no-trafficking.org/reports_docs/siren/uniap_2010ht_data sheets.pdf.

———. 2014. "Counter-Trafficking in Thailand." Last accessed July 2014. http://www.no -trafficking.org/thailand_action.html.

UNICEF (United Nations Children's Fund). 2016. "Maternal and Newborn Health Disparities: Nigeria." Accessed January 4, 2022. https://data.unicef.org/wp-content /uploads/country_profiles/Nigeria/country%profile_NGA.pdf.

———. 2019. "Ending Child Marriage: A Profile of Progress in India." Accessed January 4, 2022. https://data.unicef.org/resources/ending-child-marriage-a-profile-of -progress-in-india/.

UNISDR (United Nations Office for Disaster Risk Reduction). 2012. "Child Traffickers Thrive on Natural Disasters." Accessed May 2018. http://www.unisdr.org/archive /25934.

UN News Centre. 2014. "Opium Poppy Cultivation in 'Golden Triangle' Hits New High in 2014." December 8, 2014. http://www.un.org/apps/news/story.asp?NewsID= 49540#.V1cGPWb1ZaU.

UNODC (United Nations Office on Drugs and Crime). 2009. "Global Report on Trafficking in Persons." Accessed November 18, 2015. https://www.unodc.org/documents /Global_Report_on_TIP.pdf.

———. 2010. *The Globalization of Crime: A Transnational Organized Crime Threat Assessment*. Vienna: The United Nations Office on Drugs and Crime.

———. 2012. "Global Report on Trafficking in Persons." Accessed November 18, 2015. https://www.unodc.org/documents/data-and-analysis/glotip/Trafficking_in _Persons_2012_web.pdf.

———. 2013. "Current Status of Victim Service Providers and Criminal Justice Actors in India on Anti-Human Trafficking." Accessed May 2018. https://www.unodc .org/southasia//frontpage/2013/July/india_-country-assessment-highlights-status -of-victim-assistance-and-criminal-justice-initiatives-on-anti-human-trafficking .html.

———. 2014. "Global Report on Trafficking in Persons." Accessed November 18, 2015. https://www.unodc.org/documents/data-and-analysis/glotip/GLOTIP_2014_full _report.pdf.

———. 2016. "Global Report on Trafficking in Persons." Accessed November 2018. https://www.unodc.org/documents/data-and-analysis/glotip/2016_Global_Report _on_Trafficking_in_Persons.pdf.

———. 2018. "Global Report on Trafficking in Persons." Last accessed June 2020. https:// www.unodc.org/documents/data-and-analysis/glotip/2018/GLOTiP_2018_BOOK _web_small.pdf.

———. 2020. Global Report on Trafficking in Persons." Accessed July 2021. https://www .unodc.org/documents/data-and-analysis/tip/2021/GLOTiP_2020_15jan_web.pdf.

UN Women. 2019. "It's Election Season in Nigeria, but Where Are the Women?" February 6, 2019. https://www.unwomen.org/en/news/stories/2019/2/feature-women-in-politics-in-nigeria.

UN Women and Inter-Parliamentary Union. 2008–20. "Women in Politics." Last accessed June 2020. https://www.ipu.org/resources/publications.

US Department of Labor. 2014. "Findings on the Worst Forms of Child Labor: Thailand." Accessed June 2016. https://www.dol.gov/agencies/ilab/resources/reports/child-labor/thailand#main-content.

US Department of State. 2001–16. "Trafficking in Persons Report." Accessed June 2020. https://2009–2017.state.gov/j/tip/rls/tiprpt/index.htm.

———. 2003. "The US Government's International Anti-Trafficking Programs, Fiscal Year 2002." Accessed November 25, 2015. http://2001–2009.state.gov/g/tip/rls/rpt/17858.htm#eurasia.

———. 2017–19. "Trafficking in Persons Report." Accessed June 2020. https://www.state.gov/trafficking-in-persons-report/.

Vahini, Shakti. 2005. "Trafficking and HIV: Maharashtra." UNDP Taha Project. Accessed July 2018. http://shaktivahini.org/wpcontent/uploads/2012/03/MharastraTAHA.pdf.

Vanguard. 2018. "How WOTCLEF Supported 10,600 Trafficked Victims." October 30, 2018. vanguardngr.com/2018/10/how-wotclef-supported-10600-trafficked-victims/.

Van Klaveren, Maarten, Kea Tijdens, Melanie Hughie-Williams, and Nuria Ramos Martin. 2009. "An Overview of Women's Work and Employment in Brazil: Decisions for Life MDG3 Project No. 12." University of Amsterdam/Amsterdam Institute for Advanced Labour Studies. http://www.wageindicator.org/documents/publicationslist/publications-2009/An-Overview-of-Womens-Work-and-Employment-in-Brazil.pdf.

Vasilyeva, Maria. 2019. "Traffickers Used Russia's World Cup to Enslave Us, Say Nigerian Women." Reuters, March 6, 2019. https://www.reuters.com/article/us-russia-nigeria-sexcrimes/traffickers-used-russias-world-cup-to-enslave-us-say-nigerian-women-idUSKCN1QN1OC.

Vejar, Cynthia, and Andrew Quach. 2013. "Sex Slavery in Thailand." *Social Development Issues* 35, no. 2: 105–23.

Verma, J. S., Leila Seth, and Gopal Subramanium. 2013. "Report of the Committee on Amendments to Criminal Law." January 23, 2013. http://www.prsindia.org/uploads/media/Justice%20verma%20committee/js%20verma%20committe%20report.pdf.

ViajeroBrasil.com. 2020. "Map of Brazil Divided by Regions and States." Accessed January 4, 2022. https://viajerobrasil.com/mapa-de-brasil-dividido-por-regiones-y-estados/?lang=en.

Vivanco, José Miguel. 2019a. "Brazil's Human Rights Minister's Feigned Concern for Women." Human Rights Watch, October, 4, 2019. https://www.hrw.org/news/2019/10/04/brazils-human-rights-minister-feigned-concern-women.

———. 2019b. "A Voice for LGBT Rights Silenced in Brazil." Human Rights Watch, January 24, 2019. https://www.hrw.org/news/2019/01/24/voice-lgbt-rights-silenced-brazil.

Voice of Russia Radio. 2012. "Human Trafficking: Victim Confession to Voice of Russia Radio." July 6, 2012. http://sputniknews.com/voiceofrussia/2012_07_06/Human-trafficking-victim-confession/.

von Stein, Jana. 2016. "Making Promises, Keeping Promises: Democracy, Ratification and Compliance in International Human Rights Law." *British Journal of Political Science* 46, no. 3: 655–79.

Walk Free Foundation. 2017. "Global Estimates of Modern Slavery." Accessed November 2018. https://www.ilo.org/wcmsp5/groups/public/-dgreports/-dcomm/documents/publication/wcms_575479.pdf.

———. 2018a. Global Slavery Index. Last accessed June 2020. https://www.global slaveryindex.org/2018/data/maps/#prevalence.

———. 2018b. Global Slavery Index. "Country Data: Brazil." Accessed January 4, 2022. globalslaveryindex.org/2018/findings/country-studies/brazil/.

———. 2018c. Global Slavery Index. "Country Data: India." Accessed January 4, 2022. https://www.globalslaveryindex.org/2018/data/country-data/india/.

———. 2018d. Global Slavery Index. "Country Data: Nigera." Accessed January 4, 2022. globalslaveryindex.org/2018/data/country-data/nigeria/.

———. 2018e. Global Slavery Index. "Country Data: Russia." Last accessed July 2020. https://www.globalslaveryindex.org/2018/findings/country-studies/russia/.

Wall Street Journal. 2013. "Brazil: The Social Media Capital of the Universe." Last accessed March 2021. https://www.wsj.com/articles/SB10001424127887323301104578257950857891898.

Weitzer, R. 2014. "New Directions in Research on Human Trafficking." *ANNALS of the American Academy of Political and Social Science* 653, no. 1: 6–24.

Wilkinson, Daniel. 2019. "Awaiting Justice for Rio Human Rights Defender." Human Rights Watch. https://www.hrw.org/news/2019/03/12/awaiting-justice-rio-human-rights-defender, March 12, 2019.

Wooditch, Alese. 2012. "Human Trafficking Law and Social Structures." *International Journal of Offender Therapy and Comparative Criminology* 56, no. 5: 673–90.

World Bank. 2009. "Governance Matters: Worldwide Governance Indicators." http://info.worldbank.org/governance/wgi/Home/Documents.

———. 2011. *Poverty and Social Exclusion in India.* Washington, DC: World Bank.

———. 2014. "Thailand Economic Monitor." Accessed February 2014. http://www.worldbank.org/en/country/thailand/publication/thailand-economic-monitor-february-2014.

———. 2016. "Overview: Thailand." Accessed June 2016. http://www.worldbank.org/en/country/thailand/overview.

———. 2017a. "Country Profile: Nigeria." http://databank.worldbank.org/data/Views/Reports/ReportWidgetCustom.aspx?Report_Name=CCountryProfil&Id=b450fd57&tbar=y&dd=y&inf=n&zm=n&country=NGA.

———. 2017b. "Poverty and Equity Data India." Last accessed March 2021. http://povertydata.worldbank.org/poverty/home/.

———. 2018. "Country Profile: Thailand." Accessed January 4, 2022. https://www.world bank.org/en/country/thailand/overview.

World Data Lab. 2020. "Methodology." World Poverty Clock. https://www.worldpoverty .io/methodology.

World Economic Forum. 2018. "The Global Gender Gap Report." Accessed October 1, 2018. http://www3.weforum.org/docs/WEF_GGGR_2018.pdf.

World Travel and Tourism Council. 2015. "Travel and Tourism: Economic Impact 2015: Thailand." Last accessed July 2021. http://www.wttc.org/-/media/files/reports/economic%20impact%20research/countries%202015/thailand2015.pdf.

Younus, M. A., R. D. Bedford, and M. Morad. 2005. "Not So High and Dry: Patterns of 'Autonomous Adjustment' to Major Flooding in Bangladesh." *Geography* 90, no. 2: 112–20.

Zaluar, Alba. 2000. "Perverse Integration: Drug Trafficking and Youth in the 'Favelas' of Rio de Janeiro." *Journal of International Affairs* 53, no. 2: 653–71.

Zillman, Claire. 2016. "Brazil's New President Just Selected an All-Male Cabinet." http://fortune.com/2016/05/13/brazil-new-president-temer-cabinet/. Accesed May 13, 2016.

Index

The letter *t* following a page number denotes a table. The letter *f* following a page number denotes a figure.

About the Authors

Heather Smith-Cannoy is an associate professor of political science at Arizona State University. She directs ASU's Global Human Rights Hub and the undergraduate degree program on Social Justice and Human Rights. She has published two books: *Insincere Commitments: Human Rights Treaties, Abusive States, and Citizen Activism* with Georgetown University Press (2012); and *Emerging Threats to Human Rights: Resources, Violence, and Deprivation of Citizenship* with Temple University Press (2019). She has also published fifteen peer-reviewed articles and book chapters on sex trafficking, human rights treaties, and the International Criminal Court.

Patricia C. Rodda is assistant professor of international relations at Carroll University in Waukesha, Wisconsin. She teaches international relations, comparative politics, international law, conflict and security, and political theory. Her research often focuses on vulnerable populations and the challenges they face seeking human rights protections.

Charles "Tony" Smith received his PhD from the University of California–San Diego (2004) and his JD from the University of Florida (1987). He is a professor in political science and law at the University of California–Irvine. His research is grounded in the American judiciary but encompasses work in comparative and international frameworks using a variety of methodologies. The unifying theme of the research is how institutions and the strategic interaction of political actors relate to the contestation over rights, law and courts, and democracy. He is the author or coauthor of seven books and thirty peer-reviewed articles and chapters.